RANGERS FC
in the
1980s

The Players' Stories

RANGERS FC
in the
1980s
The Players' Stories

ALISTAIR AIRD

First published by Pitch Publishing, 2019

Pitch Publishing
A2 Yeoman Gate
Yeoman Way
Worthing
Sussex
BN13 3QZ
www.pitchpublishing.co.uk
info@pitchpublishing.co.uk

ISBN 978 1 78531 527 5

Typesetting and origination by Pitch Publishing
Printed and bound in India by Replika Press Pvt. Ltd.

Contents

This book is dedicated to the
memory of the man who took me to
Ibrox for the first time and planted
the first seeds of my love affair
with Rangers FC … Scott David
Alexander or, as I knew him, Mr A.

Acknowledgements

There are a number of people I owe a debt of gratitude to when I reflect on the writing of this book. First and foremost, I have to extend my thanks to all the players who took time to speak to me and share their memories of playing for Rangers. From Stuart Beattie back in July 2018 to Ian Durrant in February 2019 I have been fortunate to spend time with gentlemen who have lived out my dream of donning a Rangers jersey. Their recollections have made me laugh and cry in equal measure but the one common thread through all the interviews was the pride these individuals had in having played for the club.

Thanks also go to Jane and Paul Camillin at Pitch Publishing for firstly having faith in my project and also for their guidance throughout. Duncan Olner from Olner Design deserves a huge amount of credit too for the outstanding jacket design.

On the home front my kids, Eva and Finlay, and my fiancée's son, Cameron, have been tolerant and supportive from day one and I love them dearly for that. And by the time you are all reading this I will have another addition to the brood, Aurla Georgina Wills Aird gracing us with her presence in April 2019.

Finally, to my fiancée and soulmate, Leona, my Lady Ranger. I simply could not have done it without you. Better, stronger, ALWAYS together.

Alistair Aird
March 2019

9

Introduction

The genesis for this book can be traced back to the autumn of 1986. My eight-year-old self was sitting at the kitchen table doing my school homework when my dad, a secondary school teacher, came home and dropped what looked like a small magazine in front of me. Emblazoned on the front cover in yellow capital letters were the words 'Dundee United' and 'Rangers' alongside the crest of the Scottish Football League. There were pictures of two footballers – I'd later learn they were United's Kevin Gallacher and the magnificent Davie Cooper of Rangers – and, at the top, a picture of the Skol League Cup. Further analysis told me that this was the match programme for the previous evening's Scottish League Cup semi-final tie between a resurgent Rangers and Dundee United. The programme had been gifted to me by Scott Alexander – or Mr A as I called him – a man who would become a dear friend and to whose memory this book is dedicated. Prior to that I had taken an interest in football – like my peers, I loved nothing more than having a kickabout in the streets with jumpers for goalposts – but the arrival of this gift rubber-stamped my affiliation to Rangers Football Club. The obsession began there and then.

Rangers' 2-1 victory that evening had taken them through to the first domestic cup final of the Graeme Souness era. The suave, sophisticated and hirsute Souness had been appointed player-manager four months earlier in a revolutionary bid by chief executive David Holmes to rouse the sleeping giant from what had become an almost decade-long slumber. It's fair to say that the 1980s had been one of the most doleful periods for Rangers and two colossal figures in the history of the club – John Greig and Jock Wallace – had tried unsuccessfully to meet and defeat the challenges posed by Celtic, Aberdeen, Dundee United and, latterly, Hearts. In truth their hands had been tied to an extent. Greig had the unenviable task of breaking up an ageing squad at the start of the 1980s, many of whom had been team-mates of his prior to his appointment as manager in May 1978. He and Wallace also had to contend with financial constraints, with the redevelopment of Ibrox in to a state-of-the art seated football arena and a rigid wage structure making it difficult to recruit the standard of player required to compete consistently for the Premier Division title.

David Mason, club historian since 1986, recalled, 'Greigy took over in 1978 but by 1980 things had started to turn. He started to get rid of players he could probably have retained like Sandy Jardine and Alex MacDonald, as they weren't exactly at the end of their careers. He tried to turn over the squad but it just didn't work out. He brought in players who weren't at the same level as the ones who were leaving. We did have Davie Cooper but even he was in and out of the team. Greigy used to say he was a bit of an enigma but even under Jock he wasn't really a regular. Then there were guys like Ally McCoist, John McClelland and Bobby Russell, although Bobby was starting to suffer with a knee injury at that time.

'When big Jock came in it didn't get off to the best of starts as it looked to those on the outside as if he was third choice [Alex Ferguson and Jim McLean were offered the role prior to Wallace's appointment]. But that didn't matter to Jock. I think he suffered the same problems that Greigy did. He didn't have the players he needed to sustain a title challenge and in the three years he was there, Rangers finished fourth, fourth and fifth. The expectation at Rangers is not just to challenge for the title but win it so, despite winning a couple of cups, we were just drifting along and there didn't seem to be any confidence that that was going to change. Aberdeen and Dundee United were starting to emerge so it wasn't just down to beating Celtic and there were new challenges there. We did have good players so in a one-off match, like a cup tie, we could always come through. But we didn't have players that had anywhere near enough quality to make an impact.'

As David alluded to, there was success, notably in the cup competitions, but Rangers were bedevilled by inconsistency. All too often a run of victories would be terminated by a draw or a defeat that would sap confidence from the playing squad and signal a spell where precious points would be dropped at venues like Cappielow, Firhill and Broomfield, grounds where Rangers sides should have been securing maximum points.

The results and inconsistent performances resulted in an inevitable downturn in attendances. Aside from Old Firm matches, the new Copland Road, Broomloan Road and Govan stands would have swathes of empty red, brown, orange, yellow and blue seats when Rangers played at Ibrox, making for an eerie atmosphere. For futile end-of-season matches – by the time the title race entered the home straight Rangers were out of contention – crowds would dip as low as 5,000.

Tom Miller, commentator on Rangers TV, recalled journeying to Ibrox at that time.

He said, 'I used to go to games with friends from Drumpellier Cricket Club in Coatbridge and you could leave there about 2.20pm, park the car and be in your seat before the 3pm kick-off. The crowds, by comparison, were still decent but there was a flatness about the club. I think Jock Wallace's departure [in 1978] set us back about four or five years. John Greig, the obvious replacement, took over and his time in charge was a real conundrum. In the European arena he could put out teams that would compete with the best of them but domestically there were occasions where they just seemed to lack spark. John Greig did manage to pluck some top-notch, technically gifted footballers from abroad like Robert Prytz and Jim Bett. But he couldn't get the correct blend.

'At that time, Aberdeen and Dundee United were building excellent sides from their own youth academies but you have to be an exceptional young player to come through at Rangers. It's the same now, over 30 years later. We did have some youngsters at that time that were a bit special – Ian Durrant and Derek Ferguson stood out – but the pressure and expectations at Rangers mean that you can't just flick a switch and run with a youth policy.'

Tom added, 'I had a cousin who played for Aberdeen and there was a perception at that time that they were superior to Rangers. We played them at Ibrox in one match during the 1980s and drew 1-1. My cousin and I went out that night and met a couple of guys we knew who supported Rangers. They were drinking champagne and my cousin thought they were doing that by way of celebrating the draw that afternoon. He asked them, if they were drinking champagne after drawing a game, what were they going to be drinking if Rangers had won? I guess that summed up what people thought about the club then.'

The financial outlay for the stadium meant young talent had to be blooded perhaps sooner than expected and that in itself breeds inconsistency. Something had to give and that meant a resignation for Greig in October 1983 and a sacking for Wallace in April 1986. For fans like Rick Plews this was a frustrating time to be a Rangers follower.

'Watching Rangers in the 1980s was the proverbial game of two halves,' he said. 'I went to my first game at Ibrox a few months after my fifth birthday, an end-of-season midweek clash against Kilmarnock. The date was 30 April 1980 and John MacDonald ensured it was a winning start in front of a crowd of just 8,000.

'Over the next couple of seasons I attended home games regularly, often taking in reserve matches at Ibrox when the first team played away. My earliest recollections are of sitting on the old wooden seats in the Main Stand looking over at a building site where the Sandy Jardine Stand now fills the skyline. The other great thing about being in the old Main Stand was being able to peer down to a warm-up area and see the players preparing before emerging down the tunnel.'

Trouble between rival fans at the 1980 Scottish Cup Final between the Old Firm meant that young Rick was not allowed to go along to Hampden so he missed the chance to see Rangers win their first silverware of the decade in 1981. And when he eventually did get to go to a showpiece match at Hampden, Rangers lost.

'I vividly remember listening to the 1982/83 League Cup Final against Celtic on a radio in the Main Stand at Ibrox as Rangers Reserves played Celtic Reserves at the same time, but my first cup final was in 1983 when we lost to Aberdeen in the Scottish Cup,' he recalled. 'I grew up in Lenzie, about 12 miles from Glasgow and also the home of then manager John Greig and vice chairman Jack Gillespie, but there were very few Rangers fans in my class at that particular time. The majority of those showing any real interest in football gravitated towards the 'New Firm' and Aberdeen in particular, to the extent there was an Aberdeen Supporters Club in Lenzie running a full bus to most games. It's hard to imagine now but I guess it demonstrates how much young kids are influenced by instant success.'

Rick's point here illustrates where Rangers were at that time and, in an attempt to rekindle the glory days of the 1970s, Jock Wallace came back to Ibrox in 1983. However, despite getting the turnstiles clicking again, he could not reinvigorate Rangers.

'The return of Jock offered hope for a period and I finally saw us lift a trophy in person in the 1984/85 League Cup Final,' said Rick. 'Whilst I was too young to really appreciate all that Jock Wallace had achieved first time round, it was clear to me just how much he meant to the fans when he returned. The support were desperate for him to succeed. There were some memorable home matches and two that stick out are the second leg of the 1983/84 League Cup semi-final when we beat Dundee Utd 2-0 and also the second leg victory over Inter Milan in the UEFA Cup the following season. Ibrox was rocking on both occasions and it demonstrated that we could, at least in one-off games, compete with the best.'

Things would change for Rick and his fellow fans from 1986 onwards when they would gorge themselves on a diet of sumptuous football played by players who would ascend in to the pantheon of great Rangers. That is not to say that the playing squad in the success-starved early 1980s was shy of good players.

Rick recalled, 'My boyhood heroes were Bobby Russell and Davie Cooper, two players who would grace any Rangers side of any era. But there were other very good players during the 1980s, guys like Robert Prytz, Ian Redford, Jim Bett, Iain Ferguson, Ally Dawson, John McClelland and Ted McMinn. It was a time of transition as the older players were gradually replaced and funds were diverted towards stadium redevelopment. However, Aberdeen and Dundee United both had excellent sides in that era in addition to the usual challenge from Celtic. Throw in a rejuvenated Hearts side and there was a truly competitive feel about the league midway through the decade.'

Then came the revolution. Lawrence Marlborough, grandson of former chairman John Lawrence and the majority shareholder, stepped in to arrest the decline, recruiting David Holmes as CEO in November 1985 then boldly appointing Graeme Souness as player-manager some six months later. Rangers and Scottish football were changed in an instant.

David Mason commented, 'I started at Ibrox in 1986, six weeks after Graeme Souness was appointed. A few weeks earlier, before Jock was sacked, I was in the Bellahouston Hotel talking about where the club would go from here as there was no way forward with Jock. I was talking to a mate who was [Rangers director] Jack Gillespie's son-in-law and I reckoned we needed to be a bit radical and go for someone like Graeme Souness. He said he was going to mention that to his father-in-law. Shortly afterwards David Holmes announced that he had also come up with that idea when he was lying in his bed one night but the most important thing was that Lawrence Marlborough recognised the club was going nowhere. Crowds were dropping off markedly so money needed to be spent to make a change. When Souness came in everyone got a lift and the profile of Scottish Football was lifted too. Bringing in world-class players reinvigorated the place and it was a refreshing change. I had been in the directors' box three or four times before I started with the club but when I came in, I could sense the positive change in the atmosphere. It wasn't just the team that got a lift, the commercial side got a boost too. The Thornton Suite was opened and one of the directors, Freddie Fletcher, was dedicated to generating some commercial income.'

Tom Miller could also sense a change for the better was happening.

He recalled, '[reserve-team coach] Donald Mackay looked after the team when Graeme and Walter were away with Scotland at the World Cup in Mexico. He told me that something special was happening at Ibrox and the change would be enormous. If players weren't going to embrace what the new manager wanted to do, some of which was alien to the lifestyle of a Scottish footballer, then they wouldn't be at the club.'

The appointment also meant exciting times for supporters like Rick Plews.

He said, 'It was a fantastic time to be a young supporter. Suddenly I was watching Chris Woods, Terry Butcher, Graham Roberts, Graeme Souness, Ray Wilkins and Trevor Francis in the flesh – top stars who I would only previously have seen in the pages of *Shoot!* magazine. We also had some of the best Scottish players – Ally McCoist, Ian Durrant, Derek Ferguson and Ian Ferguson – so we really were spoilt.'

Tom Miller was also in awe of the talent that was on show at Ibrox but one player in particular stood out.

He said, 'There were players at that time that came in and immediately got an understanding of the football club and one of them was Ray Wilkins. He was a thoroughbred in everything he did, on and off the field. He hosted a party for all his team-mates one night at his home in Bothwell and I'm told it was wall-to-wall champagne. But he was a champagne footballer. Many thought he played too many square passes but he made the ball a prisoner and he saw things that other players could only dream of.'

Lawrence Marlborough's radical and revolutionary move paid dividends and signalled the start of arguably the most successful era in Rangers' history. The launch pad for the success that followed was the Premier Division title win in May 1987 and suddenly Ibrox was once again a magnet for Rangers fans the length and breadth of the country. Fortunately for Rick Plews he had taken steps to ensure he would be part of the capacity crowd every other Saturday.

He recalled, 'During Souness's first season I spent numerous Sundays queuing for tickets for the next home game. On a number of occasions, the queue snaked all around the stadium. Such was the demand for tickets it had become almost a necessity to purchase a season ticket and I acquired my first during season 1986/87. It was in the recently launched Premier Club situated in the Govan Rear and that's where I've sat every season since.'

It is evident from what Tom, David and Rick have recounted that the 1980s was a decade of fluctuating fortunes for Rangers followers. But what was that era like for the players that were involved? What were their memories and recollections? In *Rangers in the 1980s – The Players' Stories* you will hear from 21 players who pulled on a blue jersey for the Rangers first team between the first match of the decade against St Mirren on 1 January 1980 and the last one against Hibernian at Easter Road on 28 December 1989. The mixture is eclectic, with the recollections of celebrated figures who have played over 300 games for the club combined with those whose appearance tally is in single figures. Each one has their own, unique story to tell of one of the most turbulent and tumultuous eras in Rangers' 147-year history.

SAFE HANDS
THE
GOALKEEPERS

Just Jim
Jim Stewart (1981–1984)

James Garvin Stewart's football career was stuck in a rut in March 1981. Aged 27 he was languishing in the Middlesbrough reserve team, his two caps for Scotland in 1977 and 1979 a seemingly distant memory. Enter John Greig. The Rangers manager was looking for a goalkeeper to provide competition for the timeless Peter McCloy and he looked to Teesside to find one.

'I got a phone call from Davie Provan, who was on the coaching staff at Ibrox at the time, to ask me if I'd be interested in signing for Rangers,' said Stewart. 'There was no question about that for me, it was 100% yes. A day later the Middlesbrough manager, John Neal, told me a bid had been made and would I like to speak to Rangers. There was no hesitation. At that time, I wasn't playing for Middlesbrough – Jim Platt was playing well – and my son had just been born so all the boxes were ticked. It was always a boyhood ambition to sign for Rangers. I had been linked with Rangers a couple of times when I had been with Kilmarnock and I thought it might never happen. But to sign for the biggest team in Scotland was a no-brainer.'

The transfer fee was £115,000 but, after signing his contract, Stewart barely had time to draw breath before he was donning the yellow goalkeeper's jersey.

'It wasn't like nowadays with the transfer window but there were still transfer deadlines,' said Stewart. 'I came up from Middlesbrough on the Sunday and agreed terms on the Sunday night in Joe Mason's house in Kilmarnock as everything had to be registered for the Monday. We were due to play Dundee United on the Wednesday night and Greigy told me I was playing so I guess he saw me coming in to be first choice.'

He continued, 'I was happy with how I played but after the game [Rangers lost 4-1] there was a lot of soul-searching. I just had to regroup and recognise it wasn't always going to be as bad as that. We actually played United a few weeks later in the league and beat them, so that levelled things out a bit. When I had left Kilmarnock to go to England in 1978 United and Aberdeen were starting to come to the fore so it was a challenge for us.'

Stewart retained the gloves for the remaining nine league matches, making his Old Firm debut in a 1-0 defeat at Ibrox on 18 April 1981. Rangers won only half of the ten Premier Division games Jim played but he enjoyed better fortunes in the Scottish Cup.

'Charlie Nicholas scored the winner for Celtic in the Old Firm game but it was a great experience,' recalled Stewart. 'But it's about winning. There wasn't much in the game or much between the teams but I'd have rather we were poor that day and won. The strange thing about that game was that there were only three stands as the Govan Stand hadn't been completed by then. That made for an eerie atmosphere.'

He added, 'The Scottish Cup Final was incredible. My last game for Middlesbrough was for their reserve team at Lincoln City yet 12 weeks later I was playing in a cup final. It was great to get that opportunity so quickly but when Reddy [Ian Redford] missed the penalty in the last minute I wasn't too happy! But Coop [Davie Cooper], who was a great pal of mine, was brilliant in the replay. He had come on on the Saturday and done a couple of bits of magic but he was superb on the Wednesday night.'

Success is supposed to breed success so hopes were high at Ibrox that the cup win would be the catalyst for Rangers to re-establish themselves at the forefront of the Scottish game. To prepare themselves for the rigours of season 1981/82 they welcomed high-calibre opposition to Ibrox. Friendlies were arranged against UEFA Cup holders Ipswich Town, and European champions Liverpool, and

Everton and Southampton also came north for testimonial matches for Colin Jackson and Sandy Jardine.

'Liverpool was a busy night,' recalled Stewart with a smile. 'It was exciting to get the opportunity. I had played against them when I was with Middlesbrough so I knew what standard of team they were. They were packed with internationalists including Dalglish and Souness. We had gone to Sweden earlier in pre-season and played a number of lower league teams to build our match sharpness but when we got nearer the competitive action we were up against better calibre opposition. At that time the season started with the old League Cup section which came on the back of those games.'

In season 1981/82 Rangers were drawn alongside Morton, Dundee and Raith Rovers in their League Cup section. Stewart was between the sticks for the opening five matches – Rangers won four and drew the other – but he missed the final fixture against Raith and the first four league matches when he sustained an injury in training.

'I turned my ankle at The Albion,' said Stewart. 'The grass park had been resurfaced but during a game I went over on my ankle and it blew up like a balloon. I knew it was going to be about three or four weeks out. I came back against Brechin City then played against Dukla Prague but I wasn't fully fit. I lost a poor goal against Dukla and I was disappointed with that. But I played most of the season after that.'

Stewart played in all but six of the remaining 32 Premier Division matches. Included in that run was a first Old Firm victory – a Jim Bett penalty giving Rangers a 1-0 win at Ibrox on 9 January 1982 – and Jim was also the custodian when Rangers returned to Hampden for another rendezvous with Dundee United. The prize at stake this time was the League Cup.

'Peter [McCloy] got injured the week before the final in a match against Celtic so I ended up playing,' said Stewart. 'I enjoyed it and it was good to get the feeling of being a winner again. I felt I had been fortunate to win two medals so early but we always competed in the cups at that time. At the start of the league season we tended to be decent but there was always a tailing off. That might have been down to having guys that weren't used to going the distance. The older guys like Colin Jackson and Tom Forsyth were top players and they would pass on good habits to us. But the players who came in at that time didn't really fulfil their potential and I include myself in that too.'

Rangers enhanced what was becoming an unwanted reputation of being a cup team by reaching the 1982 Scottish Cup Final. Stewart played in all six cup ties but would be on the losing side for the first time when Rangers faced Aberdeen at Hampden. Rangers were leading 1-0 through a John MacDonald goal when a speculative effort from Alex McLeish restored parity. Three further goals in extra time saw the cup bedecked in red and white ribbons.

'Big Alex keeps telling me he did the same thing in training that week,' laughed Stewart. 'It was a total surprise when that happened, because I felt overall in the game we played well. Extra time took its toll on us a wee bit but I felt we had a real chance of beating Aberdeen that afternoon. I was also disappointed as it was the first time I'd played in a cup final and we hadn't won.'

A further dampener was put on the season when Stewart was not selected in the Scotland squad that travelled to the World Cup finals in Spain.

He recalled, 'I was fortunate enough to go to the 1974 World Cup but I never got to another one. I was in the provisional 40 in both 1978 and 1982 but I never made the 22-man travelling squad. It was a major disappointment as, in 1978, I felt my form was good enough with Kilmarnock and in 1982 I felt I'd had a decent season with Rangers. Unlike today they weren't as conscious of people's feelings so I only found out I wasn't going when the final 22 was announced.'

At the outset of season 1982/83 Jim Stewart was still the man in possession of the gloves at Ibrox. He played in each of the first 18 Premier Division matches and all 11 League Cup ties – tasting cup final defeat for a second time when Celtic won 2-1 in the final – but after shipping three goals in a defeat against Motherwell at Fir Park, Stewart was dropped.

'I have to be honest and say I wasn't playing as well as I should have been,' is Stewart's honest reflection. 'I lost a bad goal in the

Old Firm game a couple of days before Motherwell which was well documented as I should have done better with it. Overall, I thought I played well in the Celtic game but no one remembers that. Brian McClair scored a hat-trick for Motherwell at Fir Park and I knew I was struggling and needed a wee bit of help. But at that time there weren't any specialist coaches.'

He continued, 'Greigy was good with me. He told me he felt the change would benefit me and the team. It would give me a chance to get my confidence back and I could understand where he was coming from. I didn't have any complaints.'

Season 1982/83 should perhaps have been the campaign that Rangers kicked on and won the league title. At the start of the campaign the team were confident and playing good football – albeit too many draws were having a detrimental impact on the title push – but confidence was shattered one night in Germany's fourth most populous city, Cologne.

'Europe was always more exciting,' said Stewart. 'For the players it was a release from the Premier Division and European nights at Ibrox were always special. We played Borussia Dortmund and did well against them home and away. We played well against Cologne at home but when we went there it was like the Blitz! We were 3-0 down inside 20 minutes. John McClelland and Craig Paterson had come in to the team, both decent players with good ball retention, and we had Davie MacKinnon and Ally Dawson too. Our midfield had good ball players but it just didn't work, even though there were so many good players. That season, up until we played Celtic at Celtic Park, we hadn't been beaten but we drew too many games. For example, we went to Cappielow and drew 0-0 and these were games we should have been winning.'

Jim Stewart did not make a first-team appearance for over eight months. He was eventually recalled for the comprehensive 10-0 win over Valletta in the European Cup Winners' Cup in September 1983. In a European Cup fixture against the same opposition seven years later goalkeeper Chris Woods took, and missed, a penalty. Back in 1983 Rangers were also awarded a penalty but Jim was not tempted to step up.

'I never even thought about it,' laughed Stewart. 'We had gone to Malta and won 8-0 and Greigy told me I would be playing in the second leg. It was good to get back in.'

Two appearances in the Premier Division followed in October but they would be the last Jim Stewart would make for the Rangers first team. The first of those league appearances was in a 2-1 defeat against Motherwell at Ibrox in what proved to be John Greig's last Premier Division match in charge.

'I was put back in the team for the Motherwell game which gave me a chance to establish myself again,' recalled Stewart. 'We were leading 1-0 [courtesy of an Ally McCoist penalty] but there was a lack of confidence about the place and it affected us.'

He added, 'Greigy had a lot of good ideas and was proactive in terms of a lot of the things he did in European games. He got dossiers of different teams and he was quite thorough. I just think at the time, as a team, we didn't gel. But he could have walked away with the Treble in his first season.'

Appearances for the reserves in season 1983/84 were not guaranteed either. Stewart spent the early part of the campaign sharing the gloves with young Andy Bruce and by the season's end had played just 14 times for the second string. His final appearance in a Rangers jersey came at Muirton Park on 1 May 1984, a 3-3 draw against St Johnstone in the Reserve League West.

'I was surprised I didn't get an opportunity under Jock as he had tried to sign me when I was at Kilmarnock,' said Stewart. 'I think because Jock knew Peter [McCloy] and had worked with him and been successful, that gave him the edge. There was never any animosity. Peter and I used to travel together and we got on well. There wasn't a lot of dialogue with Jock but soon after he arrived, I went in for a cartilage operation which meant I'd be out for eight or nine weeks. Nicky [Walker] was signed so by February 1984 I knew I wasn't going to play. I went to Dumbarton on loan and they were competing for promotion to the Premier Division. I played three or four games for them. I knew at that time it was the end of the road at Rangers.'

When his contract expired in the summer of 1984, Stewart joined St Mirren but game time at Love Street was limited.

'It was a major disappointment to leave Rangers,' reflected Stewart. 'Initially things went well, with the cup finals but, overall, I was disappointed, particularly with myself. There were occasions where I could have done better than I did and there will always be disappointment for me that I never played in a team that won the league. Ultimately, as a Rangers player you are judged on winning the league.'

He continued, 'Alex Miller was the manager at St Mirren and he phoned me to say he was looking for experienced back-up for Campbell Money and for someone to help him try and progress. I was happy with that arrangement.'

In his two seasons in Paisley, Stewart made nine league appearances. He made his debut in a 4-0 defeat against Aberdeen at Pittodrie in October 1984 and his last appearance came on the infamous final day of the 1985/86 season. Alex MacDonald's Hearts had led the title race for most of the season. All they needed to do to clinch the title was avoid defeat against Dundee at Dens Park. Meanwhile, at Love Street, nearest challengers, Celtic, had to rack up a high score against Stewart's St Mirren in the hope that defeat for Hearts would allow them to nick the title on goal difference.

'It was the worst day of my life,' said Jim. 'I hadn't been playing at the time but Campbell pulled out with an injury a couple of hours before the game. We lost 5-0, Celtic won the league so it wasn't pleasant, what with me being an ex-Rangers player.'

The Celtic match was Stewart's last for the Buddies. Ahead of the 1986/87 season former Rangers team-mate and now Partick Thistle player-manager, Derek Johnstone, took Jim to Firhill. He joined other ex-Rangers, Kenny Watson and Colin McAdam, in the player pool but was limited to just eight league appearances. His final match as a professional was on 27 January 1987, a 3-0 win over Queen of the South at Firhill.

'At that time, I felt the chances of me signing for a club in the top league were remote so I decided to retire,' said Stewart. 'Goalkeeping coaches were beginning to become a new thing so I started to look into that. I also joined the Ministry of Defence as a police officer and

I was there for about eight or nine years. I then got a chance to go into freelance goalkeeping coaching and I really enjoyed it.'

The coaching role earned Stewart a return to Ibrox. In January 2007 Paul Le Guen left Rangers and Walter Smith, then manager of Scotland, returned to the helm. Stewart had been part of Smith's coaching team with the national side and in the summer of 2007 was invited to take on a similar role at Ibrox.

'I enjoyed working with Walter because his man-management was first class,' recalled Stewart. 'There was a coach in situ when Walter took over but I was with Hearts doing pre-season in Germany when Walter called me and asked me to come back. For me, there was no question about it.'

Stewart would hold the role of goalkeeping coach for ten years, working under Smith, Ally McCoist, Stuart McCall, Mark Warburton and Graeme Murty. He worked with a number of excellent goalkeepers, helping to hone and develop the skills of a young Allan McGregor, and his time at Ibrox was eventful. During his decade there, the club made a UEFA Cup Final appearance, won three successive Premier League titles and endured the darkest day in the club's history when they went into administration in February 2012.

'Working with Allan was an experience,' laughed Stewart. 'People talk about the off-the-park stuff but he was the first guy in each morning and he was diligent doing his work. When it comes to making saves that win games he's right up there with the best.'

Of the tumultuous end to his first season as coach, Stewart reflected, 'The games mounted up but Walter's way was to take it a game at a time. We had won the League Cup, qualified for the Scottish Cup Final and were in contention for the league. We played Zenit in the UEFA Cup Final and they were a top team. The aim was to try and stay in the game as long as we could but once they scored the goal, it was really difficult to turn it around.'

After clinching a third successive title in 2010/11, Walter Smith stepped down and his assistant manager, Ally McCoist, moved up to the top job. It was the natural progression and Jim Stewart was a trusted member of McCoist's coaching entourage. However, just eight months into his first managerial job, the Rangers icon saw his beloved club plunge to the depths of despair.

'At one stage of the [2011/12] season we were actually 15 points ahead of Celtic,' recalled Stewart. 'Everything was going well but behind the scenes we weren't getting the players we targeted pre-season and there wasn't a good feeling about the new owner. When all hell broke loose, we couldn't believe what was happening.'

He added, 'Although it was really serious, we had a great bunch of lads and the football humour helped get us through. One day Coisty came out the shower claiming he'd had a "Bobby Ewing" moment and that administration and liquidation hadn't happened. We all told him it hadn't and to get back in and have another shower! He knew the club and had a focus on what he wanted to do. You could see how much it was affecting him. He was so desperate for the club to succeed and for him to succeed as a manager as well. I wasn't privy to a lot of it but you knew things weren't right. Ally spent more time putting out fires than he did with the team.'

Rangers ended up demoted to the bottom tier of the Scottish game but Jim Stewart was part of the journey back to the top. He remained as goalkeeping coach after McCoist left Rangers in December 2014 and worked under Mark Warburton and Davie Weir in the season that the club clinched their return to the top flight.

'Every time a new manager came in I thought my time was up,' said Stewart. 'When Alistair took over from Walter we had the continuity, but when Mark came in there was always a concern over whether I'd be kept on. I knew Davie Weir well and I got a phone call from him and he told me they wanted me to stay. It was really enjoyable and I had a good working relationship with Mark and Davie. I thought that at last the club was turning the corner and we were building a team.'

Warburton and Weir left Rangers in February 2017 and although Stewart stayed at the club under interim manager, Graeme Murty, he eventually departed when Pedro Caixinha took over in July 2017.

'Pedro decided to bring his own staff in so I met with [managing director] Stewart Robertson and was told my services were no longer required,' recalled Stewart. 'It was hard to take but that's football.

When I came in in 2007, I would have taken ten years' service so I don't have any qualms about it. I had the chance to put ideas into place and there are four or five goalies now coming through the system that we identified. A lot of people aren't afforded that length of time so I was very lucky.'

Having served his boyhood heroes in two capacities, Jim Stewart's part of the story concludes with reflection on his time at Ibrox as a player.

'The highlight was winning the Scottish Cup; that would be the one that stuck out,' reflected Stewart. 'The Saturday game was disappointing but to win by the margin we did in the replay was fantastic. My biggest regret is that I didn't do as well as I thought I should have done. I wouldn't change anything, though. In our history the goalies we've had have always been top drawer and I got great support from the fans, they were first class. When I left in 1984 I was 30 and felt there was plenty of life in me. I took it quite badly when I left as it was my ambition to go to Rangers. But, looking back now, I was just delighted to get the chance to play for Rangers.'

Jim Stewart made 107 appearances for Rangers and recorded 39 shut-outs (36.4%). He won a Scottish Cup winners' medal in 1980/81 and a League Cup winners' medal in 1981/82.

Shortbread Fingers

Nicky Walker (1983–1989)

Every successful team needs a strong, dependable goalkeeper and when Jock Wallace replaced John Greig as Rangers manager in October 1983, he had three at his disposal. Peter McCloy, the longest-serving player at Ibrox, had vied with Jim Stewart for the number one jersey in 1982/83 and young Andy Bruce was also on the books. Wallace, however, felt he needed another option and he knew exactly where to find it. Joseph Nicol 'Nicky' Walker had worked under Wallace at Leicester City and Motherwell and he arrived at Ibrox in December 1983 in a cash-plus-player deal worth £100,000.

'When the gaffer left Motherwell it came as a shock to most of us,' recalled Walker. 'We were building a fairly decent team with the likes of Gary McAllister and Ally Mauchlen. It came right out of the blue, he never even said cheerio! It was in the papers the next day and that was the first we had heard of it. About three weeks after he left he phoned me and told me there were clubs sniffing about me but not to sign for anybody as he was coming to sign me.'

Walker did as he was asked and the wheels were set in motion for a dream move to Ibrox. After Wallace had reacquainted himself with the manager's office he was true to his word and approached Motherwell to snare their young goalkeeper.

'Bobby Watson was Motherwell manager at the time and we didn't see eye-to-eye,' said Nicky. 'On the day it happened Motherwell were due to play St Johnstone at home and, on the morning of the game, I was out walking the dog in Strathclyde Park. The gaffer phoned and said, "Get yersel' in here [to Ibrox]". When I got in, Bobby Watson was already there with Kenny Lyall and Kenny Black who were part of the deal. Jock said, "Sign that" so I signed the contract, but had no idea what I had signed. There was no negotiation. After I signed I asked what I had just signed and he said, "You've got a four-year deal son, now get out of here!" I had complete trust in him – I had known him my whole football career – and I knew he'd do the best he could by me. For me to get the opportunity to go to a club like Rangers was just unbelievable. You didn't knock that back, I'd have gone there for nothing.'

Having ironically played his last match for Motherwell against Rangers on 10 December 1983, Walker made his Rangers debut just over two weeks later when Wallace's side travelled to Easter Road to face Hibernian. He recorded a clean sheet too, as goals from Bobby Williamson and Davie Cooper saw a Rangers side languishing in sixth place record a much needed two points.

'Myself and Bobby signed on the same day and made our debuts at the same time,' said Walker. 'It was ironic as I grew up a Hibs fan. In the village I grew up in you supported either Rangers or Celtic so, at the time, to be different, I started following Hibs. We won 2-0 but it was a whole different scale. I remember the big bank [of terracing] at Easter Road and, playing with Motherwell, you maybe got four or five thousand people so to see the Rangers travelling support it was just unbelievable, a different world for me.'

Walker stayed between the sticks for the next five Premier Division matches and, following two weeks out of the side, took the gloves again for a home draw with Hibernian (0-0) and a win over St Johnstone (4-1). In that run of games, Rangers conceded just seven goals and Walker also had the opportunity to share the Ibrox arena with a future star of the world game, Ruud Gullit, and the iconic Johan Cruyff when Rangers faced Feyenoord in the KLM Challenge Cup. Gullit, in the embryonic days of what would be a glittering career, had a fine match, his performance capped off with a stunning goal from 25 yards.

'It was a high-scoring game [Rangers won 7-6 on penalties after a 3-3 draw] and I still have some photographs from the game,' said

Walker. 'The gaffer tried to arrange as many games as he could to get us more experience. As well as Gullit there were some others played that night that went on to play for the Dutch national team but I remember that Gullit stood out a mile.'

However, Nicky's appearance against St Johnstone proved to be his final Premier Division one of the season. Four days later Rangers drew 2-2 against Dundee at Dens Park in the Scottish Cup and when they lost the Ibrox replay 3-2 seven days later, Walker lost his place to Peter McCloy. The experienced McCloy played in each of the final ten league matches and was also selected for the League Cup Final against Celtic.

'I had played for Motherwell earlier in the League Cup so I was cup-tied,' recalled Walker. 'Big Peter [McCloy] played in the semi-final and the final. Even just going to a cup final was a great experience. I was part of the squad so I got a chance to sit back and see what it was about for Rangers and so many people. There was no pressure so I was just sitting taking it all in.'

Despite not playing for the first team as the season drew to a close, Walker was selected as part of the party that embarked on a post-season world tour. Nine matches were played in Australia, Canada and the USA, with Nicky donning the gloves in five of them.

'Big Jock did that to try and help the boys get to know each other,' recalled Nicky. 'I was a wee boy from a wee village in the Highlands and all of a sudden I'm going with Glasgow Rangers around the world. After four weeks, for some of the married boys with families it was a long time to be away, but for single lads like me it was paradise!'

He continued, 'We flew from Glasgow to London, London to Oman in the Middle East then on to three or four stops in Australia, the likes of Brisbane, Melbourne, Sydney and Adelaide. We then went to New Zealand, Hawaii, Los Angeles, Denver, Toronto then back to London and home.'

Travelling across the globe or otherwise, the traditions of the club still had to be respected. Collar and tie in the airport were a must and Walker fondly remembers what happened once on board the aircraft. He said, 'Big Jock insisted as we were representing the club we had to be in collar and tie when going through the airport but once we got on the plane we could change. So once on board we had about 20 guys – including big Peter at 6ft 5in and big Slim [Dave McPherson] at 6ft 2in – trying to get in to the toilet to change then going back in again to get the collar and tie on before we landed!'

Walker must have impressed on the tour as it appeared at the outset of season 1984/85 he had won the battle for the number one jersey. After playing in all the pre-season matches, including a 2-2 draw against former club Leicester City, Nicky was selected in the team in each of the opening six Premier Division matches. He kept five clean sheets in those games, shutting out St Mirren, Celtic, Dundee, Hibernian and Aberdeen. However, a dreadful evening in Dublin on 18 September 1984 brought the stellar start to Nicky's season to a shuddering halt.

'That was a disaster,' was Walker's rueful recollection. 'I felt I was settling in the side and was building a decent rapport with Craig Paterson and big Slim so I felt quite comfortable. We went out to Dublin and it was just a poisonous atmosphere. The gaffer told us that there would be some trouble. The first half was okay, a lot of crowd noise, but it all flared up at half-time. We were in the dressing room and our subs [Iain Ferguson and Hugh Burns] came in and said it had all kicked off and the second half was really horrible.'

As goalkeeper, Walker found himself, literally, in the firing line.

'There was a 20-metre-high fence behind the goals to stop people throwing things but all they did was pick up things that had been thrown and threw them at me,' winced Walker. 'I spent most of the time about 20-30 yards from my goal line, five to ten yards outside my box. There was stuff like bricks and boulders, bits of masonry, bits of terracing. At one point I was standing on the penalty spot and something came past my face. I looked down and it was a dart. They were chucking all sorts so when they got a corner I spoke to the ref and he could only say "what the hell can I do?"'

Understandably under such a barrage Nicky did not have the best of performances that night.

'I didn't cover myself in glory,' said Walker. 'For one of the goals I rolled the ball out to big Craigy [Paterson] but he had turned away and never saw it. He reacted at the last minute but the boy took it off him and scored. I didn't have a great game so when we came back the gaffer said he was leaving me out. I respected his decision as I knew myself I hadn't played well. That was probably the first time I had been dropped in my career which was hard to take, as I missed the next series of games which included the return leg against Bohemians, the double-header with Inter Milan, the League Cup semi-final and the League Cup Final against Dundee United.'

Walker was relegated to the reserves and his time in the second team was not without incident. He sustained a bad leg injury in a home match against Celtic Reserves, bravely completing a match that took place on the same day as the League Cup Final and ended in a 1-0 defeat. That injury counted him out of reserve matches against Dundee and Hibernian and when Walker returned to action, he was joined in the second string by one of his closest friends in the dressing room, Ally McCoist. Late goals from Paterson and Redford had seen off Bohemians in the UEFA Cup and Rangers drew Inter Milan in the second round. The first leg in Milan had ended in a 3-0 defeat but McCoist had spurned a golden chance to score a crucial away goal and that, allied to a somewhat barren start to the season, resulted in a spell in the second team.

'We got a real pasting in the San Siro, one of the biggest doings I've seen a Rangers team get,' said Walker. 'Coisty missed a chance for us and ended up having a spell in the reserves too. It was all part of learning what it meant to be a Rangers player and what the expectation was. With the likes of Coisty, Ally Dawson and Iain Ferguson, we had a great bunch of guys, living in and around Glasgow, socialising and playing together for Glasgow Rangers. It doesn't get much better!'

He continued, 'Back in those days Coisty wasn't the megastar he ended up being, he was having a hard time. He always had a glint in his eye, though, and was a really nice chap who was always up to pranks.'

Nicky was eventually reinstated to the first team on 19 January when Rangers faced league leaders Aberdeen at Pittodrie. However, it was an afternoon to forget for those of a light blue hue as Frank

McDougall scored four times in a comprehensive 5-1 win for the home side.

'In those days Dundee United and Aberdeen were really good teams,' said Walker. 'Celtic were okay and we were okay. Pittodrie and Tannadice were very hard places to go but Jock stuck me back in. One of McDougall's goals was a near-post header and I think Tommy McQueen scored a penalty. We didn't play particularly well but by that time of the year we were never really contending for the league. We had started really well because we came back from the world tour and we were all buzzing. The tour caught up with us by Christmas time, though, and we felt absolutely done in.'

Appearances for the first team between then and the end of the season were sporadic for Nicky. He played in seven of the last 12 league games; Rangers only won four of those 12 games in a meek finish to the season. Walker also played in a 3-3 draw against Morton in the Scottish Cup at a snow-bound Cappielow. Such were the treacherous underfoot conditions, Rangers considered lodging a protest but they progressed to the next round, winning the replay 3-1.

'They wouldn't even consider playing that game nowadays,' said Walker. 'Dougie Robertson, who used to play for Rangers, scored a couple of goals. It was like playing on concrete and we didn't have all the fancy footwear they have nowadays; you had your studs or your trainers. It was an awful game and that's when big Slim got the nickname "Bambi" as he was sliding about on the ice.'

Season 1985/86 proved to be Nicky Walker's breakthrough year. At the age of 23 he finally claimed the number one jersey, missing only two of the 36 Premier Division matches. He was an ever-present in the Scottish Cup, League Cup and UEFA Cup too. However, this would prove to be a season of change at Ibrox. League form was wretched, Hearts eliminated Rangers at the first hurdle in the Scottish Cup and Hibernian won the Skol League Cup semi-final 2-1 on aggregate. Matters came to a head on 6 April 1986 when Tottenham Hotspur came to Ibrox for a friendly.

'The two league games I missed, I was due to go for an operation on my pelvis,' recalled Walker. 'We didn't have a great season by

Rangers standards, we were very workmanlike, and the gaffer decided I would go for the operation to allow me to recuperate over the summer to go again the following season. I played the first half of the Tottenham match and I was going for the operation after that. I remember the game as I played against Ray Clemence, who was my hero growing up, and [assistant manager] Alex Totten had heard about this and arranged for me to have my photograph taken with Ray, which was a really nice touch.'

Come the revolution, though, all plans were ripped asunder. A few days after the Tottenham match Wallace was dismissed, Graeme Souness arrived and the transformation at Ibrox was immediate.

'Jock was unbelievable, just a fantastic fella,' said Walker. 'Back in those days there were motivators and tacticians but there were none better at man-management than big Jock. He knew how to get the best out of his players. I'm still in touch with his son, John, who is the same age as me.'

In those days there was not the same media frenzy around the game as there is now. The players found out about the shift in power at Ibrox through word of mouth.

'Ally Dawson phoned me and told me the gaffer had gone and Souness had got the job,' said Nicky. 'I couldn't believe it but the reporter Doug Baillie, who I knew through his connections with Rangers and his son Lex who played for Celtic, phoned later that night to confirm and that's when I knew it had happened. It was a big shock for everyone.'

The Souness era started with silverware. Six days after clinching the Premier Division title, Celtic arrived at Ibrox for the Glasgow Cup Final intent on capping a miserable season for their Old Firm rivals. Walker wore the number one jersey in front of a full house at Ibrox and watched his buddy Ally McCoist net a match-winning hat-trick.

'That was the best, or loudest, atmosphere at any game I've played at in my life,' recalled Walker. 'I came in after the game and my ears were actually ringing because of the noise. It was a great game and the atmosphere was the best ever, helped, of course, because we won.'

He continued, 'I didn't think I'd be playing. Big Peter had played in the first game [at St Mirren] when Walter Smith picked the team but I was picked and it was great to get a winners' medal. But the writing was on the wall for me.'

The close season was an exciting time for Rangers fans as Souness set about the task of rebuilding the playing squad. Amongst the new recruits was England international goalkeeper Chris Woods, who arrived from Norwich City for £600,000.

'Souness basically came in wielding a sword,' recalled Walker. 'One of the first players he signed was big Woodsie [Chris Woods]. I was on holiday in Spain with my mates and in those days you got the paper a day late. I went and got the paper and read that we had signed Chris and thought that confirmed I wouldn't be getting a game the following season. Rumour was Souness had sent someone to watch us towards the end of 85/86; I think it was against Clydebank when we lost 2-1, and the advice he got was that other than Cooper and Durrant, the rest should be shown the door.'

In what proved to be a Championship-winning season for Rangers, Walker made just two appearances in the league. Supplanting Woods was an impossible task. The genial Englishman went 1,196 minutes without conceding a goal between November 1986 and January 1987 and the only action Walker saw was in a 2-0 win over Motherwell in September and a 4-0 win over Clydebank a week later, deputising when Woods injured his back. He had to bide his time in the reserves and was even given the responsibility of captaining the second team. It was a reserve side that boasted a defence that would not have been out of place as a first XI for most other Premier Division sides. In front of Walker were the likes of Hugh Burns, Craig Paterson, Stuart Beattie and Colin Miller, a quartet that collectively boasted over 100 first-team appearances for Rangers.

'I'd love to say something bad about Woodsie but I can't,' said Walker. 'He was a very good goalkeeper. We came back for pre-season and played in Paul Miller's testimonial against Tottenham and after the game Souness said I had had a good game. It was one of the few times he actually spoke to me. He didn't have very much time for the guys that had been there originally.'

The lack of top team game time eventually saw a loan deal set up in January 1987, with Nicky joining Falkirk.

'I was one of the only guys who knew he wouldn't be playing, which I found hard, to be honest,' said Walker. 'I thought I should have been playing but then I watched Woodsie and realised that I was a bit short [of his standard]. I had three years left on my contract when Souness arrived and his advice was to watch Woodsie and learn, as you never knew what could happen.'

He continues, 'There was talk of a move to Chelsea – myself and Derek Ferguson were supposed to be going as part of a swap deal for Tony Dorigo – but that fell through, as did a move to Tottenham. I was delighted that a club of that stature had come in and big Peter [McCloy], who was taking our reserve team to Queen of the South, asked me on the bus if the manager had called. When I said he hadn't he said I had to call Tottenham's chief scout, Ted Buxton, that night about a move. I did as Peter asked and called Mr Buxton but he told me I had missed Terry Venables, the manager, as he was travelling to Liverpool to do the commentary on the Merseyside derby. He asked me to call back the following evening to make arrangements but when I did, I was given an apology and told that they had decided to sign Bobby Mimms from Everton instead. I was gutted.'

Eventually the best course of action for Walker was to seek a temporary move away to play regular first-team football. In January 1987 he secured such a move, joining Premier Division strugglers, Falkirk.

'It was inevitable I was going to be leaving at some stage so I went to Falkirk on loan for about a month and really enjoyed it,' said Walker. 'They had a good bunch of guys and although we lost most of the matches I played, I had plenty to do and I felt I acquitted myself well.'

It was much the same in 1987/88. Another loan deal was struck in January 1988, this time with Dunfermline Athletic, but it was cut short after just one match. Woods fractured his ribs in a 2-0 defeat at Parkhead so Nicky was recalled to Ibrox.

'I went to Dunfermline for a month but Woodsie got injured,' recalled Walker. 'The only game I played was against Dundee. I got a phone call on the Sunday to tell me I needed to get back to Ibrox as I would be playing midweek for Rangers back at Dens Park against Dundee.'

Walker started four successive league matches to add to his only other appearance that season. This had come in October against Aberdeen at Hampden.

'In those days when the first team played at Ibrox the reserves would play away so I was playing for the reserves at Parkhead but I got injured,' said Nicky. 'It was my knee but I was told I needed to get it sorted as Woodsie had just been sent off at Ibrox so I'd be playing in the cup final next week! I didn't train but when Souness asked if I'd be fit I said I was. I should have said no but you might never get a chance like that again so I said I was okay.'

The final was among the most memorable in the history of the competition. Rangers took the trophy by edging a nerve-shredding penalty shoot-out after an epic 3-3 draw. One of the stand-out moments, though, was a stunning free kick from Davie Cooper.

'I still remember the noise when the ball hit the net, just unbelievable,' recalled Nicky. 'Wee Durranty was amazing in that game, absolutely brilliant. I had mixed emotions. For the first goal I gave away a penalty but, to this day [I swear], Willie Falconer stood on my hand and went down. That wasn't a great start to a cup final!'

A further league appearance followed in a 1-1 draw with Hibernian at Ibrox in April to take Walker's tally of first-team appearances to six. He would enjoy more game time in season 1988/89, though. Woods was struck down by labyrinthitis in November and Walker took the gloves for 12 successive league matches, including the 4-1 win over Celtic in January.

'I came in and played 12 games and played okay,' said Walker. 'I was under a lot of pressure because no matter what I did or didn't do I knew I wouldn't be playing [when Woods was fit again]. I had some good games and some bad games but I remember the one at Tannadice. There was a long punt and it hit Gary Stevens on the shoulder and went past me. I got caned but I didn't think it was my fault. There was a similar incident at Tynecastle when I shouted for big Butch [Terry Butcher] to leave it and Fergie [Iain Ferguson] tapped it in.'

Season 1988/89 was Nicky Walker's last in a Rangers jersey. With his contract expiring, he signed for Hearts on 23 August 1989.

'It came to the summer and after my run of games I didn't think Mr Souness was that enamoured with me,' said Nicky. 'However, he offered me a new two-year contract and he expected me to sign it. I said no. I told him I loved Glasgow Rangers and would love to be here for the rest of my career but I wasn't going to get a game. I told him if I couldn't find another club I'd chuck it and go and work with my dad [in the family business].'

He continued, 'My last involvement with Rangers was the Scottish Cup Final. I had said to my wee brother to come down to the game. I knew I wouldn't be in the squad, goalkeepers weren't on the bench in those days, but told him we would go back to Ibrox after the game and have a party. But we got beat 1-0 and I had never experienced it before, it was strange. My overriding memory from that day was the canteen staff, who I got on really well with, and they presented me with a colour team photograph and I left Ibrox with that tucked under my arm. Apart from Masters games in the future, that was my last involvement for Rangers.'

The question now was, at the age of 26, where to go next. Nicky Walker elected to head down the M8 motorway to Edinburgh.

'I was supposed to go to Ipswich but that didn't happen so I was training by running round Strathclyde Park myself,' said Nicky. 'The season actually started and I still didn't have a club but, right out of the blue, wee Doddie [Alex MacDonald] phoned me and asked me if I wanted to come to Hearts. I went to meet him and thought he was a fantastic wee guy, straight as a die. He told me he had a decent goalie [Henry Smith] but that there was a place to be fought for.

'That was all I could ask for and was not the prospect I was facing at Ibrox. I knew a few of the guys there from Rangers and the international teams like big Dave McPherson, Fergie [Iain Ferguson], Davie Kirkwood, Gary MacKay and wee Robbo [John Robertson]. For me it was an easy choice.'

Remarkably Walker did not make a league appearance for Hearts until 16 February 1991. His arrival galvanised Henry Smith and it was season 1992/93 before Nicky enjoyed a decent run in the team, playing 18 times in the league. He vied with Smith for the gloves again in season 1993/94, making 17 Premier Division appearances and also playing in the 2-1 defeat against Rangers in the Scottish Cup semi-final.

'The first year I went to Hearts, Henry was unbelievable,' recalled Walker. 'It was the first year of my senior career that I never played. I still ended up there five-and-a-half years but it was weird the first time I played against Rangers.'

Following a serious injury, Walker had a loan spell at Burnley in 1992 but his performances for Hearts eventually earned him international recognition, winning his first cap for Scotland against Germany at Ibrox on 24 March 1993. He would earn his second cap three years later in a warm-up match against the USA for the European Championships in England. He was one of three goalkeepers selected for the tournament itself but was not selected for the matches against the Netherlands, England and Switzerland.

'It was amazing to play for Scotland,' said Nicky. 'It was at Ibrox and I would have loved for it to be at Hampden but it was great it was at Ibrox. The Germans had a helluva team playing and we had a team with no Anglos [players playing in England]. We lost 1-0 in the salmon pink strip but the talk of the game was Duncan Ferguson's overhead kick. We held our own, though, and the German keeper, Andreas Kopke, had a great game.'

By the time Euro 96 came around, Walker was plying his trade on pastures new. He left Hearts in October 1994 to join Partick Thistle, with Craig Nelson leaving Firhill to move to Tynecastle.

'I was supposed to go to Portugal [in 1993] on the night Coisty broke his leg but I got injured so I pulled out,' said Walker. 'After that Henry got back in at Hearts so I went to Thistle and ended up back in the Scotland squad. I was on the bench for most of the qualifying games. I thoroughly enjoyed it, the whole Scotland thing, loved being involved, so proud for my family as much as anything. At Euro 96 I knew I was never going to get a game ahead of Andy Goram or Jim Leighton but I trained hard and loved it.'

Coming back from the Euros, Nicky spent a season with Aberdeen and then wound down his career in the Highlands with Inverness Caley and Ross County before retiring in the summer of 2004 at the age of 42.

'After Euro 96 my contract was up at Thistle but I was getting a house built back up north, my wife was pregnant with twins and my eldest son was due to start primary school,' said Walker. 'I'd had a good season at Thistle and there was a lot of interest in me. There was a Spanish club that tried to sign me, Dundee United were on the phone, Aberdeen were on the phone. I was ending my career but Aberdeen were persistent. Roy Aitken was the manager and I thought that Aberlour was only an hour from Aberdeen. I could train in the morning then go back and work [in the family business] in the afternoon. It was never a match made in heaven, though, but I signed a three-year deal. Ironically Jim Leighton was brought in after I had been there less than a year. I had sold a goal to Robbie Winters when we got beat 4-0 and Brian Laudrup also caught me off my line in a game at Pittodrie.'

He continued, 'I remember it like it was yesterday. There was a centre-half playing for Aberdeen called Toni Koumbaure. He was getting towards the end of his career but he couldn't run, so he kept pushing up to the halfway line trying to play offside. I was trying to play as a sweeper-keeper which I was uncomfortable with. Rangers played the ball through to Laudrup and I've come out and reached the point of no return. I tried to slide tackle him but got nowhere near him so he skipped past me and I was saying "please miss it" but he just dinked it into the net and I got pelters.'

Walker was only part-time with Inverness and Ross County, splitting his time between football and the family shortbread business and he is still based in Aberlour today as production director.

'When I went to Ross County I had never played a game outside the top flight,' said Nicky. 'For my first game I met the bus at Aviemore and we played Dumbarton in December at Boghead. It was snow and ice and three men and their dog were there! It was certainly an eye-opener but I really enjoyed it and in my second year we won promotion from the Third Division.'

Nicky Walker made a total of 130 appearances for the Rangers first team. He kept 42 clean sheets (32.3%) and won a Skol League Cup winners' medal (1987/88) and two Glasgow Cup medals (1985/86 and 1986/87).

'I'm just a wee boy from a village in the Highlands so to be honoured to have played for Glasgow Rangers makes me and my family proud to this day,' recalled Nicky. 'The whole institution that is Glasgow Rangers was absolutely mind-boggling. I loved it. Regrets? That we didn't do better the season before Souness came, because things could have been different. Scottish Football wouldn't have been the same but Mr Wallace may have got a bit longer. That said Scottish Football needed a good kick up the arse and it got that!'

CASE FOR THE DEFENCE
THE DEFENDERS

The Larkhall Masher

Hugh Burns (1980–1987)

Hailing from the Rangers hotbed of Larkhall, one may have suspected that it would have been a dream come true for Hugh Burns when two Ibrox scouts approached his parents to say they were keen for him to sign schoolboy forms with Rangers. On the contrary, the then 13-year-old was initially disappointed.

'I was actually a Motherwell fan and my grandpa used to take me to Fir Park,' said Burns. 'We used to go across the Garrion Brig in the Wishaw bus and my mates used to shout "spot the loony" at me as I sat with my Motherwell scarf on! I was genuinely delighted then when Motherwell signed me on an 'S' form.' However, an administrative error meant that Burns was never registered as a Motherwell player and Rangers did not hesitate, snapping up the highly sought-after youngster on schoolboy forms in 1980.

Hugh recalled, 'The scouts approached my mum and dad at Loch Park, George Runciman and, I think, Ian Mason, and said they wanted to sign me as I hadn't officially been signed by Motherwell. I was devastated initially but then when I thought about it on the journey from Carluke back to Larkhall, it was a no-brainer. I went through to Ibrox soon after and signed the 'S' form with Davie Provan who was chief scout at the time. He was a real unsung hero for the amount of players that he brought through: me, Fergie [Derek Ferguson], Durranty [Ian Durrant], Fleckie [Robert Fleck], Kenny Black, Andy Kennedy, Billy Davies and Davie McPherson, we all became first-team players.'

Burns soon realised that there were no airs and graces at Ibrox in that era. Although overawed to be in the presence of John Greig, he recalled that the manager treated the young players in the same manner as he would the experienced first-team regulars like Jardine, Johnstone and MacDonald. He was soon working hard in and around the stadium too and making an impression.

'Just going in the front doors in the morning was great,' recalled Hugh. 'As an 'S' form you would be in during the summer holidays doing the boots and stuff like that. You wouldn't be in every day but you would train at night on the ash park at The Albion under the lights. At that time the boys that they had high expectations for were asked in and I was fortunate enough to be in that category.'

The set-up for youngsters like Burns in those days was very much different to what it is today. There was no youth team and instead youngsters were farmed out to boys' clubs to get valuable game time. 'Initially I played for Gartcosh United who had players that were all 'S' forms at different clubs,' said Hugh. 'They had a fantastic set-up. They were one of the best in the country and I was up against the likes of Peter Grant when we faced Celtic Boys Club. As you can imagine I took a bit of stick when we went there as they knew I was an 'S' Form with Rangers!'

Burns would train one night a week with Gartcosh and play on a Saturday and spend another night at The Albion. He was lucky that a Rangers legend was on hand to ferry him to and from training.

'Tommy McLean lived near me then and he looked after me,' said Burns. 'He eventually moved onto the coaching staff and he used to get me on a Tuesday and take me in to training. My school teacher used to let me away early because he knew I was going to train at Ibrox. There was no favouritism from Tommy – I would get it tight off him if I wasn't doing things right – but he would give me wee pointers as we drove to and from training. He obviously saw something in me and would tell me that "they [the first-team staff] are telling me this about you" so I was on the radar and that advice was a massive help for my career.'

Despite misgivings about signing for Rangers, Hugh Burns was now forging a path towards a full-time contract at Ibrox. He was in the presence of greatness on a daily basis and he cemented his reputation as a promising youngster when he was part of a strong side that won the prestigious Croix tournament in 1981, beating Dynamo Kiev 8-7 on penalties in the final. Travelling to northern France with Burns for what was the 25th anniversary of the youth competition were: Gordon Marshall, Alan Pirie, Billy Davies, Dave McPherson, David Scott, Andy Kennedy, Derek McFarlane, Eric Ferguson, Gordon Brown, George McNeil, Gordon Sutherland, Andy Bruce, Kenny Black, Kenny Lyall and Dougie Robertson. From that squad only Messrs Pirie, Scott, Brown, McNeil and Sutherland failed to make the step up to the first team.

Manager John Greig, who had made it his mission early in his tenure to redevelop the youth system at Ibrox, went with the squad too as did his assistant, the legendary Willie Thornton, or Mr Thornton as Hugh refers to him. 'The hairs on the back of your neck stood up when you talked to him,' recalled Burns. 'He was a legend of the club, yet he was so down to earth and he loved being in with the kids. I had him doing The Birdie Dance after one of the games which was brilliant!'

At the age of 17 Burns broke into the reserve team after playing in the junior ranks. An initial stint at Benburb, whose Tinto Park ground is within a stone's throw of Ibrox, was cut short. Alistair Marshall was the resident right-back at the time. He had been capped for Scotland so with opportunities limited for the 16-year-old, Rangers instead sent him to play for Cambuslang Rangers. 'I went to Sommerville Park and played under a really good manager called Davie McCulloch, who played middle of the park for Ayr United,' said Burns. 'He brought me on and I had a brilliant year at Cambuslang, learning my craft there.'

As season 1983/84 dawned Burns was happy to continue learning his trade in the reserve team. Indeed, when the first-team squad photograph was taken in August, Hugh was not included. In October 1983, though, it was all change. John Greig resigned and Jock Wallace took over in the Ibrox hot seat.

'The first day Jock came in he was, as always, immaculate,' recalled Burns. 'He wore a grey suit and a Rangers tie and he went out of his way to speak to the ground staff. We knew what Jock had done for the club previously but from day one he would talk to you the way he spoke to Coop, Derek Parlane, John MacDonald, Sandy Jardine, everyone was spoken to in the same manner. He looked after you. I used to cramp a lot so Jock used to phone my mum on a Friday night to make sure I had taken my salt tablets.'

Burns was prominent in the reserve team's stunning start to the 1983/84 season, making 11 appearances and scoring once (against Motherwell on 10 December) as the second string won their first 18 league fixtures. He represented his country too, playing for Scotland's U18s in front of 40,000 in Mainz as the Scots drew 1-1 with West Germany. However, although he had been playing consistently well as Christmas 1983 approached, he did not expect to receive the present he did. After starting the 6-0 friendly win over Ross County on the day of his 18th birthday, Burns was included in the matchday squad for the trip to Edinburgh to face Hibernian two days after Christmas Day.

'At that time the team was put up in the home dressing room where the first team changed,' said Burns. 'I was in the away dressing room and Fleckie [Robert Fleck] came in and said I'd better go and check the team sheet as I was on it. I thought he was kidding but I had played well at Ross County on my debut and I had felt comfortable. It was an honour for a Larkhall boy to be travelling up there on the bus.

'When I saw my name on the team sheet I felt like jelly. You just keep staring at this bit of paper with the Rangers Football Club heading that Laura [Tarbert, the manager's secretary] had typed up and you ask "is that actually me, is there another Burns?"'

Rangers won 2-0 at Easter Road and Burns came on for Sandy Clark after 68 minutes. He said, 'There was a massive crowd [20,820] that day. I remember the enclosure was full of guys I went to school with and it was a brilliant experience.'

Burns appeared as sub the following weekend too, his home debut, in a 1-1 draw with St Mirren, and although a return to the reserves followed, he was now part of the first-team picture. If his confidence was on the rise then it received a further boost when Jock

Wallace announced in January that he expected Burns to be pushing for a place in the first team before the end of the season.

Included in that run in the reserves was a second goal of the season for Burns, Rangers' eighth in an 8-0 demolition of Dundee at Ibrox on 10 March, and just a fortnight later he was back in the first team. On this occasion he would not be playing in the Premier Division, instead he would be gracing the turf at the National Stadium as he was selected in the 13 for the League Cup Final against Celtic. Burns had appeared as sub in the second leg of the semi-final against Dundee United but he could scarcely have believed that just a month later he would take on a similar role in the final.

However, a week prior to the Old Firm showdown, Ian Redford and Robert Prytz had been ordered off in a tempestuous Scottish Cup replay defeat against Dundee which left Jock Wallace short in midfield and Hugh got the call.

'I was selected as part of a first-team squad of about 17 or 18 players that went to Turnberry before the final,' said Burns. 'I never thought for a minute I would be part of the 13. Derek Ferguson was there too and I thought he was still ahead of me at that time. I still maintain, though, I made the 13 because I trained really hard. We drove down to Troon and trained at Portland Park and because I showed the gaffer I was delighted to be there and had a willingness to be involved, I got picked. He simply said in his normal authoritative manner in the Hampden dressing room "12 McAdam, 14 Burns". I couldn't believe it and couldn't get my top on quick enough!'

With Rangers leading a fairly evenly contested final 1-0, Burns was called upon to replace John MacDonald early in the second half. His arrival prompted a tactical change, with Ally McCoist moving up front alongside Sandy Clark and Hugh taking up position in midfield.

'I came on and the gaffer told me to go and express myself,' recalled Hugh. 'I never felt nervous going on and Coisty then got himself on the end of a long ball and made it 2-0. But you're never home and hosed and Celtic scored two late goals to take it to extra time. The rest is history as in extra time Coisty got his hat-trick and we won 3-2.'

The celebrations that followed were memorable. Burns was in dreamland and as he walked round the pitch on the lap of honour he was intent on gathering as many Rangers scarves as he could. He recalled, 'I remember grabbing Jimmy Nicholl as soon as the final whistle went. I then went and got Coop who I had a special bond with.'

The mercurial Cooper lived in Motherwell and, as he did not drive at the time, Burns used to drive him to training each morning. Having had Tommy McLean for company in the fledgling days of his career, here was an 18-year-old Hugh being asked by the club's star player for a lift to Ibrox. 'After the game Coop said to me, "right Mash" – I was the Larkhall Masher – "Christine [Cooper's partner] is taking us up the road,"' said Burns. 'Coop didn't really mix then so we went back to the ground, the gaffer said a few words, we sang some songs then headed back to Larkhall. With my winners' medal in my inside pocket I went into the pub I drank in at the time and got a standing ovation from the full pub.'

Burns was living the dream and retained his place on the bench for the next two Premier Division matches, both of which were significant. He scored his first top-team goal against Motherwell at Fir Park six days after the League Cup triumph and a week later, he replaced Davie Cooper in a 3-0 defeat against Celtic, a result which ended Rangers' 15 match unbeaten run in the league.

Thereafter Burns went back to the reserves and by the season's end had made 22 appearances for the second string, helping them to retain the Premier Reserve League title. A seventh and final substitute appearance followed for the first team in the final league match at Tannadice and Burns looked all set for a trip to Russia to represent his country. Scotland U18s had beaten Wales 8-2 on aggregate in March to seal qualification for the European Youth Championships, due to be held between 25 May and 3 June. However, whilst he would be on his travels between those dates, it would be on a round-the-world trip with the Rangers first team.

'Jock took me up the stairs to his office and asked me where I'd rather be, in Russia with Scotland or on the world tour with the first team,' said Burns. 'It was a big choice for me and I said I would rather be with Rangers. Had I done that now I'd have been slaughtered in the press and although the gaffer said there were no guarantees I'd be going, I chose my club over my country.'

Prior to the tour, Burns had predominantly played in midfield for the first team. In the matches played in Australia, Canada and the USA, though, he was selected in his preferred role of right full-back. He missed only two of the nine matches and scored the second goal in Rangers' 4-2 win over Australia B in Newcastle.

'I had played at right-back in the Croix tournament but Davie MacKinnon was in that position at the time,' said Burns. 'I was comfortable playing there, though, and I liked that I could see everything in front of me. I was flying at that time and playing well and big Jock spoke to me after a game in Newcastle and told me he wanted my first international cap. I'll never forget that. I still think about the world tour today and what an unforgettable experience it was.'

Burns was hailed as the find of the tour. He was a marauding full-back, really good at going forward – a 1980s James Tavernier perhaps – but was sometimes found wanting defensively. 'I had ability and I was good on the ball but I used to get turned a lot,' said Burns. 'I got a reputation for being solid and wholehearted but I liked to whip the ball in like Coop did and I learned a lot training with him.'

Although still only 18, Burns continued at right-back when the team returned for pre-season friendlies in West Germany and also the opening two league matches against St Mirren and Dumbarton. Memories of pre-season training in 1984 were painful, though.

'We went through to Gullane on the bus in collar and tie, no facilities there, got changed on the bus, then I saw the hill,' said Burns. 'My first thought was "you're having a f*****g laugh."

'I used to struggle on the sand because of my big legs. I got to the top where big Jock stood and I was in tears, telling him I was going to be sick. He told me to "feed the f*****g seagulls" as once we started the run we weren't allowed to stop. We got breaks but we were there for about two hours.'

This pre-season event only happened once a year but the players would feel the benefits of it as the season progressed. However, the burgeoning Rangers career of Hugh Burns stalled somewhat at that time. After replacing Bobby Russell in a 0-0 draw with Celtic at Ibrox on 25 August, Burns did not play for the first team in the Premier League again until a 1-1 draw against the same opposition on 22 December.

When he returned to the team Rangers were handily placed in the title race. Only two defeats in the first 18 league matches placed them third, eight points behind leaders Aberdeen at the halfway stage. However, a lacklustre second half of the season – Wallace's men lost nine of their last 18 matches – saw Rangers finish fourth, a colossal 21 points adrift of champions Aberdeen. Burns appeared in 12 of those matches and was again a shining light amidst the gloom. His performances and maturity drew praise from his manager in the close season, with Wallace commenting in the *Playing for Rangers* annual:

> I expect him [Burns] to consolidate. He has matured a lot. He had a great tour in Australia and then he was outstanding in the U21 international [for Scotland] in Spain. But, to be honest, he lost his way a little bit last year, the way a lot of young players do. We had to work on him and be very firm with him and make him into a better professional. He has to be more disciplined but he has shown, particularly towards the end of the season, that he can play for the first team.

Burns wore the number two jersey in each of Rangers' four pre-season fixtures ahead of season 1985/86, scoring in the 5-1 win over Ross County in July. It was a jersey he would don for all but ten of the Premier Division matches in the season ahead. The campaign started superbly, with five wins in the opening seven matches placing Rangers at the top of the table ahead of the visit of champions Aberdeen to Ibrox on 28 September. Burns was magnificent in this spell. He scored two goals in Ibrox wins against Hearts (3-1) and St Mirren (3-0) and nutmegged Tommy Burns as he surged down the right wing to provide the assist for Ally McCoist's goal in the 1-1 draw against Celtic at Parkhead. He also provided a pinpoint delivery for Craig Paterson to score the only goal of the game at Ibrox against Osasuna in the UEFA Cup on a night when the Ibrox turf resembled a swimming pool. The latter match had earned Burns another three points in the race for the Rangers Player of the Year award too, with his tally of 16 points being ten better than second-placed Nicky Walker.

Indeed, his form was so good that Burns was being touted for a call-up to the Scotland squad. However, the splendid start to the season for both Rangers and Hugh Burns was derailed in that September meeting with Aberdeen. In the early 1980s there was always a bit of 'needle' in matches against The Dons but this encounter was borderline barbaric. After a number of robust tackles, Burns saw red when he fouled John Hewitt.

'My thought at the time was that he was going past me but he wasn't getting far,' recalled Burns. 'I wasn't over the top of the ball but I've done him with quite a violent challenge, it was a lash. You could talk to referees in those days, they weren't governed by someone in the stand, and the likes of Brian McGinlay and the Hope brothers were a different class. If you were playing well they'd tell you. The referee that day, though, was George Smith, who it emerged later on was a Celtic fan. I thought I might have dodged the red and got a yellow as we were at home but I didn't.'

Craig Paterson soon joined Burns for an early bath and a pitch invasion followed. Calm was restored and the nine men eventually succumbed 3-0 and Rangers recorded a second successive home defeat in the league. Burns was automatically suspended for the next league match, a 3-0 win over Motherwell, and after returning to the team, he was then injured during a 2-1 defeat against St Mirren at Love Street. A miserable spell was rounded off when a booking in the final minute of a 3-2 defeat against Dundee in November meant he had accrued 11 penalty points and the SFA imposed a four-match ban.

Burns eventually returned to the first team on 4 January, ironically against Dundee. Thereafter he played the full 90 minutes in all bar one of the remaining 15 league matches. For good measure, he took his goals' tally for the season to three when he scored the equalising goal in a 1-1 draw against Aberdeen in February.

'Coop slipped me in and I was expecting the stand-side linesman to put his flag up for offside,' recalled Burns. 'I looked right across but he never flagged and I sclaffed it with my left foot beyond [Jim] Leighton. My goal against Hearts earlier in the season was better, though. I got the ball around the halfway line, worked a couple of one-twos and Coop put me in again and I scored past Henry Smith at the Copland Road end.'

However, before the season had reached its conclusion, it was all change at Ibrox. Jock Wallace, who had done so much for Hugh's career, was dismissed and Graeme Souness was appointed player-manager.

Burns had no reason to doubt that, aged 20, he would have a pivotal role in the new era. He said, 'I thought it would go on forever. I was flying, knew I was playing, I was doing everything right. I could even have gone to the World Cup in Mexico in 1986. Walter Smith told me that I could have gone but there were concerns over my fitness so big Goughie [Richard Gough] played right-back instead.'

However, the early signs did not bode well for Burns. Although he had been selected at right-back for the Glasgow Cup Final at the end of the 1985/86 season, providing the assist for the first of Ally McCoist's three goals, on the ten-day pre-season tour of West Germany, he started only one match – against Wurzburg Heidingsfeld. It was on that tour that Burns witnessed the beginning of the end of his Rangers career.

'We were all sitting playing games one night in what was a loft conversion in a house,' recalled Burns. 'I was sitting with Coop and Souness asked me to take part in one of the games. I didn't want to and told him I wasn't comfortable doing so and, just like flicking a light switch, everything changed. Souness was raging with me for not taking part and tore in to me in front of the rest of the players. I was angry and upset about it and went to see him the next morning. I wanted to go back home but Walter [Smith] told me Souness was having a sunbed and he advised me to stay with the team.'

Ally Dawson continued at right-back for the two friendlies on British shores against Tottenham Hotspur and Bayern Munich, with the latter match being Terry Butcher's first for Rangers.

'He was a gentleman and the best centre-half I've played with,' recalled Burns. 'Pound for pound he was the best signing Souness made. He really bought into the Rangers culture. At that time some of the players that came in from England would come across as if they really cared for the club but they didn't. Terry was different, though, and sometimes he'd come back with me to Larkhall and go to supporters' functions.'

Burns was brought on as substitute in the Bayern match, replacing Dawson, but once again he incurred the wrath of his new manager. 'At the end of the game Souness came in to the dressing room and, although it was a friendly, he was raging,' said Hugh. 'He booted one of those big Gatorade bottles and it spilled all over Donald Mackay's grey suit but no one laughed. Next thing I know the manager is over at me and shouting at me for defending badly during my time on the park.'

The front door at Ibrox seemed to be constantly revolving in those early days of the Souness era, with players coming and going. Hugh Burns remained initially, but when Souness signed the experienced Jimmy Nicholl from West Brom, he looked to have fallen down the pecking order for his coveted number two jersey. He spent much of the early part of the season in the reserve team and by November had played 13 times for the second string and scored eight goals. In that timeframe Burns had played just twice for the first team, at right-back in a 2-1 league win over Hamilton Academical on 23 August and a 0-0 draw against East Fife in the Skol League Cup four days later.

It later emerged that the incident in West Germany had blotted the Burns copybook but it was allegedly something Hugh had said at a supporters' function that had angered Souness too. 'I was at the top table and I was asked what I thought about Graeme Souness becoming my manager,' recalled Burns. 'I said I was delighted. The guy had an aura about him and I was looking forward to working with him. As I said, I was flying at the time and thought I would have a big part to play. I then said, tongue in cheek, that I was hopeful that we would now be allowed moustaches and beards as this was something big Jock didn't allow. The chairman, David Holmes, was at the table and reported this back to Souness who took that as me bad-mouthing him. I believe that comment was a major contributor to ending my Rangers career.'

By now Burns, among the top earners at the club, had suffered the indignity of being asked to leave the home dressing room where the first team changed and go to the away dressing room with the reserves. He played 14 of the opening 17 1986/87 Premier Reserve League games, scoring nine goals. Included in his goal haul were strikes against Hibernian, Dundee United, Aberdeen and Hearts, and although he played at right-back, Burns was the top scorer in the second team.

His form in the reserves was eventually recognised and he was brought back into the first-team fold when Hearts visited Ibrox on 29 November. 'When Souness told me I was playing, I was delighted and let out a roar when I got back to my car,' said Burns. 'We went to the Grosvenor Hotel on the Friday night and stayed over. Souness did that for all the home games. Big Jock would get us to come to Ibrox at 1.45 on a matchday but under Souness we went to the hotel, had dinner about 6.30 then played cards before our rooms were checked at 11pm.

He continued, 'I played really well against Hearts on the right-hand side of midfield in a 4-4-2. We won the game 3-0 and I got a standing ovation when I was subbed towards the end of the match. I was in the team again the following week when we beat St Mirren and Souness also picked me when we went to Easter Road to play Hibs.'

However, the run of three successive games proved a false dawn and that appearance in his coveted number two jersey at Easter Road on 6 December 1986 proved to be the 97th and final time Hugh Burns donned a Rangers first-team jersey.

'I was asked in to see the manager not long after the Hibs match and told that Bradford City wanted to sign me,' said Burns. 'I travelled down but I didn't want to sign for them. This also upset Souness as they were offering good money for me and terms had been agreed.'

A loan spell at Leeds United followed and this looked to be a more promising proposition. Burns had an affinity with the Elland Road side as his uncle had played for them. 'I knew my Rangers career was over so I went down to Leeds, played in four reserve games and did really well,' recalled Burns. 'John Sheridan was playing midfield for the first team and when we went out for a few beers he told me I was a much better player than the boy who was right-back then and I should be in the team. The fact that Billy Bremner was manager was another positive so I really wanted to sign. However, when I spoke to Billy he told me that Leeds couldn't afford what Souness wanted for me so I was back up the road again.'

Hugh returned to Scotland and ended up back in the Rangers reserve team. He featured in matches against Dundee United, Celtic, Hibernian, Falkirk and Aberdeen before eventually securing a loan move when the eccentric John Lambie took him to Hamilton in March 1987. 'It was a shock to the system,' said Burns. 'We used to train on the ash in the car park and the dressing room was really small. John Lambie was just like big Jock though, and Hamilton had a good team, with the likes of Gerry Collins, Gerry McCabe and John Brogan. I made my debut against Celtic at Douglas Park and although we lost 3-2, I played well.'

Burns made a total of five appearances during his loan spell, scoring once against Dundee United at Tannadice. However, with Hamilton unable to afford a permanent deal, Hugh was back at Ibrox where it soon emerged he was still surplus to requirements. Just a year earlier Burns had been on the verge of being on an aircraft bound for the World Cup in Mexico, yet here he was, a Rangers player in name only. Understandably he was disillusioned at the time and he admits he had started to fall out of love with the game. 'I wasn't training as hard as I should have but my agent, Bill McMurdo, phoned me up and said that Hearts were interested,' said Burns. 'They were doing well at the time so I decided that since I was finished at Rangers, I would go for it.'

Burns admitted he did not make the most of his time at Hearts. 'I later found out that Hearts didn't really want me,' said Burns. 'They were interested in big Slim [Dave McPherson] and Souness said he would only let Davie go if I was part of the deal. I had gone from being out of favour at Rangers to being second choice behind Walter Kidd at Hearts. I look back now and regret that I didn't kick on when

I was there. Davie improved as a player and Walter took him back to Ibrox a few years later and I often wonder if he would have done the same with me had I played well too.'

Burns found it difficult playing against Rangers too. He made his Hearts debut in a 0-0 draw against the Light Blues at Tynecastle on 3 October and took his place in the away dressing room at Ibrox for the first time as a visiting player eight weeks later. 'The first time was when Ray Wilkins made his Rangers debut,' recalled Burns. 'I got a great reception from the fans and we went ahead through Mike Galloway but eventually lost 3-2. It just didn't feel right, though, and I should have done what Peter Grant did when he left Celtic. He went down south as he knew he couldn't play against Celtic and I should have done the same by either going to Bradford or Leeds. Had I done that I may have kicked on and my career may have got back on track.'

Burns would last just over a year at Tynecastle. He made 24 Premier Division appearances in season 1987/88 but did not play at all for the first team in the opening gambit of the following season. He did make a scoring return to Ibrox, netting twice in a 3-2 win for his side in the Premier Reserve League in September 1988, but left Edinburgh soon after and turned into something of a nomad. Burns spent time at Dunfermline, Fulham, Hamilton (on a permanent deal this time), Kilmarnock, Ayr United and Dumbarton.

'Apart from Rangers the best time of my career was when I was at Ayr,' admitted Burns. 'George Burley signed me and I was made captain and I started to enjoy my football again.'

However, in 1996 Hugh Burns decided to call time on his professional career at the age of just 32. He had a spell with Larkhall Thistle and a stint as player-manager at Benburb but cut his ties with football completely soon after. 'I should have got my coaching badges as I think I'd have been a good manager,' said Burns, 'but I was done with the game then so decided to concentrate on my business interests and golf.'

Fast forward almost 20 years, though, and Hugh Burns is back in the game. Although he does not sign up for legends matches – a troublesome shoulder means he would rather not compromise his golf game by playing football again – he is now ingratiating himself with a new generation of Rangers fans as a co-commentator on Rangers TV.

'I really enjoy it,' said Burns. 'I'd far rather do Rangers TV than anything else as I'm a Rangers man and the club have been really good with me. I'm excited about the new era under Steven Gerrard and there is a more positive feeling about the place now than there has been for the past few years. I'm hoping to do some matchday hospitality in the future but for now I'm quite happy to work alongside Tom [Miller] and I still feel that surge of excitement when I come in through the front doors.'

For Hugh Burns, his Rangers career will always be a story of what might have been. As an integral part of the first team at 20, he should have carved out his own place in Rangers history over the next decade as the club enjoyed one of the most successful eras. Instead he was overlooked by a new manager and a promising football career was sadly compromised.

Hugh Burns made a total of 97 appearances for Rangers. He scored eight goals and won a Skol League Cup winners' medal (1983/84), a Reserve League Championship medal (1983/84) and a Glasgow Cup medal (1985/86).

Dozy

Ally Dawson (1975–1987)

In the spring of 1975, the Rangers family was a happy one. A bullet header from Colin Stein at Easter Road had brought the league title back to Ibrox for the first time in 11 years and, in the process, had prevented Celtic from winning ten-in-a-row. Alistair John Dawson had celebrated his 17th birthday just over a month before the glorious day in Edinburgh, yet within two months he was playing alongside luminaries like John Greig, Derek Johnstone and Tom Forsyth in the Rangers first team.

'It was a strange time,' recalled Dawson. 'I was just coming out of school and I was playing for the reserves and eventually signed full-time. School work unfortunately went downhill after that! I was very fortunate to go on tour with the first team to the likes of Australia and New Zealand. It was out of this world but the police had to get involved. At that time because I was under 18 years of age, the club needed to inform the police to get my parents' permission for me to leave the country. That was the first I knew about going on the tour when the police came to the door.'

Dawson made an impression on the tour. Following a good performance against British Columbia on 29 May 1975, he played in a further five matches, all in the left-back position. The trip also afforded him the opportunity to rub shoulders with his hero, Colin Stein.

'Colin Stein actually asked me one afternoon what I was doing and said to come out with him for a walk,' said Ally. 'Whether he was told to do it or did it off his own back, it didn't make any difference. For him to take me under his wing was great.'

He continued, 'The tour was fantastic. I didn't particularly like flying and there were some dodgy internal flights but we stopped off in places like Toronto and Vancouver as part of it. I think either John [Greig] or Alex Miller got injured so where I might have only got one or two games, I ended up getting four or five. Just to experience the whole buzz of everything going on, the antics of the players off the pitch, it gives you that insight into the lives that they have. Everyone looked after me and I never felt alone at any time.'

Three Premier Division appearances followed in the treble-winning 1975/76 season and a further four top-team matches over the next two seasons suggested Dawson had been identified as one for the future.

'I came to the club as a centre-back but ended up playing left-back after I had played there in a tournament over in France after someone got injured,' said Dawson. 'I was up against John Greig and Alex Miller as Willie Mathieson was coming to the end of his career and wasn't playing a lot. That gave me an opportunity. Jim Denny was another lad who could play centre-back or full-back. Looking back, that was probably a good way to do it [playing periodically] whether it was by design or through injuries. There were a few young boys around the same age group – Chris Robertson, Gordon Boyd and myself – trying to break through at the time. It was a learning curve but you could see the changes starting, certain players coming in and the older players moving out as they came to the end of their career.'

He continued, 'I had the likes of Davie Cooper or Willie Johnston in front of me and, in the reserves, there was the likes of Willie Mathieson, Dave Smith and either Peter McCloy or Stewart Kennedy. They had vast experience and you learned a lot from them. Johnny Hamilton was a great help too. It was a great mixture, a great balance and we got decent crowds for the reserve games since some of the supporters didn't want to go to the away grounds so went to Ibrox instead.'

In the summer of 1978 there was a changing of the guard. In a shock move Jock Wallace left Ibrox for Leicester City and John Greig took over the managerial reins. Dawson profited from the change, establishing himself as the first pick at left-back midway through season 1978/79. After sporting the number three jersey in a 0-0 draw against Aberdeen at Pittodrie on 18 November, Ally played the full 90 minutes in all but one of the remaining games the first team played. This run saw him collect his first winners' medal – a late Colin Jackson header securing the League Cup against Aberdeen – and make appearances in both legs of the European Cup quarter-final against Cologne.

'I used to come in to Ibrox about two or three weeks before we returned for pre-season training to do a bit of running and John was already in, although it wasn't official at the time,' said Dawson. 'Jock was probably the best man-manager I've worked with. He had a great knowledge on the park but he knew how to deal with things off the park and how to cope with it. He was the guy who had this bravado but he wasn't always like that, he was a father figure. He would bark at you if he needed to or he could put his arm around your shoulders. He had a knack of knowing when he needed to do that. John was different. He was cutting his teeth and it wasn't a normal thing to do at the time, take an ex-player and put him right into a management role. It nearly worked, as in his first season we could have won the Treble.'

Dawson added a Scottish Cup medal to his collection in May 1979, playing in all nine matches in the competition, including the marathon three-game final against Hibernian. However, the abiding memory from that campaign is of a fateful night at Parkhead in May when the dream of a double Treble died.

'The Aberdeen match was like a blur but the Hibs match went to two replays,' recalled Dawson. 'We needed extra time to win 3-2 in the second replay and after that it was decided the final would go to penalties. I don't remember a lot about the games but the biggest thing for me was the first touch, the first pass, the first tackle. I always felt if I could do something positive right away it would set the tone for the next part of the game.'

Ally continued, 'The Celtic match was a strange one. Johnny Doyle was sent off but Celtic won [4-2] and won the league. If we had got a draw, we had two games left [against Partick Thistle and Hibernian] where we could have won the league instead.'

A third winners' medal was earned when Dawson was part of the reserve team that beat Celtic 3-1 in the Glasgow Cup Final, but a wretched 1979/80 season followed. The team were perhaps still suffering a hangover from losing out on what, at that time, was an unprecedented back-to-back Treble. Dawson was again a mainstay in the team, playing in 32 of the 36 Premier Division matches and also featured in the infamous Scottish Cup Final which was lost 1-0 to Celtic.

The season was not completely barren, though, with Rangers winning the Drybrough Cup. The final against Celtic was memorable for two splendid goals, one from Ally's fellow full-back Sandy Jardine, and the other from the mercurial Davie Cooper.

'Sandy picked the ball up on the edge of our 18-yard box, ran about three-quarters of the length of the pitch and scored with his left foot,' said Dawson. 'The game is remembered for Davie's goal when he flicked the ball over and over then tucked it in the corner. That's what you could get from Davie. He had everything. I knew if I gave him the ball, he could keep it for a while. If I went by him [on an overlap] I wasn't sure if I would get it back or not.'

Dawson received recognition for his performances when he earned his first full Scotland cap in a friendly against Poland in Poznan. A second cap followed three days later in a 3-1 defeat against Hungary in Budapest. Ally would gain a further three caps for his country, against Northern Ireland at Hampden in the British Home Championships in May 1983 and twice against Canada a month later.

'I came on as sub against Poland and played the whole match against Hungary,' recalled Dawson with pride. 'I had been in a couple of squads and didn't get on but this was an incredible experience. There are defining points that you look back on with pride – family, marriage, kids – and playing for my country was up there alongside them for me.'

A post-season tour of Canada followed, with Ally patrolling his usual beat on the left-hand side of the Rangers defence in the opening match, a 3-3 draw against Nancy in Calgary in the Red Leaf Cup. However, when Rangers faced Italian side Ascoli in their next match in Toronto, Dawson suffered an injury that threatened to bring a premature end to his burgeoning playing career.

'I was looking forward to a good wee tour,' said Ally. 'I loved going away because you were going to different countries and playing against different opposition. We were over in Toronto, the Varsity Stadium; I played in the game and the next thing I know I'm in hospital. I couldn't tell you what happened but I've been told it was a cross-field ball from Tommy McLean, there was a clash of heads and that was it. I found out the following day I had a fractured skull and perforated eardrum. I didn't think about it at the time but it was career-threatening.'

However, within six months of sustaining the injury, Ally was back in the Rangers first team. After a couple of games in the reserves he donned the number three jersey for what proved an embarrassing 3-0 defeat against Chesterfield in the Anglo-Scottish Cup on 28 October 1980.

'I was probably the only one that didn't care about the score,' said Dawson. 'I couldn't train, couldn't do contact to begin with but eventually I got the all-clear from a hospital in Leeds. I remember once in the reserves at Airdrie, the ball came out the air, I went up to header it and did it without a problem. I didn't feel anything, didn't get dizzy so I knew I was fine. I didn't shirk out of anything and the only physical impact is that I've only got about 15-20% hearing in one ear.'

Rangers bounced back immediately from the Chesterfield humiliation, Dawson playing at left-back in an emphatic 3-0 win over Celtic four days later. He retained that berth in the team for the next 22 Premier Division matches and played in all Rangers' Scottish Cup ties too. The road to Hampden culminated in a final against Dundee United and it was there that Ally Dawson enjoyed the proudest moment of his Rangers career.

The first game at Hampden was turgid. It ended 0-0, although Rangers should have won it when they won a penalty in the last minute. Ian Redford missed from 12 yards but Rangers were rampant in the replay four days later. Cooper and Russell were immense, terrorising United from start to finish. The scoreline was the reverse of the one experienced in the Premier Division a few weeks earlier. And Ally, aged just 23, led his team up the stairs at Hampden to lift the Scottish Cup.

'One of the greatest achievements in my career was being captain and picking up the Scottish Cup,' recalled Dawson fondly. 'I was first made captain against Dundee United when they beat us 4-1 in the league a few weeks before the final. Sandy [Jardine] must have been a candidate and that would probably have been the easiest thing for John to do. I don't know why he picked me but, with Sandy coming to the end of his career, maybe he was looking at the longer term. I wasn't going to say no – it was the opportunity of a lifetime – and very rarely would you get a second chance. It was difficult, I was young, and there were a lot of senior players in the team. It had an effect to begin with as now you weren't just looking after yourself but having to encourage others in the team. It stood me in good stead, though, as when I went to Blackburn I was made club captain.'

Appearances were more sporadic for Dawson in 1981/82. In a stop-start season, he made 25 league appearances but missed the League Cup Final against Dundee United with a persistent pelvic injury. Competition at left-back had intensified, with the experienced Alex Miller and young Kenny Black deputising in Ally's absence. Indeed, towards the end of the season, Dawson showed his versatility by playing three league matches at right-back.

'The advantage of playing in so many positions – I had a spell in midfield too – was that you learned how other people played,' recalled Dawson. 'I was naturally right-sided but I could play on the left and I was comfortable at left-back. My left foot was okay but I worked hard on my left side, a lot more than what I would have had I played at right-back. I did a lot of crossing and finishing in training as I could cut in and have a shot at goal with my stronger foot. I felt it was a necessity to move around and play in other positions to understand how other players – team-mates and opposition – played.'

He continued, 'As a full-back I made sure I would defend first rather than look to support the likes of Cooper, Bobby Russell and

Ian Redford. I tended to tuck in and provide cover for the two centre-backs as Sandy was an attacking full-back. That meant if the move broke down you had three to beat. I would sometimes go on an overlap but Sandy would then cover for me.'

The next two seasons followed in a similar vein, with Dawson alternating between the full-back positions. As an example of his dexterity, he played right-back in the 1983 Scottish Cup Final against Aberdeen and left-back in the 1984 League Cup Final victory over Celtic. Rangers were struggling, though, and by the time they faced their Old Firm rivals, they were under new management.

'I was surprised and disappointed when John left,' said Dawson. 'I would have loved him to have stayed and been successful and I wondered if I had let him down. I don't think John had the right people around him. We had a team at that time that could win games, win a cup tie as was proven in the Scottish Cup and League Cup, but we never had consistency in the league over a long period of time. We brought in good players like Jim Bett but I don't think the team had the right balance. That and the fact crowds were starting to decline probably resulted in the board making the changes.'

Dawson remained a regular under Jock Wallace, adding another League Cup winners' medal to his collection when Dundee United were defeated 1-0 in the 1984/85 final. However, by now Craig Paterson had taken over the captaincy. Prior to Paterson, John McClelland had skippered the side to victory in the 1984 League Cup Final.

'I was still bothered by the pelvic injury so Jock told me that he was going to make John captain,' said Dawson. 'John was ideal. The crowd took to him straight away and moving out to full-back helped him.'

As season 1985/86 dawned, the preferred full-back pairing was Hugh Burns and Stuart Munro and Dawson had to wait until the October meeting with Motherwell for his first league start. He replaced the suspended Craig Paterson at centre-half after drawing praise from reserve-team coach John Haggart for his influence on youngsters like Stuart Beattie during his spell in the reserves.

'If I wasn't playing for the first team, I had no issue playing for the reserves,' said Dawson. 'No one has a right to play so the only way I knew I was going to get out of the reserves was to train hard and play well. I was only in my mid-to-late twenties but I could help and encourage the young ones that were breaking in at that time, like Stuart Beattie and Ian Durrant.'

His form in the second team must have been good as Dawson missed just one of the next 20 league matches. He played in all positions in the back four, including a run of games at sweeper when Wallace reverted to a back three. However, a booking in the 1-1 draw with Aberdeen in March took Dawson beyond the disciplinary points threshold, earning him a four-match ban. When Ally returned to action against St Mirren at Love Street on 19 April, it was all change in the visitors' dugout. Jock Wallace had been dismissed earlier in the month, with Graeme Souness recruited as player-manager and Walter Smith, who took charge in Paisley, as his assistant.

Dawson recalled, 'I was out at a dinner in Glasgow and Andy Cameron was compere and he talked about Graeme coming. That was the first we really heard about it. Graeme came in the next day and spoke to us and pulled me aside. I had suffered a displaced cheekbone and fractured jaw a few weeks prior so he asked how I was doing. We played in a closed-door game and I must have done okay as he told me, as I was experienced, he was making me captain until the end of the season.'

Dawson scored Rangers' goal in Paisley, one of 11 he scored in a blue jersey, but a 2-1 defeat saw Dundee leapfrog the Light Blues into fifth place in the ten-team Premier Division. Qualification for Europe now looked a forlorn hope but a draw at Pittodrie and a 2-0 win over Motherwell at Ibrox on the final day of the campaign ensured a UEFA Cup place for season 1986/87. Just six days later the season ended on a high when Dawson added a Glasgow Cup winners' medal to his collection when champions Celtic were beaten 3-2 at Ibrox.

'You can relate what was happening then to what's happening now [under Steven Gerrard],' said Dawson. 'Both looked at who was there, who wasn't there, who was going to be playing, who wasn't going to be playing. Graeme felt the players should have been of a better standard as he had been used to that. He demanded and expected everything from you and if you didn't do it you were moved aside. My contract was due up at the end of 1987 but I thought that now I was back in I was okay. However, I had a horrible pre-season and eventually Jimmy Nicholl came in at right-back.'

Prior to Nicholl's arrival Ally had been chosen ahead of Hugh Burns at right-back and was also appointed tour captain when the first team journeyed to West Germany in pre-season. He retained the number two jersey when the curtain was raised on the Premier Division season. All eyes were on Easter Road for the first competitive match of the Souness era and those eyes witnessed an explosive 90 minutes.

'My memories of the match are just the melee after Graeme Souness was sent off,' recalled Dawson. 'I was booked but I was just in the middle of it trying to pull people away. I turned round and Alan Rough was sitting against the post and he ended up the only one not booked as he was the only one not near the incident. I think the referee could have just given two or three cards out and that would have been it as the majority were, like me, trying to pull people apart.'

He continued, 'I didn't notice how bad Graeme's tackle actually was but when I went to Blackburn, Donald Mackay, who was on the coaching staff, told me he had told Graeme not to play in the game. He told him he was going to encounter a totally different game and to sit on the bench and come on. Graeme decided to play but Donald was proven right.'

When Jimmy Nicholl returned to the club it signalled the beginning of the end of Ally Dawson's season and, indeed, his Rangers career. Nicholl slotted in at right-back and with the other back-four berths claimed by Messrs Munro, McPherson and Butcher, even Ally's versatility could not get him more game time. Rangers won the league for the first time in nine years but Dawson featured in just seven league matches. The League Cup was also secured and Ally claimed his fifth winners' medal in the competition when he partnered Terry Butcher at centre-half in a 2-1 Hampden win over Celtic.

'I was frustrated not to be playing but Davie McPherson was suspended for the cup final so I played centre-back,' recalled Dawson. 'I just wanted to know that if I was going to be there [at Ibrox] that I would get a chance to play. I was offered a new contract but I wanted to know that, if I got in, I would stay in the team if I was playing well. I was told there would be no guarantees I would even get in, so I decided it was time to move.'

In August 1987 Ally Dawson's Rangers career was over. By then the second longest-serving player at Ibrox, he played in pre-season friendlies against Deveronvale, Inverness Thistle (scoring a penalty in a 3-3 draw) and Falkirk but left soon after to join Donald Mackay, at Blackburn Rovers.

'I had opportunities under Graeme but I probably didn't take them,' reflected Dawson. 'I would have loved to have stayed, I didn't want to go. Before going to Blackburn I had an opportunity to go to Switzerland. Robert Prytz's agent said he knew a club over there would take me if I could get away on a free [transfer]. I would have doubled my wages but Graeme refused as he wanted money for me.'

He continued, 'Donald had been in at Ibrox the previous year and took the reserves so I got to know him. Graeme told me that Donald wanted to take me down to Blackburn, what were my thoughts? As I wasn't going to get on at Rangers I decided if he was happy then I would go. We never fell out. Graeme was a single-minded person and he had his thoughts on what he wanted to do. It's probably the same as Steven Gerrard now.'

Rangers received £25,000 for Dawson and he swelled a Scottish colony at Ewood Park, joining the likes of Colin Hendry and Steve Archibald, who was on loan from Barcelona, in the first-team squad. At that time Rovers were in the old Second Division and at the end of season 1987/88 they narrowly missed out on promotion, losing to Chelsea in the play-off semi-finals. However, Dawson's time in Lancashire was blighted by injury – he partially ruptured his Achilles tendon – and after making 40 league appearances he left Blackburn at the end of season 1989/90.

A short stint with Limerick followed, then, after a trial with Motherwell, Ally joined Airdrie in September 1990, making his debut in a 4-0 win over Ayr United at Broomfield. Nine further appearances followed – his last was in January 1991 – as Airdrie finished runners-up in the First Division and won promotion to the Premier Division.

Dawson knew he could no longer cope with the rigours of top-flight football – he was now hampered by the injury sustained at Blackburn – so he went to Malta to play and coach for two years. He finished playing thereafter but his time on the island was made more special as he met his wife there. Between 1999 and 2002 he was manager of Hamilton Accies – under his stewardship they won the Third Division title in season 2001/02 – and thereafter he worked with Rangers as a community coach.

Ally's contribution to the Rangers cause was recognised in 2011 when he was inducted into the Club's Hall of Fame. Introduced by then chairman, Sir David Murray, in 2000, the Hall of Fame honours the contribution its inductees made to Rangers during their time at Ibrox, taking cognisance of the number of appearances, honours and international caps won and exceptional ability. His name is now embossed in gold alongside luminaries like Moses McNeil, Alan Morton, Willie Waddell, Jim Baxter, John Greig and Ally McCoist on a mahogany panel that sits above the famous marble staircase at Ibrox.

Dawson said, 'It was Sandy [Jardine] that phoned me up one day to tell me I had been inducted in to the Hall of Fame. It was a great honour. I was fortunate to lift the Scottish Cup as captain of the team I supported and not many people can say that. Playing for your country was fantastic but in my football career that was the highlight.'

Ally Dawson made 391 appearances for Rangers, scoring 11 goals. He picked up two Scottish Cup winners' medals (1978/79 and 1980/81), five League Cup winners' medals (1978/79, 1981/82, 1983/84 and 1986/87) and five Glasgow Cup medals (1978/79, 1983/84, 1984/85, 1985/86 and 1986/87).

Jimmy Nick
Jimmy Nicholl
(1983–1984, 1986–1989)

There were three teams James Michael Nicholl wanted to play for. In 1974 he signed for one of them, Manchester United, and two years later he played for the second, his country Northern Ireland, winning the first of 73 caps against Israel in a 1-1 draw. But it would be October 1983 before he completed the Treble, signing for Rangers on loan from Toronto Blizzard. The timing of his arrival was less than perfect, however.

'My contract with Toronto was all year round and there used to be indoor soccer but it got stopped,' said Nicholl in his beautiful Belfast brogue. 'That meant I could only play summer football for Toronto so I had to find myself a club in Britain for the winter if I wanted to keep playing for Northern Ireland. I was supposed to go to Burnley but I got a phone call from [former Rangers player] Iain Munro, who I'd played with at Sunderland. He told me John Greig had phoned him and asked if I would go to Rangers. Dundee United, Celtic and Aberdeen were winning everything and the crowds were down. That didn't bother me, though, I just wanted the opportunity to play for Rangers.'

He continued, 'I stayed at the Bellahouston Hotel across the road from Ibrox, signed with John on the Thursday night then he resigned on the Friday morning! I was kicking a ball about with the boys on the red ash when wee Tommy [McLean] came out and told us we had a meeting. We thought it was to discuss the game that weekend but John told us he was calling it a day.'

Thus, before Jimmy had even trained with his new team-mates there was a change at the helm. After making his debut on 29 October against St Mirren and making his Old Firm debut the following week under the caretaker charge of Tommy McLean, Nicholl met his new gaffer, the indomitable Jock Wallace. Wallace did not take long to preach to his new player about the traditions at Ibrox.

Nicholl recalled, 'The morning after I signed I went for breakfast in the hotel. There was a bloke at the table and he wished me luck at the Rangers. When big Jock arrived there was a meeting and he called me over. He told me I was the luckiest man in the world. I thought he meant being at Rangers so I told him I knew that. But he then told me I didn't know what I was talking about. He said that when I had come in that first morning for training I wasn't wearing a tie [a tradition at Ibrox at that time was to report for duty wearing a collar and tie]. Cardigans were the trend so I had one of them on with an open neck-shirt. I told him I didn't know that at the time but I did now. How did he find out? It was the boy in the restaurant at the hotel; it was Eric Caldow [a Rangers stalwart in the 50s and 60s].'

The return of Wallace had an immediate impact. After losing his first match against Aberdeen at Pittodrie, Rangers embarked on a 22-match unbeaten run in the league that lasted until April 1984. Crowds had been dwindling and unrest had grown among the supporters but Wallace's return brought a buoyancy about Ibrox that had been absent for a few years.

'After the Celtic game [which Rangers lost 2-1] big John McClelland came up to me and said I had to go with him,' recalled Nicholl. 'I asked him where we were going as I was just going across the road to the hotel. He told me I couldn't go through the front door and when I asked why he said I'd get strung up. He took me down corridors and tunnels and outside so we avoided the supporters. The team weren't doing well so the fans were angry.'

Nicholl played a significant role in the unbeaten run, playing at right-back, and he thrived under Wallace's guidance.

'After the first meeting you knew what he was going to demand of you and how he was going to be,' said Nicholl. 'He was brilliant. At the end of the meeting, Davie Cooper said that the big man was quieter this time around so he must have been mental the first time, because after he spoke to us I was pumped to the eyeballs.'

He instilled discipline in the squad too and Nicholl recalled one incident in the dressing room that illustrated the standards that Wallace had.

Pointing to the facial hair I was sporting when we met, Nicholl said, 'You wouldn't get away with that. Jock used to come in and rub his fist into your face and tell you that you hadn't shaved close enough and that it would need to be closer the next day. When you left the front door to go to The Albion your socks had to be up and you weren't allowed to walk, you had to jog. It was discipline like that that made me a better player and made us a better team. Billy Bingham did the same thing when he took over with Northern Ireland. It's sadly lacking at clubs today but I enjoyed it as you had to shape up and sort things out. If you couldn't put up with the demands that Jock put on you there was no room for you. He had good football men with him too like Alex Totten and Stan Anderson.'

With Rangers back on the rails, Wallace took his side to Easter Road two days after Christmas in 1983 to face Hibernian. Rangers won 2-0 and Nicky Walker, Hugh Burns and Bobby Williamson made their debuts. But it was a less memorable day for Nicholl who earned himself not just one but TWO red cards.

'I clashed with their left-back and the referee that sent me off was Allan Ferguson,' recalled Nicholl who was laughing heartily as he recounted the story. 'In those days you used to get the referee's profile in the programme and Allan Ferguson was from Giffnock and sold women's lingerie. He used to wear a gold bracelet, gold chain and a big sovereign too. Unbeknown to me and big Jock there was a new rule that had been brought out. If you got sent off and then did something else while you were still on the park that was a sending-off offence, you could get a second red card. Well, when I got sent off I turned round to the referee and told him to go away and sell his women's knickers, bras, thongs, negligees; I must have mentioned every type of women's underwear. But big Jock came to me during the week and said I would be missing two games as I had been sent off twice. The second red had been for the abuse I gave the referee!'

Nicholl ended up with double doses of training as his penance but he was back in the team in the New Year. And he was selected at right-back for the season's first major showpiece, the League Cup Final against Celtic on 25 March 1984.

'Occasions like that were the reason why I had come to Rangers,' recalled Nicholl. 'I was 26 years of age and I thought I could handle it. But I got so wrapped up in the fear of losing that I didn't play my natural game. You might look calm on the outside but you're nervous on the inside, hoping you make a good pass or a good tackle.'

'You would be confident without being over-confident going into other games but when it comes to Celtic, it's true what they say, the form book goes out the window. In other matches if eight or nine players are on their game they can pull the others through. But against Celtic everyone has to be at it and if players couldn't handle the occasion, we weren't going to win the game. Everybody had to give everything they had but you had to be careful not to be reckless with it, you needed to control it.'

Ally McCoist stole the show at Hampden with a hat-trick but Nicholl had played alongside the man of the moment before, during his time with Sunderland.

'He was hopeless at Sunderland,' joked Jimmy. 'He got a bit of stick from the fans as he had decided [in 1981] to go to Sunderland instead of Rangers so it wasn't a great start for him. But typical Coisty, he was just one of these fellas and if you're going to win over the supporters then what a way to do it. After the game we were all back at Ibrox having a party when big Jock told everyone to get on the bus. We got on the bus and took the League Cup into Glasgow and into the Panama Jacks nightclub and got a huge cheer. Imagine doing that these days!'

Nicholl's next experiences of Old Firm games were somewhat less enthralling. Just six days after winning the League Cup, Celtic won 3-0 at Parkhead in the league and although Rangers won the next encounter 19 days later, it was a bittersweet experience for Jimmy. It was to be the last appearance of his loan spell so Jock Wallace made him captain for the day but he once again fell foul of officialdom.

'When Jock made me captain I was pumped to the eyeballs,' remembered Nicholl. 'I was flying to Toronto on the Monday and I didn't know what was in the future so this looked like being my last game for Rangers. I took a couple of late challenges after playing the ball up the line and after one of them, Brian McClair caught me and I kicked out at him. It was half-hearted but the referee sent me off. Bobby [Williamson] scored an overhead kick [the only goal of the game] and big Jock came in [to the dressing room] and there was a great atmosphere. I was a wee bit subdued. Jock came over and told me I was the luckiest man in the world. He said I had been captain but I had let the team down and if we hadn't won the game, he'd have kicked my arse so hard that I wouldn't have needed a plane to fly to Toronto! Then he told me he loved me and that was the last contact I had with him.'

He added, 'There was no finesse about Jock on the training pitch but I enjoyed working with him. We used to have meetings every Friday and at one of the first ones, we were all sitting in the dressing room. I was sitting next to the door but he started at the other side of the room. He just wanted to talk football and he asked Davie Cooper what he thought the game was all about. Coop said it was all about teamwork then Bobby Russell said it was about knowing your job. By the time he got to me there wasn't much left I could say! You had to come up with something different too, because if you said what someone else said he'd bark that we'd had that answer. By the time it got to the third meeting, Jock turned to me and said, "Nicholl, what do you think the game's all about?" and I answered, "Does it really matter what we say? At these meetings somebody might say something constructive about what would make us better but we never do anything about it." I told him he just dominated everybody and my face was getting redder and redder. Next thing we knew Jock was shouting, "Dominating? Dominating? I'll give you dominating, now get across to that training pitch."

'Soon after, we went to Majorca for a wee break and you had to be at the bar for 7.30pm to have a drink with big Jock and all the staff.

When we were in the airport he was walking with Alex Totten when all I heard was "Nicholl, Nicholl, come here you!" I walked up to him and he said, "See you in that meeting about three or four weeks ago, you said that you found me too dominating and domineering, what exactly did you mean? Tell me the truth." I then told him that what I would rather do was sit and listen to him talking about football and he grabbed me in a big bear hug and told me he'd known that all along.'

During his loan spell, Jimmy Nicholl made 29 appearances for Rangers. He had ticked another box on his list of footballing dreams and returned to Canada satisfied to have contributed to a successful spell for the club, albeit only short-term. He was soon back on British shores, though, signing for West Bromwich Albion in July 1984, but his time there was not a happy one. Despite a lack of first-team action, Nicholl was still selected for the Northern Ireland squad that went to Mexico for the 1986 World Cup. And it was on the journey back from South America that his return to Ibrox was plotted.

'Northern Ireland were on the same plane as Scotland coming back home,' recalled Nicholl. 'We had a few drinks and it was a brilliant trip. During the flight I found myself in the galley at the back and Graeme [Souness] was there. He asked if I had been to Rangers before and I told him I'd been there for six months under big Jock. At that time I had no idea he was going to Rangers [as player-manager] but the Thursday before the first game against Hibs, a phone call came in. It was Ron Saunders [manager at WBA] telling me Souness wanted me up at Rangers and Bobby Williamson was going to West Brom. It was a straight swap and I came up and signed.'

Nicholl was in line to make his second debut for Rangers in the opening fixture against Hibernian at Easter Road. However, there was concern that he would still be subject to a suspension following his red card against Celtic in his last spell. Secretary Campbell Ogilvie spent much of the Friday before the game trying to confirm Nicholl's eligibility and he was eventually cleared to play. In the end he had to wait until the following Wednesday evening to pull on a Rangers jersey again, as injury ruled him out of what proved to be an explosive match in Edinburgh.

The appearance at right-back in a 1-0 win over Falkirk at Ibrox would be one of 34 Nicholl would make in Rangers' run to the league title in season 1986/87. He had a spell on the sidelines in December and January, missing seven matches, but returned for the run-in. He spent much of that spell wearing the number seven shirt as part of a four-man midfield that included Souness, Durrant and the mercurial Davie Cooper.

'Coop was always a clever player,' noted Nicholl. 'As he got older he wasn't going to run past the full-back but he could still beat them just by dropping his shoulder. There would be wee disguised passes [like the one for Ian Durrant in the 1-0 win over Celtic in August] and sometimes he'd go to cross and just slip a clever pass instead. People think the game is all about pace so does that mean Cooper couldn't play today? Of course he could, he was brilliant.'

He added, 'They called him the Moody Blue but he was far from it. Sometimes he'd get the train and the tube to Ibrox with the supporters as he couldn't drive. I also used to pick him up and we'd go up Sauchiehall Street in the morning and go into a café for a croissant and a cup of tea. He would talk away to the supporters. He used to wind the English boys up in the dressing room too.'

Part of that wind-up would be taking the mickey out of his English team-mates in the often feisty Scotland v England matches on the training pitch. As part of the non-Scottish contingent, one would have suspected Nicholl would have turned out for England in these encounters, but his Scottish heritage meant otherwise.

'My mother's from Greenock so I played for Scotland,' he announced proudly. 'In one training session I was going down the left and I crossed the ball in by putting one foot behind the other. McCoist headed it in and it was one of the best things I ever did. In another session Souness, Fergie and Durranty were getting stuck into each other.

'It was a Friday morning and we had a game the next day. It started getting out of hand and for the first time that I can remember the assistant manager blew the whistle, picked up the ball and stopped the training. That shows the respect that Walter had in that dressing room.'

That fighting spirit and competitiveness on the training pitch soon bore fruit and in May, Nicholl was part of the side that secured the point at Pittodrie that was needed to annex the Premier Division title. Earlier in the campaign he had doubled his tally of League Cup medals too, playing at right-back in the 2-1 win over Celtic at Hampden.

Nicholl was less involved in the first team in season 1987/88. After missing just two of the first 17 Premier Division matches, he figured in only seven of the final 18 games. The manager felt there was a need to inject some youth in to the team and Nicholl was the man to make way.

'Graeme brought me in and said he wanted to give Scott Nisbet more games,' said Nicholl. 'He had been doing well in the reserves at centre-half but Graeme said he wasn't going to get into the team there. He was a good young player so Graeme asked if I would talk to him about playing right-back. I did that, taking time out with him at training to give him advice, then after a couple of reserve games, Graeme told me he was going to play Nissy in the first team.'

Nisbet's game time meant a spell out of the team for Nicholl. He went into the reserves but spent a bit longer out of the first-team picture than he expected.

'I still felt I could have done a better job than Nissy so I thought Graeme would give him a couple of games then I'd get back in,' said Nicholl. 'However, it lasted a lot longer than that [between 21 November and the final league game at Brockville on 7 May, Nisbet wore the number two jersey in all but six matches] so I went to see Graeme. I ended up back in the team not long after but I heard later that some of the lads had been going to him saying that I should be back in the team. Graeme didn't tend to do what the other players told him – he would usually do the opposite – which is probably why I was out for so long.'

It was not just the form of Nisbet or the stubbornness of Souness that kept Nicholl out the side; he had a spell out through illness too.

'I couldn't run or lift my legs,' said Jimmy. 'Davie Provan at Celtic had something similar and when I told him about the tablets I was on, he told me to get off them as they broke down my immune system.

For a long time all I could do was come in, get changed and then go out and do a couple of laps round the park at Ibrox. Eventually I came okay but it was something in my system and no one could understand what it was.'

Nicholl added another League Cup medal to his collection that season. With Terry Butcher suspended, he played at right-back in the final against Aberdeen, with Richard Gough moving inside to partner Graham Roberts in central defence. In an epic encounter the Dons led 3-2 in the dying minutes before Nicholl lofted a long ball forward in search of an equalising goal. Roberts won the ball in the air and his header bounced off Durrant and was clinically despatched into the net by Robert Fleck. Rangers claimed the trophy by virtue of holding their nerve in the penalty shoot-out but Nicholl felt it prudent to point out that the third goal was not the only one he was involved in that day.

'I'm claiming an assist for Coop's free kick,' he said laughing loudly. 'Me and him were standing over the ball and he asked me what I thought we should do. I told him just to hit it and he did!'

Although there was disappointment in the Premier Division – Rangers finished third, 12 points adrift of Celtic – and an early exit from the Scottish Cup, the season was memorable for a run to the last eight of the European Cup. In their first sojourn into the continent's premier club competition for nine years, Souness's side defeated European Cup Winners' Cup holders, Dynamo Kiev, and Polish champions, Gornik Zabrze, before succumbing to the 1986 winners, Steaua Bucharest. Souness leant on the experience of 30-year-old Nicholl in this arena, with the Northern Irishman playing in five of the six ties. Although these matches would see Nicholl err more on the defensive side of his game, he still managed to forage forward, witnessed by a one-two with Mark Falco followed by a precise cross to set up McCoist for the opening goal against Gornik at Ibrox.

'It was the Dynamo Kiev game that we brought the pitch in,' remembered Nicholl. 'It made the pitch tighter which meant you had to be more accurate with your passing. I remember at one point their outside-left controlled the ball but he was off the park! I just walked over and picked the ball up as he had no idea he was off the pitch.'

He added, 'The European nights were different. In the league at Ibrox the fans would give you a clap and a cheer but by twenty past three, they expected you to be 2-0 up. But on European nights they were with you all the time and I loved those games.'

If Nicholl thought he would slot back in at full-back for season 1988/89 then all he needed to do to confirm that would not be the case was consult the front cover of the first edition of the *Rangers News*. Its headline quoted Graeme Souness as saying that he had 'signed the best right-back in Britain'; Gary Stevens having arrived at Ibrox from Everton for a fee of £1 million. Clearly the athletic Stevens would be first choice – over the season he missed just one first-team game – but although he only made three appearances – the 1-1 draw against Cologne in the UEFA Cup, a 3-1 league win over Dundee and the 1-1 draw against Raith Rovers in the Scottish Cup – there would be a new role for Jimmy Nicholl in the Rangers hierarchy.

'When Graeme told me he had signed Gary I asked him, "Do you not think he might be too good for the reserves?"' laughed Nicholl. 'Gary came in and was great, getting up and down the line. Graeme and Walter told me to keep myself fit but also asked if I'd like to help big Peter McCloy take the reserves. In those days the first team and the reserves would usually both play on the Saturday and there would be about seven or eight senior players in the reserve squad. There were good young players too like wee Johnny Morrow, [Gary] McSwegan and [John] Spencer. Because the first team were playing at the same time, Graeme and Walter couldn't see the reserves play so on the Monday they'd ask me about the players' application and attitude and on the basis of what I said, they'd decide who would be considered for the next first-team game.'

He continued, 'Although I was only 31, I decided that I was going to pack it in and concentrate on coaching. I initially thought I would play at centre-half in the reserves but there was a young English lad, Nigel Howard, and I thought that I wasn't going to deprive him of a place. I used to get really down after reserve games but if Coop was playing for us I'd go back to Hamilton with him for a beer. He said he couldn't do what I was doing. I told him you had to encourage players but he would say "if you can't play, you can't play, get them out the door!" He eventually started coaching at Motherwell and Clydebank and also with Charlie Nicholas and Cooper would have been a good coach.'

The fledgling steps of what would become an excellent coaching career were trodden at Ibrox. The reserve team finished third in the Premier Reserve League table, with notable victories chalked up over Celtic (twice) and eventual title winners, Dundee United. But the lure of playing proved too much to resist and in August 1989, Jimmy left Rangers to join Dunfermline Athletic.

'I was sitting in the house and I got a phone call from [Dunfermline manager] Jim Leishman,' said Nicholl. 'They had just been promoted and he was looking for experienced players to help keep them in the Premier Division. Every decision I have made has been on my initial gut reaction and I fancied playing again. I spoke to Graeme and Walter the next day and they didn't stand in my way. Graeme even said if it hadn't been for the Rangers job he'd still have been playing in Italy.'

He added, 'Dunfermline was the polar opposite from what I had come from. All they wanted to do was stay in the league and when they drew with Hibs to stay in the Premier Division, there was a party upstairs. It was all straw hats and trumpets just because they had avoided relegation. That meant just as much to them as winning the league and cups did to Rangers. There was a different type of pressure at Dunfermline too. You look at the fixtures and, if you lose a couple, the next run of games could mean it could be another month before you pick up a point. But your determination could see you pick up a point at Easter Road that you weren't expecting to as well. That put things in perspective. That's not success in the eyes of Rangers but it is in the eyes of Dunfermline. And you're part of that success.'

Nicholl stayed at Dunfermline for 18 months, making 24 league appearances, before an opportunity arose that allowed him to continue playing and develop his credentials as a manager. In

November 1990 he was offered the role of player-manager with Raith Rovers.

'I planned to play for Dunfermline until I was 35 so I would travel up and down from Manchester where I was living at the time,' said Nicholl. 'After that I was going to go down to the north-west and play for Burnley or Oldham but then all of a sudden I got the Raith Rovers job. I went there on the Thursday night for the interview and 20 minutes later I had the job!'

Under Nicholl, Raith enjoyed one of the most successful periods in their history. They won promotion as First Division champions in season 1992/93 but trumped that achievement two seasons later when they came from behind to defeat Celtic on penalties in the League Cup Final.

'I started off trying to work the players hard in training but my assistant manager told me I couldn't do that,' recalled Nicholl. 'He reminded me that these lads had been working all day so I couldn't put those demands on them and it was a good bit of advice.'

He added, 'I played my last game for Raith in 1995 against Hamilton at Firhill. I was 39. We only needed a draw to get promotion for the second time [Raith had been relegated from the Premier Division at the end of season 1993/94]. We beat Celtic in the League Cup in November but were 15 points behind Dundee. We couldn't really get going after getting relegated but I knew we'd be alright. We went unbeaten from December until the end of the season and at the end of the Hamilton game I came off and big Dave Narey, who played centre-half, told me it was his last game. So that was the two of us packing it in as we both felt we couldn't do it in the Premier Division.'

Concentrating solely on management, Nicholl led Raith into European football for the first time in their history in season 1995/96. They entered the UEFA Cup and enjoyed a fairy tale run that culminated in the grandiose Olympic Stadium in Munich. Eventual winners, Bayern Munich, boasting the talents of Jurgen Klinsmann and future Ranger, Christian Nerlinger, won 2-0 at Easter Road but Nicholl's novices looked like overturning that deficit in Germany. Danny Lennon's goal had them ahead at the interval but second-half goals from Klinsmann and Babbel took the German giants through.

Jimmy left Kirkcaldy in February 1996 to join Millwall, returning to Raith a year later. Spells as assistant manager to Jimmy Calderwood at Dunfermline, Aberdeen and Kilmarnock followed before Nicholl returned to management, with two spells in charge of Cowdenbeath sandwiching time as assistant manager to Kenny Shiels at Kilmarnock and Pat Fenlon at Hibernian.

During his second stint with the Blue Brazil, Nicholl had been appointed as Northern Ireland manager Michael O'Neill's number two and, in January 2018, he was back at Ibrox. With Graeme Murty given the Rangers manager's job until the end of season 2017/18, he persuaded Nicholl to leave Falkirk, where he was assistant manager to Paul Hartley, for a similar role with Rangers. The arrival of Nicholl seemed to galvanise Rangers but a 3-2 defeat to Celtic was the catalyst for a cataclysmic time that featured two heavy Old Firm defeats, player unrest and an eventual third-place finish in the Premier League. When Murty was dismissed before the end of the campaign, Nicholl was placed in caretaker charge.

'The highlight of my managerial career will always be Raith Rovers,' stated Nicholl. 'We beat Celtic in the League Cup Final, got into Europe and won two league titles. Managing Rangers at my stage of life was a great opportunity. We were still in a difficult position but as long as you've done the best you can and been true to yourself, you can't ask for any more. There were a few harsh words when Graeme left and we had a meeting and I never missed them. I asked them why all of a sudden they were training harder, working harder. I couldn't get my head around that. If they had no respect for the previous manager then they certainly weren't going to have respect for me. There were good ones, like Bates, Dorrans, McCrorie, Candeais, but I told them all I was a supporter in charge for three games and told them, as a supporter, what I expected from them.'

He concluded, 'I definitely have no regrets about my playing career at Rangers. I was lucky to get there on two occasions [as a player] and to be part of the staff, taking the reserves then to go back to help Graeme. My biggest memories are the first cup final with Jock Wallace and winning the league at Aberdeen. Before that, Rangers were finishing third, fourth and fifth so for the turnaround to happen in the first season with Souness and Walter and for me to be part of that was excellent.'

Jimmy Nicholl made 124 appearances for Rangers. He won a Premier Division championship medal (1986/87) and three League Cup medals (1983/84, 1986/87 and 1987/88). He managed Rangers for three matches at the end of season 2017/18, registering a win and two draws.

The Unsung Hero
Stuart Munro (1984–1991)

Stuart David Munro was undoubtedly one of the unsung heroes of the 1980s. A strong, industrious and dependable left-back, he survived numerous challenges for the number three jersey to make over 300 appearances for Rangers. He did, however, encounter a tough start in his quest to become a professional footballer.

'At the age of 15/16 I was training a couple of nights a week with Falkirk at Brockville,' said Munro from his home in Australia. 'I joined Bo'ness United when I was 17 and played with them for about six months. I then went to St Mirren on trial and ended up signing for them. I had a couple of good years with them but there was so much travel. I was working full-time at BP in Grangemouth where I lived but I wasn't driving at the time. I used to finish at 4.15 then grab a bite to eat and get a bus from Grangemouth to Falkirk. It was then the train from Falkirk through to Glasgow Queen Street followed by a run down to Glasgow Central where I'd get the train to Paisley. I'd then run down Love Street to the ground to train and I would do the same on the way back. I did this three times a week.'

There would be no reward for Munro's dedication. Although he was at St Mirren for two years, during which he played a lot of youth and reserve-team football, he never turned out for the first team. He was eventually released when the management team in Paisley felt he was not going to make it as a Premier Division player.

'I just wanted to be a footballer and Jimmy Bone, one of the senior players at St Mirren, helped me out by getting me fixed up at Alloa,' recalled Munro. 'Alex Totten was the manager there and two of my best mates were playing for them at the time. It was part-time football, training a couple of nights a week, but I started to really enjoy myself and play pretty well.'

Stuart's form was soon attracting interest and a possible move to Dundee was mooted only for it to be scuppered by an especially harsh Scottish winter. By then, Willie Garner had taken over from Alex Totten at Recreation Park and Munro eventually ended up with two of the top teams in the country chasing his signature.

'We played Hamilton in the Scottish Cup in January 1984 and I played up front,' said Munro. 'I scored a goal and we got beat 3-1 but I didn't know that in the stands that night was big Jock [Wallace]. After the game Willie Garner told me Jock wanted to speak to me about going to Rangers. However, he also said that he was going to Aberdeen the following week to be assistant manager to Alex Ferguson and that he wanted me to go there. Now I had two of the biggest clubs in Scotland – and Aberdeen were probably the biggest at the time – interested in me.'

He continued, 'Willie said that I couldn't really tell big Jock I wanted to think about it so I'd need to make a decision on what I wanted to do. My dad was out in the car park so I didn't speak to him but my gut feeling told me Rangers. I went outside to the changing room corridor at Hamilton and here was this man, this colossus of a man, big Jock, his presence was unbelievable.'

Sanctuary was then sought to negotiate Munro's move to Ibrox. He recalled, 'He walked into the home dressing room and there was a wee physiotherapy room at the back. There was a physio giving a player treatment and Jock simply said, "You … you … oot!" They left and he closed the door and he told me I was coming to the Rangers. I said "aye" and he asked me how much I was getting paid by BP and Alloa. He added the two figures together and he said I would be paid that and that was the end of it.'

Munro's first Rangers appearance was against Clyde in the Reserve League West on 8 February 1984 and it did not take long for him to make his debut for the first team. However, it was not in the left-back role that he would make his own a few seasons later.

'I was signed as left-winger or left-midfielder,' said Munro. 'That's where I played at Alloa. I had a wee bit of pace at the time and used to like getting up and down the touchline and getting crosses in. At the time Jock was trying to build the team but the resources he had were nothing like the Souness era. Ally Dawson was the left-back, although he could play anywhere across the back four, and Davie Cooper was left-winger so I wasn't going to take his position. I made my debut [as sub against Dundee in a 3-1 win at Dens Park on 25 February 1984] at inside-left because of that. I was always a hard-working player and I think it was that honesty and hard work that eventually got me a position at left-back.'

Two further substitute appearances followed before the end of the season and there were two appearances in the starting XI too, against St Johnstone and Dundee United. Munro also made 25 appearances for the reserve team, scoring two goals against Airdrie and Hibernian. Stuart was part of a stellar reserve team that season, one which won the Reserve League title, and he played in some thumping victories, notably 8-0 against Dundee, 9-1 against Ayr United and two 6-0 thrashings of Motherwell.

At the end of season 1983/84 Jock Wallace took the squad on a world tour. Munro was included in the 18-man player pool and the trip proved memorable for him both on and off the park.

'That was where I met my wife,' said Munro fondly. 'Big Dave Mitchell was a good friend of mine and we were out in Sydney one night when I met her in a club. These were the days before phones and emails so we were writing letters every couple of weeks to keep in touch. That went on for a wee while before eventually she came over and we ended up getting married. We've been married for over 26 years and had two kids, both of whom were born in Australia.'

On the park Munro played a part in seven matches, turning out three times in Australia, twice in Canada, once in New Zealand and once in the USA.

'I had only been at the club three months so I was still very nervous and starstruck around the players,' recalled Munro. 'I shouldn't have been as the boys were brilliant, a great bunch of guys. On the tour itself three players got bad injuries and that seemed to be the story of the tour. But when you look back on it, it was a fantastic trip in terms of what we put in, the amount of games we played and the travel that was involved. I was hoping the tour would have got me integrated into the first-team squad but when we came back for pre-season I suddenly found that I wasn't involved.'

While Wallace took the first team to Switzerland, Munro was in the reserve team that played against a Stornoway Select, Troon Juniors and Dalbeattie Star. It would be 9 October before Stuart's name was on the first-team team sheet for the second leg of the League Cup semi-final against Meadowbank Thistle. And over the course of the 1984/85 season he made only 13 Premier Division appearances, albeit all of them being in what would become his preferred position of left-back.

'I just had to knuckle down and try and win back my spot but it took me about a year and a half to find my feet,' said Munro. 'In season 1985/86 I was left-back and Shuggie Burns was right-back. I was 21/22 at the time so while I wasn't a kid any more, I wasn't experienced but we did well. We both had energy and we could get up and down all day. But it was an inconsistent period and eventually big Jock got sacked. Then there was the shock when they went out and got Souness.'

Munro missed just eight first-team games in season 1985/86. He was absent from 11 January until 15 March as he had picked up pneumonia.

He recalled, 'We played a game one night and it was horrendous weather and I ended up in my bed with a virus for a few weeks. I moved into my parents' house as they were looking after me and big Jock arrived at the door one day to see me. He had come all the way through to Grangemouth to see how I was, which was brilliant. Jock was like that. Not long after I had signed he took me on a tour of Ibrox and there was the Blue Room, a blue snooker table, blue table tennis table and then we walked out on to the park. For me it was incredible as it was the first time I'd walked out the tunnel. We were standing there and Jock said to me, "You know what son, I've tried to get blue grass but I can't get blue grass." It was so funny but that was big Jock, a great man.'

Big changes were afoot at Ibrox, though. Graeme Souness was appointed as the club's first player-manager in April 1986 and the rebirth of the Blues began.

'Straight away we knew he was going to be signing players,' said Munro. 'We had a big squad but there were a lot of younger guys round about the same age as me. A lot were left with the decision of staying or going as they didn't know if they were going to get a game. There was a huge turnover in players but although I hadn't really cemented a first-team place, I always had this belief and I was a fighter, so I decided to stay. I knew I was going to be one of the first players under the microscope. But Souness liked a hard-working, honest type of player and although he tried to replace me a few times at left-back, I had that work ethic and eventually found consistency to win him over.'

Staying at Ibrox proved an inspired decision as Munro missed just one of the 44 Premier Division matches played in season 1986/87. He took his place in a solid back-line alongside Dave McPherson, Terry Butcher and latterly, Graham Roberts and that defence was the bedrock upon which the foundations of the title charge were built.

'Butcher had such a presence and willingness to win,' recalled Munro. 'You couldn't have asked for a better captain. Terry was a great help to me and I had Davie Cooper in front of me. He was such a Rangers man and, to this day, he's the greatest player I ever played with. His standards were so high that if you passed the ball to him and it wasn't right on his foot, he wouldn't stretch for it. He would look at you and growl to say that the next time you passed it to him you knew you had to make it perfect.'

He continued, 'To be fair to big Jock, there were a lot of changes in the squad but Souness brought with him a belief and improved the standards as well. No disrespect to big Jock but Souness's standards were very, very high in terms of the ability of players and in Walter Smith he had a fantastic assistant. He was the man-manager. Souness wasn't like that. He had an aura about him and you never really mixed with him but Walter was the day-to-day contact and you couldn't have asked for anybody better.'

Although the start to the 1986/87 season was uneven – Rangers only won 11 of the first 19 league matches and lay nine points adrift of Celtic in December – the team was getting stronger and stronger. Souness's men dropped a mere six points (this in the days of two points for a win) in their last 24 league matches to claim the title. Runners-up Celtic trailed in their wake, finishing six points adrift.

'Souness was very fortunate that the English clubs were not playing in Europe at the time,' said Munro. 'In the early 80s we had good players but they maybe weren't the best and that's why Rangers were finishing second, third and fourth in the league. But when Souness came he could go out and sign Terry Butcher when Manchester United were trying to get him. He could sign Chris Woods too as Rangers were just as big a club, if not bigger, than them and could offer European football as well. The likes of Davie Cooper were at their level, international class, so could just thrive.'

The League Cup was won in October, the first piece of domestic silverware in the Souness era, and a first winners' medal as a professional for Stuart Munro. The match was memorable too for an altercation with a future team-mate. Munro and Maurice Johnston clashed off the ball. Both players were booked but Johnston, yellow carded earlier in the match, was subsequently ordered off by referee David Syme.

'It was great to get my first medal and that made everybody realise that Souness was there to win things,' said Stuart, 'although there was no day bigger than going to Pittodrie and winning the league in the second-last game of the season. That would probably be my highlight of my career at Rangers.'

The only black spot on the season for Munro was a red card in a European tie against Borussia Monchengladbach. Rangers had comfortably beaten Ilves Tampere in the opening round of the UEFA Cup and negotiated their way past Boavista next before being drawn against the West Germans. A 1-1 draw in the first leg at Ibrox left the tie hanging in the balance ahead of the return leg.

Stuart recalled, 'I was on the ground and the ball got stuck beside my legs. This guy was whacking my legs, right in front of the referee. I remember looking up at the referee with my hands out but he didn't do anything. Next time the player lifted his leg to kick me, I flicked his standing leg and he fell down and started screaming like a banshee. I got sent off but it was a soft red card. It was a long walk to get to the tunnel to the changing rooms but about ten or 15 minutes later in came Davie Cooper. I thought all the guys were coming in and the match had finished 0-0 but Coop had been sent off as well.'

Munro hoped that the title win would see him and Rangers kick on and enjoy more success but season 1987/88 was an anti-climax for both parties. Having been a model of consistency in the championship-winning season, Munro made just 17 appearances in the Premier Division. He also played in just two of the six European Cup ties.

'Souness brought in the likes of Jimmy Phillips, Avi Cohen and Jan Bartram to play left-back,' said Munro. 'I never felt the position [at left-back] was mine at that point. Then one day Hibs came in with an offer and Souness pulled me into the office. At that time there had been a few guys who, if Souness wanted rid of them, he'd try and make it difficult for them if they didn't accept it. He would ban them from training with the seniors and it happened to Graham Roberts and a few others. When he spoke to me he said that everyone had their price and Hibs had come in with an offer that had been accepted. He asked if I wanted to speak to them but I said no. He said that was okay and I gained so much confidence from the fact that he didn't push it or question it. He never treated me any differently after that either. Soon afterwards he called me back into his office and said I was now his number one left-back and that he wasn't looking for anyone else [in that position].'

Although appearances were sporadic initially, Munro did add to his collection of medals when he played in an enthralling League Cup Final against Aberdeen in October 1987.

'I finished that game with a cut eye and a broken nose,' was Munro's initial recollection. 'I was standing in the shower room after the game and the doctor was telling me that the best time to straighten a broken nose was when it was still swollen. So there I was in front of the mirror and the rest of the lads were in the bath taking the piss out me!'

He continued, 'Any of these cup finals were just phenomenal and for many, many years afterwards I would watch the videos of them.

Doing the lap of honour was fantastic and you never got enough of it. And at Rangers we were very fortunate that we got to do it in front of such passionate supporters.'

When Rangers wrestled the title back from Celtic in season 1988/89, Munro was still in and out of the team. He made 22 appearances as he vied with John Brown for the number three jersey. Indeed it was Brown who got the nod for the League Cup Final win against Aberdeen – Munro was an unused substitute – while Munro was in position for the Scottish Cup Final defeat against Celtic in May.

Having spent two seasons playing intermittently, season 1989/90 would be completely different for Munro. He and Maurice Johnston were the only players in the first team to play in every competitive match, with Munro an integral part of a back four that conceded a mere 19 goals in the successful defence of the Premier Division championship. Munro has fond memories of Johnston.

'He was terrific for the team and was probably the only person who could have coped with that situation [being the club's first high-profile Roman Catholic],' said Munro. 'He had 24/7 security and we used to have security at Ibrox at the time. We had to park our cars inside the stadium and we had to go out with the security guys to get our cars checked for bombs before we drove home. When we went to the training ground the security guys would also check the perimeter for snipers too. Mo would sit in the corner of the dressing room and he'd open up these envelopes that were full of mail written with newspaper cuttings spelling things like, "We're going to kill you." He was a terrific lad and he just laughed it off. And he performed too.'

After scoring in his third league appearance against Aberdeen at Ibrox, Johnston kicked on, netting 17 goals in total. His goals, allied to those from Ally McCoist, who scored 18 times, and that obdurate defence ensured Rangers secured the league title for the 40th time in their history. Munro, never one to be among the goals, rounded off the season in style too, scoring the final league goal of the campaign in a 1-1 draw against Hearts at Tynecastle. It was one of just three he would score in a Rangers jersey.

'The goal against Hearts was a good one but I don't think it was on TV,' recalled Munro ruefully. 'I scored one against Dundee United at Tannadice and another up at Aberdeen, although that wasn't really my goal! Derek Ferguson headed it and I was trying to get out the way. It was going to miss the target but it hit off my stomach and went in. Prior to that I'd scored a few for Alloa and in my younger days I was a striker but I focussed on being a defender first.'

Munro did like to get forward, though, and he developed excellent relationships with both Davie Cooper and Mark Walters.

'A lot of full-backs do an overlap behind the winger but I used to do a thing with Coop called the "underlap",' said Stuart. 'Because he hugged the touchline so much, when I gave him the ball I would go inside him. He used to just flick the ball with the outside of his left foot and I'd go forward. I had the energy to get up and down the park but big Terry used to say I was a defender first and to make sure we gave nothing away. We had such good attacking players that we didn't need to go forward all the time, we could pick and choose our moments.'

One of those attacking players who was in his pomp at that time was Ally McCoist and he and Munro became close pals in what was a tight-knit dressing room.

'I socialised a lot with him and we were really good mates,' said Munro. 'To me he was just a really nice person, really funny, always looking for the mickey-taking. He was a very intelligent guy so it didn't surprise me that he went into management. Had it been a different era I could have seen him being a really successful Rangers manager. As a player, as a goalscorer, you couldn't have asked for anyone better. He was a great player and a Rangers man through and through. There was a little spell when the partnership between Mo and [Mark] Hateley was what Souness was looking for and Coisty was pushed to the side for a few months. That got to him a little bit but he did what he did best, he came back scoring goals. When Walter took over he was always going to be the number one striker and he was one of the greatest goalscorers I've ever seen.'

Munro's consistency in season 1989/90 was appreciated by the club's supporters too but he was not afforded the same recognition at international level. He remains one of the best players of that era never to have been capped for Scotland.

He said proudly, 'That was the year I got about 90 or 100 Player of the Year awards from all the different supporters' clubs. I thought I had a good year and was getting talked about for the Scotland squad as well. I was probably more disappointed that I never got more of a chance with them. I was probably the number one left-back at the time and Maurice Malpas, who was in front of me for the senior squad, was injured. They put me in the Scotland B team which I was told was to be in preparation for going to the World Cup in 1990. I was told we'd be playing three at the back so I'd be more a left wing-back rather than left full-back. They wanted me to get forward and I thought I could do it. But I only had two games and although I did okay, I'd have played better in a back four. What annoyed me more than anything was that, at the World Cup, they never did play three at the back and that pissed me off as, that year, I felt I was the best left-back available.

He continued, 'My confidence was sky-high that year. In my early years at Rangers my thoughts during a game would be all negative but by 89/90 it was the opposite. I was now thinking how I could help win the match, could I get forward and make overlaps and get crosses in?'

That confidence augured well for Rangers as three games from the end of the season the title was secured with a 1-0 win over Dundee United at Tannadice. Trevor Steven got the goal that mattered but his header came from a cross from the left executed from the RIGHT boot of Stuart Munro.

'Walter Smith talks about that one,' laughed Munro. 'When I took the ball from the throw-in and moved it on to me right foot he says he went "Oh Jesus Christ!" but I pinged it over and Trevor headed it in. Those were the things that you look back on. That was the confidence you got being part of that squad.'

Another hallmark of that team was their superior fitness. Munro had experienced the arduous pre-season under Jock Wallace on the infamous sand dunes at Gullane but he maintains the pre-season regime under Souness in the idyllic setting of Il Ciocco in the Tuscan hills was tougher.

'I missed Gullane one year as I was captaining Rangers at the Tennent's Sixes but it was really hard going,' winced Munro. 'But Souness's pre-season training was unbelievable, so difficult. You would never do the type of things we did back then nowadays but we would do running sessions and you would wake up the next day and you couldn't walk. But we were expected to go out and do the same again. Gullane was only a one-day thing, about three or four hours, and it was pure hell, but under Souness it was 10-12 days of very, very hard running. It wasn't just running, there was a lot of ball work and small-sided football too. But when Souness came in he brought in a different perspective to the warm ups, introducing a lot of the Italian stuff, and he tried to change the culture. He tried to get us in on a Sunday after the game to do recovery sessions. But it didn't really work with us Scottish boys as we liked our Saturday nights out so it eventually got binned!'

Season 1990/91 turned out to be Stuart Munro's last in a Rangers jersey. His campaign was stop-start, hampered by injury, and ended prematurely, with Munro making the last of his 21 appearances in a tempestuous Scottish Cup quarter-final against Celtic on 17 March.

'I picked up a hernia and a groin injury just after Christmas, which meant I could hardly walk,' said Munro. 'I got all sorts of different treatment but it wasn't going away and I was struggling. They tried to get me fit for the game against Celtic and I played but could hardly move. Souness admitted afterwards that they were wrong to play me but they were desperate as we were starting to get a lot of injuries. I was eventually sent to a surgeon down in London and I had to get a Gilmore's groin operation. It was bad timing for me as my contract was up at the end of the season too.'

While Munro was recuperating, Souness left Rangers to join Liverpool and Walter Smith took over the reins at Ibrox. He guided the club to the title in a thrilling final-day battle with Aberdeen and in the summer of 1991, he set about putting his stamp on the Rangers squad. He wanted Munro to be part of his plans but the planned acquisition of David Robertson meant Munro would elect to move on.

'I got on really well with Walter and I had a conversation with him,' recalled Munro. 'The first thing he said to me was that he wanted me to stay and sign a new three-year contract. We never spoke about money but he wanted to be up front with me so he told me he was going to be signing another left-back. He never told me who it was but I asked him if he was costing £1 million or more. When he said "yes" I knew he wasn't going to be spending that kind of money to have him sitting on the bench.'

He continued, 'I was quite confident I could play in other positions. I was in midfield the day I scored against Dundee United and Aberdeen and I would be asked to do man-marking jobs in European games by stepping in there too. But I decided I was going to look around. I had been at Rangers for eight years so I felt the time was right to try something different.'

Munro elected to join Blackburn Rovers, who were managed by former Ibrox coach Don Mackay. Unfortunately, it did not work out. After a good pre-season he broke a bone in his ankle and was out for around six months. On his return Kenny Dalglish, who replaced Mackay in October 1991, had signed Alan Wright so Munro only played one game for the club.

'I moved on to Bristol City and really enjoyed it,' said Stuart. 'I was there for two-and-a-half years, playing under Russell Osman and then Joe Jordan. I then got a phone call from Maurice Johnston, who was at Falkirk, to see if I wanted to go there. They were my local team and Fergie [Derek Ferguson] was also there so I spoke to the manager, John Lambie. He wanted me to get involved as a player-coach and I had been doing all my badges so it fitted perfectly to do that. I had a season there and then finished off with St Mirren so I had almost gone full circle since I started my career there.'

Thereafter the Munros emigrated to Australia and that's where you will find the family today.

'I played for one year [at Sydney United] with big Dave Mitchell then I got involved in coaching,' said Munro. 'It used to be called the National Soccer League over here and for three or four years I was very successful as manager at a few teams. But when the NSL was disbanded and the A-League started up I started coaching at State

League level and took a full-time job at a sports school. I've been there on and off for the last ten years. I had a couple of years as assistant manager at Perth Glory with Ian Ferguson and I do some coaching with local village teams too. It involves coaching the coaches and giving them a little bit of help, which is good. I'm just enjoying life.'

Stuart Munro made 304 appearances for Rangers. He won three league titles (1986/87, 1988/89 and 1989/90), four League Cups (1986/87, 1987/88, 1988/89 and 1990/91) and one Glasgow Cup (1985/86). He misses the passion of Scottish Football but still keeps tabs on Rangers.

'The last couple of years have been rather frustrating, knowing that the board weren't making good decisions with their appointments,' he said. 'I always kept an eye on things but the interest wasn't as strong, especially after Coisty left. But Steven Gerrard has come in, and while he hasn't got the money to sign the best players like Souness did, the standards he has brought in are really, really high. While he might not have his stripes as a coach, as a man-manager, somebody that knows the game, he'll know what he needs to do to make his team successful.'

Munro cherished his time at Rangers. He was not a big money buy – he joined from Alloa Athletic for a mere £25,000 – but his work ethic, endeavour and consistency ensured he was one of the few who remained from the malaise of the mid-80s to taste the success that the club enjoyed in the latter part of the decade.

'My biggest highlight was being part of that first championship,' said Munro. 'The occasion at Pittodrie was brilliant, as it was at Tannadice [in 1989/90], but that first one, even though it wasn't the first of nine-in-a-row, it was such an important statement to win it that year. The bus journey back to Glasgow was unbelievable.'

He concluded, 'I regret leaving when I did but I was a lucky guy. I decided to stay and fight for my spot in the team when Jock left and Souness came in and it worked out well for me. I won over a lot of supporters and those four years or so under Souness were very special.'

Skippy
Dave MacKinnon (1982–1986)

David Donaldson MacKinnon was another one of Rangers' unsung heroes during the 1980s. An industrious, whole-hearted full-back, his dexterity was such that he could also play in midfield, at sweeper and at centre-back. His route to Ibrox was a circuitous one.

'I started my career at Arsenal,' said MacKinnon. 'It was great and I was there from aged 16 to 20. I was on the fringes of the first team with the likes of Liam Brady and Frank Stapleton and I played in a pre-season friendly in Holland against Dundee in 1976. [Former Rangers manager] Davie White was manager at Dundee and he asked me if I would leave Arsenal. I told him I was quite content there but I went up on loan and eventually signed. I spent two years there and was then transferred to Partick. I was their second-most expensive signing at £18,500!'

Davie's time in Maryhill was blighted by a serious injury, one which some suspected would bring his playing career to a premature conclusion.

He recalled, 'I got kicked in the back and I remember playing against Rangers in the first game of the 1980/81 season. I felt so tired and when I went to the toilet at half-time there was blood everywhere. I was taken off and underwent various tests. I lost about two stone in weight in about six weeks and eventually it was discovered I had tuberculosis. My right kidney had been damaged by the kick and I had to get it removed. I was 24 and on the evening of the operation I remember on Scotsport that the announcer said my career was over. I had just won my first cap for the Scottish League so I was determined not to give up. I was in hospital for a fortnight and I decided I was going to change my game. I was going to get more involved, run from the first minute to the last and play every game as if it was my last.'

MacKinnon returned to the first team with Partick in January 1981. Bertie Auld, the manager who had signed him, had now left and Peter Cormack was in charge. Cormack picked Davie for a Scottish Cup third-round tie against Clyde and the full-back never looked back. Come May 1982 he had a decision to make.

He said, 'I played for the rest of the season [1980/81] and the rest of the following season and Peter then said if I wanted to get another club, go and get one. I had been offered a new contract at Thistle but I got offers from Everton and St Mirren and I heard rumours about Rangers. I was in the house – ironically I'd bought it from Derek Johnstone – and the doorbell went. It was Davie Provan, John Greig's assistant manager. I remember he came in and I had low hanging lamps and he whacked his head off one of them! He told me Greigy was interested so afterwards I phoned my father [to tell him about the offers]. He was Rangers daft and had taken me to Ibrox when I was younger. He told me if I went to Everton he'd never speak to me again!'

MacKinnon then travelled to Ibrox to speak to John Greig to negotiate terms and he was immediately enraptured.

'John Greig asked me what kind of money Everton were offering and they were offering a lot more than Rangers,' said MacKinnon. 'I asked about a signing-on fee, at which stage Greigy took me to see the Trophy Room and took me on a walk down the tunnel. He told me that when the stadium was full against Celtic the hairs on the back of your head would stand up and he asked me to point out where I used to watch games from. He took me over there and that was it, I asked "where do I sign?"! When you look back over your career money isn't the main objective and when you get asked to sign for Rangers, you sign for Rangers.'

MacKinnon donned a Rangers jersey for the first time in an eventful pre-season match against a fine St Etienne side in the Tournoi du Nord. The match ended 0-0, with Rangers prevailing 6-5 in an enthralling penalty shoot-out. McClelland, Bett and McAdam missed from 12 yards for Rangers but goalkeeper Peter McCloy was the hero, saving four spot kicks.

'I was due to take the next penalty,' laughed Davie. 'Johnny Rep was the big player for St Etienne and we kept chatting to each other every time the ball went out of play. Lokeren, Jim Bett's old club, were there and Lille, in a four-club tournament. It was really good but I remember I had terrible blisters on my feet. Before the game, one of the directors, Rae Simpson, who was a surgeon, took a look at them and I went to his room and he cut everything away with a scalpel. When you're playing the game you don't think about it as the adrenaline is flowing but at the end the white socks I was wearing were red with blood. I got through the game and it was great; the first time you put on that jersey is just incredible.'

The competitive action for season 1982/83 kicked off with the sectional ties in the League Cup. Four wins and two draws saw Rangers through to the quarter-finals, with MacKinnon in his favoured right-back position for each match. It was a position he would maintain until January 1983, a run of 33 consecutive matches.

'I started at centre-forward, scored a lot of goals, and then went to Arsenal as a midfield player,' said MacKinnon. 'They converted me to a right-back and I played there for Dundee and Partick too. At Rangers Sandy Jardine had gone to Hearts and one of the first things John Greig said to me was that I was going to be his number one right-back.'

He continued, 'When you play for Rangers you would play in any position but I would have loved to have remained at right-back. You had to be flexible but my best performances were at right-back. Once you start filling in for people in midfield or at the back, though, you then get the tag of utility player.'

During that run of games MacKinnon broke his goalscoring duck when he struck against St Mirren at Love Street on 16 October 1982. Although full-backs of that era were prone to maraud forward regularly, they were not noted for their goalscoring and this was one of just three goals Davie scored in the Rangers first team.

'The ball came out to me at the edge of the box and I hit it with my left foot,' recalled Davie. 'It hit a couple of defenders and the goalkeeper and looped up into the goal but I was claiming it. What a feeling it was, getting a goal for Rangers.'

In keeping with many of the seasons in the early 1980s, season 1982/83 was another story of what might have been for Rangers. It started well – Greig's side remained unbeaten in the first 17 matches – and particularly excelled in Europe, defeating Borussia Dortmund comprehensively, following up a 0-0 draw in West Germany with a fine 2-0 win at Ibrox.

'We started the season unbeaten and they said it was the best Rangers team in a generation,' said MacKinnon. 'I thought John Greig was a wonderful coach and a great manager and his philosophy was that the goalkeeper, either Jim Stewart or Peter McCloy, would roll the ball out to the full-backs. When I got it, I looked up and I had great players like Robert Prytz, Bobby Russell, Jim Bett and Davie Cooper all showing for the ball. Up front we had Derek Johnstone and John MacDonald. Everybody wanted the ball. It was magnificent for me because once I had passed the ball I was encouraged to get forward. That was probably the best I played in my career because I had so many good players playing with me.'

He continued, 'We went up to Aberdeen and we hadn't won at Pittodrie for a few years. We beat them 2-1 and I was involved in our second goal. I gave the ball in to Coop who then found Bobby Russell with a reverse pass. Bobby played it to me, I crossed it and wee Prytzy headed it in.'

Rangers were riding the crest of a wave but another trip to West Germany delivered a fatal blow to the confidence that was surging through the side. Thereafter any hopes of a successful season foundered.

'We beat Borussia Dortmund and we were fantastic,' said MacKinnon. 'I honestly thought that that team would go on and win the league. We then faced Cologne [in the UEFA Cup], beat them 2-1 at Ibrox and there was a piece in the German press that said I would have kicked a rabbit if it ran across the park. When we got to Germany I got into my room and I had a rabbit in my bed! In the match we were 4-0 down after 25 minutes and it ended up 5-0. We actually played okay but they were sensational.'

He continued, 'Confidence is huge in football and in the next league game when I got the ball from the goalkeeper, I looked but nobody wanted it. The confidence was out the side and that caused us a lot of problems.'

Defeat in the League Cup Final followed against Celtic in early December and Rangers fell away in the race for the title. A miserable season was capped when Aberdeen won the Scottish Cup, beating Greig's men 1-0 at Hampden after extra time.

'I felt we were the better team against Celtic but we got beat 2-1,' recalled MacKinnon. 'Against Aberdeen we were almost certainly the best team. Jim Bett hit an unbelievable shot from 30 yards that Jim Leighton saved and Billy Davies, who came on as sub, scored with a header at the back post but the referee said he had fouled the defender. The odds were against us and it was a huge disappointment.'

Davie MacKinnon ended his debut season having made 46 first-team appearances. An ankle injury sustained against Aberdeen had kept him out of the side for six weeks but his committed displays won admiration from the Rangers supporters. He became a fan's favourite, earning himself 35 Player of the Year awards.

However, if season 1982/83 suggested MacKinnon would be a mainstay in the first team for years to come, season 1983/84 was the polar opposite. After missing most of pre-season, he picked up his first winners' medal as substitute in the Glasgow Cup Final against Celtic. He marked his first competitive appearance with a goal against Queen of the South in the League Cup. MacKinnon appeared in 11 of the first 13 Premier Division matches too but appearances would be sporadic thereafter. Indeed, between late November 1983 and April 1984 he only made one appearance as substitute.

He explained, 'I was suspended for the first two games of the season then John Greig left and Jock Wallace came in. Around mid-November we played Aberdeen. I was one of the only players that ate eggs and there was an outbreak of hepatitis A at the hotel in Aberdeen where we had our pre-match meal. Shortly afterwards we were playing Hibs and Jock Wallace took me for a walk around the track. He asked what was wrong with me as he felt I had lost all my energy. I then went to the toilet and my urine was black which meant I had hepatitis. That was a difficult time but Jock used to phone me every Saturday night and told me how the game went. I couldn't go out the house and my diet meant I lost a lot of weight.'

MacKinnon returned to the first-team fold as substitute for Robert Prytz in a 1-0 win over Celtic at Ibrox in April. Two further appearances from the bench coupled with two starts at right-back gave the resolute Ranger a total of 23 appearances. He had, however, missed out on a place in the League Cup Final through suspension.

'I came back after the hepatitis and the manager said if I could prove my fitness in the reserves I would be back in the squad,' recalled MacKinnon. 'I played against Dunfermline at East End Park [in the Reserve League West] and I was captain. Jock was there watching. I tackled someone, won the ball, but the referee booked me and, believe it or not, that took me past the booking threshold so I missed the cup final.'

At the conclusion of the campaign Davie thought his days at Ibrox were numbered. Hearts had shown an interest in taking him to Tynecastle and there was a reported bid from Billy McNeill's Manchester City too. However, rather than seek pastures new MacKinnon was selected in the travelling party for the post-season world tour.

'It was a crazy tour,' noted MacKinnon. 'I played most of the games but it was a strange tour. It was supposed to develop team spirit but it didn't really. There were a lot of divisions within the team. They had brought in a lot of new players and there was a definite split. There were three or four different factions within the team so I don't think it did what Jock Wallace wanted it to do.'

On their return a pre-season tour of Switzerland and West Germany was arranged but there was still uncertainty over the future of Davie MacKinnon. However, after an appearance against Solothurn at left-back, MacKinnon was restored to his favoured right-back role for a 2-1 win over Kaiserslautern. He was voted Man of the Match and, following the match, Wallace confirmed MacKinnon was back in his plans.

'That season [1984/85] was strange,' said MacKinnon. 'I played a lot but I alternated between right-back, centre-back and midfield. I think that versatility held me back but wherever I played I was the type of player who gave 100%. I would never have allowed where I was playing to alter how I played.'

Wallace, however, had been fulsome in his praise of MacKinnon. In his newspaper column in the *Evening Times* he held MacKinnon up as proof that if you have the desire and ability and you work hard enough you can get to the top with the team you want to go to. That did not excuse him from constructive feedback, though.

Davie recalled, 'All the players were in and big Jock had his arms over the treatment table that was in the middle of the dressing room. He called me out and grabbed my ear and said I made too many passes. He wanted me to have two touches, one to control it, the other to hoof it up to the front man. Everyone was looking at me and I probably made one of the worst moves I ever made; I told him I couldn't do it. I told him that I needed three touches, two to control it and the other to hoof it! I was trying to be smart but he grabbed me round the throat and then slapped me.'

Heartbreak was not far away. MacKinnon played in all the League Cup ties leading up to the final against Dundee United in October 1984. He was included in the squad that travelled down to Turnberry in the week prior to the match and was informed by Jock Wallace that he would be in the starting 11. Alas, it did not turn out that way.

MacKinnon recalled, 'We played in a practice match on the Saturday at Girvan. I played centre-midfield and was told I'd be playing in the final. I phoned my family and told them but when we got up to Ibrox and Jock announced the team, I wasn't in it. Even worse, Robert Prytz, who hadn't been at Turnberry, was on the bench. It was great that the guys won but I was still a bit upset so the next day I went to see big Jock. He told me I wouldn't miss another game that season and that I would be playing against Inter Milan on the Wednesday.'

So what had prompted the manager's change of heart? Why had MacKinnon gone from being left out of the cup final 13 to being back on the front line for a vital European tie?

'Jock showed me the team sheet he had written out on the Saturday night,' continued MacKinnon. 'I was playing. But he told me that on the Saturday night he'd had a dream about the team and I wasn't in it so that's why he dropped me!'

Wallace was true to his word. MacKinnon played centre-midfield in the epic 3-1 win over Inter Milan and between then and the final game of the league campaign against Hibernian at Easter Road, he missed only four matches, all of which were through suspension. In total he made 53 first-team appearances, during which he maintained his love affair with the Rangers support, winning a clutch of Player of the Year awards from supporters' clubs.

One of those 53 appearances was on a poisonous night in Dublin. When Rangers were drawn against Bohemians in the opening round of the UEFA Cup there was always the chance that there would be an incendiary atmosphere at the first leg in the Fair City and that proved to be the case.

'We were staying in a castle outside Dublin and there were threats made to the team and there was an armed guard everywhere we went,' recalled MacKinnon. 'We got to the ground and it was madness. I was playing right-back and I chased their winger into the corner and the ball went out for our goal kick. I went to get the ball and there was this guy running towards me with a balaclava on. He threw a rock against the fence and it splintered through and some of it went in my eye.'

The location of goalkeeper Nicky Walker also gave MacKinnon cause for concern. He was standing so far from his goal line that MacKinnon feared he would be lobbed.

'I told him to get back on his goal line,' continued Davie. 'But he showed me that there were darts everywhere! It was just a matter of getting out of it.

'I don't get scared very often but that could have potentially blown up into something.'

Political angst was commonplace that season for the Rangers first team. After elimination from the Scottish Cup in mid-February at the hands of Dundee, there were free weekends so the club's hierarchy decided to embark on a tour of the Middle East. Three matches were played, two in Baghdad and one in Amman, Jordan. MacKinnon has vivid recollections of the impromptu tour.

He said, 'We were told we were going on a tour the next cup weekend. We wondered where we were going. We were told we'd be flying to London and then flying to Baghdad! It was crazy and at the hotel we were asked to go into a room. We met Tariq Aziz and Saddam Hussein and Saddam told us to go back and tell people in the UK that the Iranians were the aggressors and that the Iraqis were peace loving. In the first game it was 1-1. Hugh Burns tackled somebody, really over the top, and big Jock took him off. He was shouting at Shuggie, "Saddam's in the stands, you're going to start World War III."'

Season 1985/86 would prove to be Davie MacKinnon's last in a Rangers jersey. Despite performing well in pre-season and being assured by the manager he was in the team for the season, MacKinnon was soon back in the reserves, playing for the second string as they walloped North Uist 13-1 in July 1985. With Hugh Burns the preferred option at right-back, MacKinnon found himself either playing in midfield when selected for the first team or covering for the injured Craig Paterson at centre-back. However, MacKinnon was soon hampered by a knee injury he picked up in the Reserve League Cup semi-final against Celtic.

'I didn't want my Rangers career to end in the reserves,' said MacKinnon. 'I got a really bad knee injury and went for a cartilage operation. Because of other injuries Jock wanted me to play centre-back against Celtic. It was the 4-4 game at Ibrox. The physio told him my knee was knackered but Jock asked me if I wanted to play and I said I did.'

It would prove to be a memorable day for the redoubtable MacKinnon as he scored one of Rangers' four goals. Although the record books credit Cammy Fraser with two goals that day, Davie will always count the looping header that edged Rangers 4-3 ahead as his goal.

He recalled, 'The *Rangers News* gave the goal to me and if we'd had VAR at that time it would have been mine! I met Pat Bonner [goalkeeper for Celtic that afternoon] at Glasgow Airport recently and he said it was my goal so I'm definitely claiming a goal against Celtic!'

Not long after the epic draw with Celtic, Jock Wallace was gone. Graeme Souness came in and Rangers were set to be aroused from their recent slumber. For Davie MacKinnon, initial hopes that he would be a part of Rangers' resurrection eventually evaporated.

'Souness actually took me aside and said he knew my knee was knackered but he wanted me to play centre-midfield,' said MacKinnon. 'We needed to qualify for Europe but Souness wanted to bring in young players like Ian Durrant and Derek Ferguson and he was looking for me to help talk them through the game. Although my contract was up Souness said it would be renewed and I would get rehab for my knee.'

Then came the U-turn. Having played in the final four league matches, including the 2-0 win over Motherwell that secured fifth place and UEFA Cup qualification for season 1986/87, MacKinnon was told before the Glasgow Cup Final against Celtic that his Rangers career was over.

'There was a full house at Ibrox but I was called in by Souness before the game and he told me my contract wouldn't be renewed,' recalled MacKinnon. 'He did tell me I was his type of player but he didn't think my knee was going to make it. He asked me if I still wanted to play [against Celtic] and I said I did. I went out and my team-mates, family and the supporters didn't know that this would be my last game for Rangers. I played centre-midfield and I set up a couple of Ally's goals in our 3-2 win.'

With his team-mates still none the wiser, MacKinnon reluctantly bid farewell to the Rangers supporters as they wildly celebrated the one memorable moment in an otherwise wretched season. Back in the dressing room Souness broke the news to the squad that the experienced MacKinnon would not be part of the picture at Ibrox for the new season.

MacKinnon noted, 'Everyone was celebrating when Graeme let the boys know that that had been my last game. The lads couldn't believe it. I collected my boots and I was wearing the number four jersey so I decided I was taking it. I was walking along the corridor when the physio, Bob Findlay, came running out. He told me I couldn't have the shirt as I would ruin a good set. We ended up with me pulling one arm and him pulling the other before I gave him a nudge – I felt like slide tackling him – and I got my jersey.'

Although it was a surreal and sad time, Davie left Rangers with only good memories. An abiding one is of his time playing alongside the late, great Davie Cooper.

'Davie Cooper was a brilliant player,' recalled McKinnon. 'You knew if you just gave him the ball, he played. We had a great relationship because I had played against him a lot of times and he told me that he was glad that I had signed [for Rangers] as I was the only player he couldn't beat. During my education at Arsenal they really taught you how to play the game and one of the key things for any defender was to keep your eye on the ball. Coop was a great guy for jaunting back and forward but by keeping my eye on the ball, I knew I could always get it. When he said that to me – and it was in front of the players – it took me to another level when you've got a wonderful player and a wonderful guy telling you he's glad you're playing in his team. I also thought Jim Bett was a magnificent player for Rangers. He had a wonderful engine and he was always looking for the ball. He had a difficult relationship with the fans at times but, like Coop, he was a world-class player.'

MacKinnon now had to decide where his future lay. He had offers from 1860 Munich, Motherwell and St Mirren but elected to go part-time, signing for Airdrie in August 1986.

'I couldn't train every day so it was a difficult time for me on the field,' said MacKinnon. 'Off the field it was a good time as I started working with Tennent's. In those days you didn't earn enough money as a player so I had 12 years there as area manager and director.'

After three seasons, 98 league appearances and two Player of the Year awards, MacKinnon left Airdrie and joined Kilmarnock. The Ayrshire side were then in the Second Division but MacKinnon etched his name in the folklore of the club when his penalty kick secured promotion in the final game of season 1989/90 against Cowdenbeath. However, two further operations on his cartilage meant it was time to call time on his football career. He left

Kilmarnock in 1991 and had a season with Forfar Athletic, making his final league appearance on 18 April 1992 in a 1-1 draw against Stirling Albion, a month shy of his 36th birthday. After pursuing his business interests, Davie returned to the football world, taking on executive roles at Kilmarnock, Dundee and Hamilton. Today he is managing director at the popular online station, Rock Sport Radio.

He concluded, 'My biggest highlights at Rangers were, collectively, the European games. We had some great games and the fans made them electric nights. I played out of my skin in those games so every European game at Ibrox was just magnificent. Regrets? I got injuries and illness at the wrong time and because you'd play anywhere when you came back, to get a game, you became known as the utility player. At the end of the day, though, I wouldn't have changed a thing.'

Davie MacKinnon made a total of 169 appearances for the club, scoring three goals, taking into account the Old Firm goal of course! Had he not had to contend with hepatitis and latterly his knee trouble, he reckons he would have played nearer 250 times in a Rangers jersey. He won two Glasgow Cup medals (1983/84 and 1985/86) and two Reserve League Championship medals (1983/84 and 1985/86).

Big Badge
Stuart Beattie (1985–1986)

When Stuart Beattie signed for Rangers in April 1985, three months shy of his 18th birthday, he set himself the target of a first-team debut within two years. This was not a lack of faith in his ability; it was merely recognition that in his position of centre-half Rangers had the likes of club captain Craig Paterson, David McPherson, Derek Johnstone, Dave MacKinnon and the versatile Ally Dawson to call upon.

'I first played for Rangers at U18 level in a match against the Scotland amateur team at The Albion,' recalled Stuart. 'I was actually meant to be sub for Scotland but John Haggart, the reserve coach, said that the Rangers team needed a centre-half and asked if I could play. I played well and scored and after the game John asked me if I would go with the Rangers team to an U18 tournament in Dusseldorf.'

Despite picking up an injury in the match – he tore his ligaments – Beattie was invited to Ibrox every day for a fortnight to get treatment before travelling with the team to West Germany. He said, 'When we went to Dusseldorf we played four matches. Jock Wallace came over on the Saturday night after the first-team game against Celtic and watched the two games on the Sunday. I was sent off against Russia in the first match but after the second match, I was invited to Jock's hotel room and offered a two-year contract on £70 a week. Jock said he had been impressed with how I'd played and that I potentially had a big future at Ibrox.'

Beattie had always wanted to play professional football but on his return to Scotland he had to make a phone call. There must be very few people in football who turned down the overtures of Sir Alex Ferguson, but Stuart Beattie did.

'I was due to go to Pittodrie for a week's trial,' he said, 'but I phoned and said I wouldn't be coming. Alex Ferguson then phoned me back and said not to sign for Rangers and come up to Aberdeen. But I was only 18 at the time and didn't want to move home and Rangers were a massive club so I decided to stay with them. Aberdeen then went out and signed Brian Irvine and I wondered if I had made the wrong choice. But when you get a chance to sign for Rangers, you don't knock them back.'

Beattie started his Rangers career with a bang. After making three appearances for the second team at the end of season 1984/85 – including a 5-0 thrashing by Celtic – he was in the reserve team that beat North Uist 13-1, Newton Stewart 5-0, Wigtown 10-0 and Falkirk 3-0 in pre-season friendlies ahead of the 1985/86 campaign. He even played alongside the future Michelin-star chef, Gordon Ramsay, in a 1-1 draw against East Kilbride. Ramsay was listed as a trialist in a match that proved to be his one and only appearance in a Rangers jersey. Stellar performances at the heart of the defence against Hearts (5-0), Celtic (1-0) and St Mirren (5-0) in the Premier Reserve League followed and Stuart was rewarded with a place on the substitutes' bench when the first team faced Queen's Park in the Glasgow Cup Final at Hampden on 9 September. He recalled, 'We were sitting having lunch after training when John Haggart came up and told me I was in the squad. There were 18 in the squad so I didn't expect to play but when the team went up on the noticeboard, I saw I was sub.'

Less than five months after signing his contract Stuart realised his ambition of playing for the Rangers first team when he replaced David McFarlane in the second half. When Beattie took to the field he did so alongside the likes of Ally McCoist, Derek Johnstone and Derek Ferguson.

'For the first five or ten minutes I was chasing shadows,' admitted Beattie, 'but we won the game 5-0 and Cammy Fraser scored a hat-trick. Then on the way home my dad drove through a red light and got stopped by the police. While he got his ticket, I just sat there in the front seat holding my wee trophy!'

Just six weeks after collecting his first medal Stuart Beattie was playing in the Premier Division. With Paterson and McPherson suspended, Stuart was chosen to start the match against Hibernian on 19 October 1985. He was part of a five-man defence: Hugh Burns was at right-back, Stuart Munro at left-back, Ally Dawson at sweeper and David McKinnon partnered Stuart at centre-back.

'It was the highlight of my Rangers career but it was a complete shock on the Friday before the game when John Haggart took me in to the Boot Room and the gaffer was there,' said Beattie. 'He said that he was going to play me the next day and I was stunned, it was like a bolt out of the blue. After we spoke, I got the tube into Glasgow and I saw an article in the *Evening Times* that said I was going to start the game, it was that quick.'

Beattie was up against Gordon Durie and Steve Cowan, both renowned goalscorers, but he acquitted himself well even though the visitors won the match 2-1. An own goal from Munro and a late strike from Colin Harris had Hibernian 2-0 ahead before an 84th-minute penalty from Davie Cooper reduced the arrears.

'The main difference between first-team football and reserve-team football was pace,' noted Beattie. 'The pace of the game was frightening, so fast. We marked differently too. In the reserves it was man-marking but in the first team we had our own wee areas to look after so it was more zonal marking.'

The atmosphere inside Ibrox was memorable too. The attendance that day was listed as 23,478 – just over half full – but Stuart remembers the noise and the buzz around the ground when the teams emerged from the tunnel. He noted, 'Before the referee tossed the coin I was doing my stretches and the fans in the Copland Road end were shouting, "Stuart, Stuart, gie's a wave." I thought they were shouting at Stuart Munro but Ally McCoist came over and asked why I wasn't waving to the fans. He explained that they were shouting for me as it was my debut. It was an unbelievable feeling; the hairs on the back of my neck and my arms, were all standing up.'

Two weeks later, with David McPherson free from suspension and back in the first-team fold, Beattie returned to the reserves. The second string was top of the Premier Reserve League and had lost just once all season. They made the short trip across the city to face Celtic at Parkhead and it was a memorable match for Stuart for all the wrong reasons.

He recalled, 'I got sent off for two bookable offences. Owen Archdeacon was through on goal so I took him out and, having been booked earlier, I knew as soon as I had done it I would be off. As I was walking up the tunnel I was spat at by a couple of the Celtic supporters so I gestured back to them. I didn't think anything of it until the Monday morning when I was called up to the gaffer's office. Jock Wallace basically ripped me to shreds. He said that as a Rangers player you had to respect every team you play and although I said I'd been provoked he said you had to expect that and deal with it. I was fined £30, which was almost half my weekly wage at that time.'

Evidently Beattie did not irk his manager too much. At the end of November he joined the first-team squad as they jetted out to Malta for friendly matches against Hamrun Spartans and Valletta. 'The reason I got on the trip was because Hughie Burns had been booked on the Saturday which meant he would be suspended for the next two games after the break,' said Beattie.

But there was an issue; Stuart did not have a valid passport! 'The one I used to get to Dusseldorf was only a one-year passport and it had expired,' laughed Stuart, 'so John Haggart and I had to go up to the Passport Office in Glasgow to sit and wait so I could get a ten-year passport to make the trip.'

Beattie roomed with David McFarlane in Malta and wore the number five jersey in both matches. Fellow reserve-teamer Scott Nisbet was the star of the trip, scoring a brace in the 4-1 win over Hamrun Spartans and a hat-trick in the 7-0 victory over Valletta. His goalscoring exploits made him ripe for a wind-up.

'Ally McCoist nailed him,' said Stuart with a smile. 'Big Nissy was in his hotel room when he took a phone call from someone claiming to be a reporter from the *Evening Times*. It was actually McCoist winding him up. Ally was a funny guy and he was asking Nissy what it was like to score the goals and play up front with Ally McCoist. Nissy was giving it "oh he's brilliant" and all that. He kept him going for about four hours by which time Nissy had told everybody that he'd had the *Evening Times* on the phone. We were in the dining room having dinner when Ally finally told him it was him on the phone. Nissy was raging but we were all laughing.'

On their return to Scottish shores Beattie remained in the first-team frame. With Craig Paterson now sidelined with an ankle injury, Stuart was at the heart of the Rangers defence for a 1-0 win over Motherwell – the first clean sheet in the league for a month – and a 1-1 draw against Dundee United at Ibrox. In the latter match David Dodds gave Beattie a torrid time. It was another step on the steep learning curve of playing for the Rangers first team. 'He punched me in the stomach,' recalled Beattie with a wince. 'Dundee United got the kick-off and Dodds ran at me, punched me and I doubled over. I tried to get back but he got ahead of me and scored, in off the post. It was only about 55 seconds in and Jock Wallace didn't see the goal as he was still in the changing room which was a bonus for me.'

Conduct like this was part and parcel of the game in the 1980s and Dodds was merely using his experience to try and put the frighteners on the young emerging centre-back. Beattie gave as good as he got. He said, 'The first half flew by but Davie Dodds had a Tubigrip on his thigh and after about 25 or 30 minutes of the game I got a chance to get him back. I caught him on the thigh and even after treatment, he was struggling.'

Dodds was eventually replaced with 20 minutes remaining and Ally McCoist earned Rangers a point, and his team-mates a bonus, when he equalised ten minutes later. 'When you played for the first team you essentially doubled your money,' said Beattie. 'As well as that you got £100 appearance money and £50 per point so, as it was two points for a win in those days, I could earn £340 if I played for the first team and we won.'

The 1-1 draw with United 11 days before Christmas proved to be Stuart's last first-team appearance until February. When he returned to the reserves he was heading back to Parkhead for another Old Firm battle, this time in the semi-final of the Reserve League Cup.

Alongside him at centre-half that Boxing Day afternoon was Derek Johnstone.

'It was brilliant playing with big DJ,' recalled Beattie. 'Every game I played in the reserves with Derek he would talk you through everything and pass his experience on. He had played in a European final at centre-half and he would sit down with you and explain things. You can't pay for advice like that.'

The reserves were chasing a league and cup double and a first Reserve League Cup since 1976/77. However, although Robert Fleck's penalty equalised an early goal scored by Lex Baillie to force extra time, a header from the experienced Alan McInally in the 114th minute put Celtic in the final. 'Big Peter McCloy had a right go at me for that goal,' said Beattie, 'but I thought that since the ball was in the six-yard box, he should have come for it.'

When Stuart returned to first-team action on 1 February 1986, he did so alongside Derek Johnstone. Reigning champions Aberdeen were the visitors and although Joe Miller scored after just three minutes, a Hugh Burns goal seven minutes after half-time earned Rangers a 1-1 draw. Six weeks later, after playing in a 1-1 draw against Elgin City in Charles McHardy's testimonial, Stuart made his ninth first-team appearance of the season. Rangers lost to Dundee in a 2-1 defeat at Dens Park. This left Beattie just one appearance short of triggering a clause in his contract that would see him granted an extension if he made ten appearances for the first team.

Next up for Rangers was the final Old Firm tussle of the season against Celtic at Ibrox. With Paterson still injured, Stuart was hopeful of retaining his place in the team and making that tenth first-team appearance, but it was not to be.

'No footage exists of my games with Rangers as there was a TV ban at the time,' recalled Stuart, 'but it was lifted the week of the Celtic game so that made me want to play even more. It was torrential rain that day and I knew the big man [Paterson] was struggling, but at 12.30 Jock took me a walk down the tunnel and said he was going with experience and was dropping me. That's the game you want to play in – the atmosphere was frightening – but the gaffer said it was nothing to do with my performances, that I had done really well, he just didn't want to throw me in at the deep end in what was an important game for us. The sweetener was that I was 14th man [in those days the matchday squad comprised the starting 11 and two substitutes] which meant I was on half bonus.'

Beattie watched as his team-mates fought out an enthralling 4-4 draw but it proved to be one of Jock Wallace's last in charge of Rangers. Indifferent league form, a third-round Scottish Cup exit and defeat in the Skol Cup semi-final meant a first season without a major trophy for five years. Just 15 days after the Celtic match, Wallace was sacked. His second spell as manager yielded just two League Cup triumphs.

'I think there was a reserve game that night and we were told the gaffer had been sacked,' recalled Beattie. 'Jock was like a father figure to the players and we were all sad to see him go. His style wouldn't survive nowadays but he would take you under his wing although he wouldn't hold back from giving you a slap if you stepped out of line. Nicky Walker was in tears but at that time we weren't told who was coming in. It was numbing and over the next few days, things unfolded.'

Beattie also recalled his one and only trip to the infamous sand dunes at Gullane. During his first spell in charge at Ibrox, the annual trip to East Lothian had entered Rangers folklore, as the players were challenged to run up and down the undulating dunes. 'That was the worst day of my life, torture,' said Stuart with a shudder. 'You basically trained until you were sick and you weren't allowed to stop. We went through on the bus, got changed, ran up and down the dunes until we dropped then washed ourselves in the sea and got back on the bus back to Ibrox. Your thighs would be killing you, real, real pain but Jock had done it for so many seasons before so you didn't question it. Managers today wouldn't get away with it, though.'

The remainder of pre-season training was carried out running up and down the stairs at Ibrox or on The Albion training ground opposite the stadium. 'I don't think we saw a ball for about two or three weeks,' is Stuart's rueful recollection.

There was a transformation when Wallace's replacement arrived, though. Within days of Wallace's sacking, the winds of change blew through Ibrox at hurricane speed. In swept the club's first player-manager, one Graeme James Souness. He quickly made his mark. Beattie recalled, 'He called a big meeting with the players in the home changing room and told us that he was new to this but he was going to improve the standards and the performances, because we were shocking, basically.'

The first change was with the training kit. 'Under Jock we were given training kit on a Monday and that was it until the Friday,' said Stuart. 'It didn't matter what the weather was, at the end of training you would put your kit in a big cage then take it back out again the next day. The only thing washed daily was our slips; the kit was only washed on a Friday.'

Under Souness the players were issued with fresh kit every day and the wearing of flip flops, or sliders as Stuart called them, was compulsory, with players fined if caught not wearing them.

Training was different too. 'Jock was a lot more inclusive, reserves and first team,' said Beattie. 'Souness's focus was the first team. A youngster like me would walk past him in the corridor and he wouldn't speak to you. As an impressionable youngster at the time that was tough to take. We would train at The Albion and the reserves would play on the ash park and the first team on the grass. Under Jock we all trained together and would usually finish the session with the first team playing the reserve team in a game. However, under both gaffers we trained as we played. Ally McCoist used to elbow me and lash out when I tried to turn him in training and one Friday I hit Ted McMinn so hard that he injured his ankle and missed the game on the Saturday.'

Beattie was fortunate enough to get some time on the training field with two of Souness's best signings. He recalled, 'When Jock was manager, training finished at 12.30 and you were told to go home and rest. But when the likes of Terry Butcher and Chris Woods were signed they would often stay back after the first team had finished training and they'd ask me and Scott Nisbet to stay back with them to practice headers and stuff like that. Butcher was brilliant that way.'

The wage structure changed too. At the time of Souness's arrival, the highest-paid players at Ibrox were earning £250 per week so with the influx of the likes of Woods and Butcher, all players were given new contracts. 'I got a wage rise,' said Beattie. 'I went from £70 a week to £110 a week with the same appearance fee and bonuses we had under Jock. We also weren't allowed to go out drinking after a Wednesday. Previous to that the likes of myself, wee Durrant, Derek Ferguson, McCoist and Nicky Walker used to go out on a Thursday. I'd stay at Nicky's flat and the dressing room on a Friday morning used to smell like a brewery!'

With the slate wiped clean Beattie recognised that Souness's remit of restoring Rangers to the pinnacle of Scottish football would mean he would likely spend the next couple of seasons playing predominantly for the reserves. However, although he had impressed under Jock Wallace, he never felt he would get the same opportunity to impress Souness. And he reckons the seeds were sown for his Ibrox departure before the 1986/87 season had kicked off.

He recalled, 'Under Jock we always came back for pre-season in the third week in July so I had booked a holiday but Souness decided to bring us back earlier. Walter Smith told me not to worry about it as I wouldn't be going with the first team to West Germany but Souness told me to cancel my holiday. I decided not to. And that's the biggest regret of my Rangers career. Scott Nisbet was in the same position as me but he cancelled his holiday and went on to do well in the first team. I often wonder if I had done the same, if things might have turned out differently.'

Although he was still doing well in the reserves, such was the consistency of Dave McPherson and Terry Butcher – McPherson missed only two of the 44 Premier League matches and captain Butcher just one – first-team chances were limited and Stuart was only involved in one first-team squad under Graeme Souness. 'Big Jock would come to most of the reserve games but in my time there Souness only went to one, against Hibs at Easter Road,' said Stuart. 'He picked me in his squad once, for a game against Aberdeen at Pittodrie but I wasn't selected as part of the 13.'

Rangers won the league for the first time in nine years in 1986/87 but Stuart Beattie was no longer on the books by then. In December 1986, his Ibrox journey was over. Ten days before Christmas he was in the reserve team that played Queen's Park. Beattie, who had received fulsome praise from reserve coach Donald Mackay for his performances in the second team, was introduced to Dave Cusack, manager of Doncaster Rovers, after the game. Cusack had been impressed and felt he would do well for Doncaster. Stuart left Hampden that night and thought nothing more of the discussion. As far as he was concerned he was a Rangers player and he did not know where Doncaster was, far less that they had a football team. However, when he arrived at Ibrox for training shortly afterwards, Stuart was summoned to the manager's office.

Beattie recalled, 'Souness was there with Walter Smith and he told me that Dave Cusack was interested in taking me to Doncaster. I was 19 at the time and I told him I wasn't interested and wanted to stay with Rangers. He told me that was my prerogative but if I stayed I would be training three times a day, seven days a week, 10am, 2pm and 6pm. Now I stayed in Stevenson at the time and didn't drive so I said I couldn't do that. The result was I was going to Doncaster.'

Beattie was gutted and it was a real wrench to leave Rangers. 'My brother-in-law took me down to Doncaster and it was a shambles,' said Stuart. 'Their stadium was like a junior ground. On my first day at training I had no boots so I had to go to a sports shop and buy a pair then get a receipt and give it to the club. Our training gear, if you wanted it washed you had to take home and wash it yourself. It was a total difference.'

Stuart made 26 league appearances for Rovers, initially under Tottenham and Scotland legend Dave Mackay, then Joe Kinnear. But at just 21 his career was over.

'I got Man of the Match in my first game against Mansfield and played another couple of games before I injured my back against Fulham at Craven Cottage,' said Beattie. 'I was getting a pain when I moved my neck, which was travelling down my left leg and into my groin. The Doncaster surgeon felt, given my age, it might be growing pains and he gave me a cortisone injection in my groin. I went back six weeks later and it was still the same so I got another injection. The third and final injection followed but there was still no improvement. I was still doing light training at this time so I was sent to Lilleshall

Rehabilitation Centre and within five minutes they had identified I had an issue with a disc in my lumber. The first disc got removed from my back on my 20th birthday.'

The back injury signalled the end of his professional playing career. However, after taking a year out, Stuart returned to play junior football for Ardrossan Winton Rovers. He also had time with Cumnock Juniors and Kilbirnie Ladeside – where he got the chance to meet his hero, Gordon McQueen – before finally quitting the game in 1995 at the age of 28.

'I had had two discs removed before I started playing juniors and then went to the Southern General in Glasgow to have a third done two days after I played for Kilbirnie against Auchinleck Talbot,' said Beattie. 'It was a risky procedure and the surgeon advised me to quit football as I could have ended up in a wheelchair. I had no alternative as by now I could hardly move my left leg.'

In April 1996 Rangers sent a team down to Ayrshire to take on an Ayrshire Junior select in a benefit match for Stuart. Ian Durrant played part of the match and Ally McCoist was also in attendance.

Although he has some regrets, notably not cancelling his summer holiday in 1986, Stuart Beattie is proud to have played for Rangers. He won a Glasgow Cup medal and was part of the team that won the Premier Reserve League in 1985/86. He made a total of nine appearances for the first team. Today he lives in Prestwick and works as a team leader with Hall's of Scotland. Although he does not attend many games these days, he remains a Rangers supporter, proudly saying, 'Once a Ranger, Always a Ranger.'

Coach
Colin Miller (1985–1986)

Colin Fyfe Miller was steeped in the Rangers tradition and dreamed of one day playing for the club he had always followed. He realised that dream when he was signed by Jock Wallace from Toronto Blizzard in July 1985, initially on a six-month contract. Unfortunately for Miller, who at the age of 20 was already a Canadian international when he arrived at Ibrox, bureaucracy and red tape meant that he ended up a victim of circumstance as a promising Rangers career was halted before it even got started.

'I was born and raised in Scotland in a little mining town called Allanton,' said Miller from his home in Abbotsford, Canada. 'My dad was a coal miner and my mum worked at Hartwood mental hospital. Like everyone at that time I played football in the street and every Christmas I would get a Rangers strip. My dad was a fanatical Rangers supporter and was actually at the Ibrox Disaster match in 1971. My grandfather was a Motherwell supporter but all my mum's family were Rangers fans too. Now, my car licence plate has 'Follow, Follow Glasgow Rangers' on it and my cell phone cover is Ibrox Park with the Rangers logo on it.'

He continued, 'We moved to Canada because it was a better way of life. My dad had some health problems and actually failed the medical twice. But he eventually passed and three weeks later the flights were booked and we moved out in February 1975.'

The Millers had to overcome a few obstacles on their arrival in Canada. The firm that were employing Mr Miller went bust and the family, mum, dad, Colin, older brother Dal and younger sisters Tracy and Sharon, had to move in with Colin's Aunt Wilma and Uncle George. And on his first day of school there was bloodshed when the locals found out that it was best not to make fun of Miller's Scottish accent! The family eventually settled in Vancouver and Miller started to play football.

'School football in Canada is not as big a deal as it is in Scotland,' said Miller. 'Instead we have a very well-organised club youth system and I played for a club in East Vancouver. I got scouted there and ended up playing in the provincial programme, representing British Columbia four times. It was actually a Rangers supporter called John McMahon who came from Toronto to watch me and I got drafted by Toronto Blizzard. Vancouver Whitecaps, Tampa Bay Rowdies and Edmonton were all interested in signing me but I was delighted to go to Toronto as they gave young footballers a chance.'

He added, 'I was actually the youngest player to play in the North American Soccer League (NASL) at that time. You couldn't sign a professional contract until your high school class had graduated. I was 17 when I graduated and the following Sunday I made my debut against Portland Timbers.'

One of Miller's team-mates in Toronto would also play alongside him when he went to Ibrox, Jimmy Nicholl.

'Jimmy was a huge influence on me, a fabulous professional,' recalled Miller. 'He's one of the funniest guys I've ever met and he actually stayed with me before his wife and kids came across. I was 17/18 at the time and it was such a thrill for me to host a guy who had played for Manchester United and played for Northern Ireland at the World Cup.

'He taught me about setting standards and I was lucky enough to have the Canadian national team captain, Bruce Wilson, as a team-mate too.'

It was while with the Blizzard that Miller first came up on Rangers' radar. With Jimmy Nicholl on the right-hand side of midfield and Miller at right-back, Toronto faced Rangers on 15 June as part of the Ibrox club's post-season world tour in 1984. Such was the quality of Miller's display, he was earmarked as one for the future. But this was not the first time he had caught the eye of the Rangers manager, Jock Wallace.

'The Blizzard manager was a chap called Bob Houghton and he was manager of Malmo when they lost to Nottingham Forest in the European Cup Final,' said Miller. 'He wanted me to go back to Scotland during the off season and asked who my local team was. The closest to Allanton was Motherwell and Jock Wallace was the manager there at that time. I came back and big Jock really took a fancy to me. What an education it was. I was there for about a month and as I was due to go back to Toronto, Jock pulled me in on the Tuesday and asked me what I thought of Celtic. I told him I was like a bull when he sees red! He then told me he didn't want me to go back to Toronto. He wanted me to rip up my contract and start for the first team at left-back against Celtic at Fir Park on the Saturday. It wasn't as easy as just ripping up the contract, though, so I went back to Toronto. But Jock said to stay in touch as you never knew what might happen.'

Wallace had the foresight to see that the NASL was in trouble and would fold eventually and, when it did, opportunity knocked for Colin Miller.

'When Rangers played Toronto in Hamilton, Ontario, big Jock was now the Rangers manager,' remembered Miller. 'My dad actually flew from Vancouver to Toronto for the match and he was all kitted out in his scarf and tammy hat. There was about 19,000 at the game and there must have been at least 15,000 Rangers supporters. Toronto beat Rangers 2-0 and after the game my dad and I went out with Ally McCoist, Peter McCloy and all the lads. It was one of the thrills of my dad's life.'

He continued, 'I saw big Jock before the game and he gave me a big hug. He was a big, hard guy but what a heart he had. He was an incredible man. At Davie Cooper's funeral [in 1995] he told me to take my coaching badges and I would make a good manager one day. That was very special to me. About a year after we beat Rangers, as Jock predicted, the NASL folded and I got a call from him at 4am asking me if I wanted to come back and play for Rangers.'

Colin and his wife, Maria, touched down in Scotland ahead of pre-season for the 1985/86 campaign. After surviving a scary ride from the airport in John Haggart's Mini Metro ['It was like an episode of *The Flintstones*, with feet hanging out the windows and no sunroof,' chuckled Miller] the couple initially stayed in the Bellahouston Hotel. Miller completed the full pre-season with the first team – Wallace had intended to take the team to West Germany but plans were changed and the club went to the Scottish Highlands instead – and the 20-year-old was part of a surprisingly small group at Ibrox. Along with Davie Cooper he was the only full international in the first-team squad. Although born in Scotland, he was a Canadian international, having won his first cap, ironically, against his birth country on 19 June 1983.

'It was a privilege and an honour to play for Canada,' recalled Miller. 'I won 61 caps and captained the team on 38 occasions. My dad's sister sponsored us to come to Canada but after a number of years you could apply to become Canadian citizens. We got our citizenship in 1982 and I captained the Canadian youth team after that. I was never asked to come back and play for Scotland but, if I'm honest, I don't think I was at that level to play for the Scottish national side at that time. I exchanged jerseys with Gordon Strachan on my debut and when we played Scotland again [in 1992], I swapped with Coisty so I have the international jerseys of two Old Firm managers.'

It was on that trip to The Highlands that Miller looked set to launch his Rangers career. Alas, red tape would put an end to his hopes of a first-team debut.

'I had played left-back in all the games in training and I was all set to start there in the first game in the Highlands,' recalled Miller ruefully. 'I was in my room sleeping when there was a knock at the door and it was big Jock. He told me he was sorry but I couldn't play as my international clearance hadn't come through. That was a huge setback. I was young and fit but it took seven weeks for the clearance to come through. That meant I couldn't play in the reserves either. There weren't many international transfers at that time so there must have been some serious mix-ups between the SFA and the Canadian FA. [Rangers secretary] Campbell Ogilivie did everything he could to speed the process up but there were no emails then like there are nowadays.'

Stuart Munro came in at left-back and hardly missed a game for the first team thereafter. Although he could also play right-back ['I could give the ball away in any position,' he joked], competition for the number two jersey from the likes of Hugh Burns and Ally Dawson was also fierce, so Miller found himself starting the season in the reserves. He was an ever-present in the second team and even got his name on the scoresheet on 14 September 1985 when he scored Rangers' seventh goal in a 7-2 win over Clydebank at Ibrox. And five days earlier he had picked up his first medal when he was selected at left-back in a strong Rangers side that defeated Queen's Park 5-0 at Hampden in the Glasgow Cup Final.

'What a thrill that was, playing for Rangers at Hampden in a cup final,' admitted Miller with pride. 'People will say that it was only the Glasgow Cup but I really don't care. There was about 15,000 there and the Rangers end was busy. Big Jock came in after the game and congratulated us all. It was a recognised first-team fixture and I was just thrilled to bits that I had helped win a cup for Rangers.'

The appearance at Hampden did not signal a change in Colin's first-team fortunes. Despite working tirelessly in training on his left foot to give him more versatility, the only glimmer of a chance had come when Miller had been placed on standby for the visit to Fir Park to face Motherwell in October. In the end, though, he remained with the reserves at Ibrox when Dougie Bell recovered from injury.

Miller admitted, 'I was never bitter about not getting enough chances, although I did chap the manager's door a number of times. It was just one of those things.'

Despite the lack of top-team action Miller was a popular figure among the Rangers following. Having moved from the Bellahouston Hotel to the Grosvenor, Miller and his wife eventually moved in with Colin's gran in Harthill.

'Harthill is as Rangers as you'll ever get so I became the town hero,' said Miller. 'I had kids watching my car but I felt embarrassed as I wish I'd played more games and been more successful at Rangers.'

Although Miller had not made inroads to the first team Wallace evidently saw enough in him to offer him a further six-month contract when his initial deal expired on 4 January 1986. The deal was sealed on Boxing Day 1985 when Rangers faced Celtic in the semi-final of the Reserve League Cup.

'I was at left-back that day and although we lost after extra time, I played very well,' recalled Miller. 'Big Jock came in before the game and you can imagine the team talk he gave. It even gives me goosebumps thinking about it now. The atmosphere was great and it was actually a very good game of football. I must have made an impression as Jock told me after the game that my contract would be extended.'

And with the ink on that contract barely dry, Miller was making his Premier Division debut against Clydebank at Ibrox a week later. Stuart Munro had donned the number three jersey in each of the 22 league fixtures to that point but Miller was drafted in to face the Bankies.

'I believe Stuart was injured,' said Miller. 'I was always training with the first team, myself, Billy Davies, big Stuart Beattie, and playing well in the reserves. But as consistent as I was, it still wasn't enough to get in ahead of Stuart [Munro] at left-back. I didn't have a car then so on the day of the game, I had to take the bus from Harthill and then the subway out to Ibrox.'

He continued, 'Whenever you got the chance with the first team you recognised the level you had to get to. In the reserves you could get away with things you would never get away with in the first team. I was still playing catch-up when it came to coming to terms with the pressure of playing for Rangers and was a bit naïve about the goldfish bowl that is the Old Firm. Big Jock was under pressure but, although we had good players who were all Rangers supporters, for some reason it just didn't click. Against Clydebank we went 2-0 up and the crowd started to get behind us. But Clydebank then had a good spell and a couple of players got a wee bit edgy. It wasn't a comfortable atmosphere as you could sense the frustration of the supporters.'

Miller retained his place the following weekend for the 2-0 home win over St Mirren and again when Rangers travelled to Tynecastle to face Hearts in the third round of the Scottish Cup on 25 January. The 3-2 defeat that day effectively ensured a barren, trophy-less season for Rangers and increased the pressure on Jock Wallace.

'The pitch at Tynecastle was like a sheet of ice,' recalled Miller. 'I kicked two off the line that day but Hearts scored with the third rebound. I thought I played very well in that game too but we lost and when you're trying to make an impact and get a run in the team, it's important to win. Maybe I was the easy one to pick to drop out the side. Before the game the following weekend the gaffer asked me if I wanted to go with the first team and sit in the stand or go with the reserves. I wanted to play. I had watched enough. I was still living my dream but I realised then I was a squad player.'

That pressure came to a head on 6 April 1986 when Rangers welcomed Tottenham Hotspur to Ibrox for a friendly. Although it was a painful night for Rangers, the match gave Colin Miller the most memorable moment of his Rangers career.

'You can only imagine the thrill I felt that night captaining Rangers,' said a proud Miller. 'Walking out alongside Ray Clemence at Ibrox was a privilege and I am thankful to big Jock for giving me that opportunity.'

The end was nigh for Wallace. David Holmes, the Rangers chief executive, had been appointed the previous November by majority shareholder, Lawrence Marlborough, and his remit was to effect changes that would drag Rangers out the doldrums. As a result, Wallace went and Graeme Souness took over. For Colin Miller, out of contract in July 1986, it was a period of uncertainty.

'Graeme Souness was my favourite player when I was growing up and I'll never forget the day he first walked in to the dressing room,' remembered Miller. 'I was due to leave to join up with the Canada squad for the World Cup in Mexico but Souness came in and said he was going to wake up a sleeping giant. I had a good relationship with him. With the greatest of respect to Jock and the staff that were there, Graeme brought different standards with him from Italy. Jock used to take us to Gullane for training – one day coming off the bus he said I'd be first to throw up and he was right – but training and game preparation under Graeme was completely different.'

Although he was going to make swingeing cuts, Souness wanted to have a look at the young players like Miller. Colin was therefore understandably delighted when he was offered the chance to extend his stay at Ibrox.

'As I had to join up with the Canada squad I didn't get the chance to see out the rest of the [1985/86] season and show Souness what I could do,' recalled Miller. 'But we had had a full-scale practice match on the pitch at Ibrox the day before I left to join up with the national team. After the game Graeme said he had heard good things about me and I was a young lad with potential so he offered me a one-year contract. He said he'd maybe see me in Mexico [the player-manager was in the Scotland squad] but, in the end, I was one of the four players that manager Tony Waiters left behind in Vancouver.'

However, despite the positive feedback and the security of the new deal, season 1986/87 was of a similar ilk to the previous campaign for Miller. When the first-team squad went to West Germany in pre-season Miller stayed at home with the reserves. And he was an ever-present for the second team throughout the early months of the season too, his run of games only coming to an end when a groin injury ruled him out of a match with Clydebank. However, such was the consistency of Stuart Munro, first-team opportunities were few and far between and by December 1986, Miller had just one top-team appearance to his name, wearing the number four jersey as a much-changed Rangers side lost 2-0 to Finnish side, Ilves Tampere in the UEFA Cup in October.

'I used to wait for Graeme to go into the sauna in the home dressing room to speak to him about playing for the first team,' said Miller. 'He told me he was impressed with my attitude and how I'd been playing in the reserves. Ironically, I used to travel through to Ibrox every day with Stuart Munro [Andy Bruce, Scott Nisbet and Craig Paterson were also in the carpool, with Colin commenting that when Nisbet drove it was frightening and that he wouldn't let him drive a supermarket trolley] but there was never any animosity. It was important for me to keep playing well, though, as I was still wearing the Rangers jersey and it still meant the world to me.'

He continued, 'I still trained with the first team and after we beat Tampere 4-0 at Ibrox, [coach] Peter McCloy asked me if I had a passport as I was travelling to Finland with the team for the second leg. Thankfully I did and I actually played centre-midfield and got Man of the Match. But we lost 2-0 and the team got changed after that.'

Something had to change and the next move in Miller's career was sealed at Lesser Hampden on 15 December 1986. He was selected to face Queen's Park in a friendly arranged ostensibly to help Souness's first signing, Colin West, regain match fitness. But for Miller it proved to be the last time he would wear a Rangers jersey.

'Hearts and Motherwell were interested in signing me but, for whatever reason, Rangers wouldn't let me go,' recalled Miller. 'Then all of a sudden Walter Smith phoned me in the house and asked me to go to the Grosvenor where the team stayed the night before a game. Terry Butcher had been sick all week so I thought I had a chance of being in the squad. I had dinner with the players and afterwards I was asked to go and see Graeme. He told me if he waited for the young players to come through at Rangers he'd be out of a job, he had to buy success. He said I was one of the players that he could move on to allow him to bring in his own players. He said that there was a chance to go to Doncaster Rovers as their manager, Dave Cusack, had watched me play against Queen's Park and was very impressed. I accepted at that point that my Rangers career was over. I wanted to play. I was never one of these players that just wanted to pick up his wages and go through the motions.'

The deal was done just before Christmas 1986, with young striker Neil Woods heading in the opposite direction, and Miller would spend 18 months in Yorkshire. He was so highly thought of that Dave Cusack sought counsel with him to recommend any other Rangers players to sign on at Belle Vue.

'After a couple of games the manager asked me to recommend any Rangers players and I said that big Stuart Beattie was a no-brainer,' said Miller. 'He wore his heart on his sleeve, was as honest as the day is long, was quick and could play a bit. I said nobody would get the better of him. Stuart came down and, before he got injured, had a terrific time. He was arguably the best centre-half in that division and Billy Bremner wanted to sign him for Leeds United. I would have recommended Billy Davies too but he had already moved on [he was given a free transfer by Souness in the summer of 1986 and had since joined St Mirren]. Myself, Billy and Stuart were always winning Player of the Year awards in the reserves and I was always surprised Billy didn't get more first-team games for Rangers as I rated him very highly.'

A brief return to Canada followed Miller's departure from Doncaster – despite captaining the side he was moved on by Dave Mackay, a legendary player with Spurs and a title-winning manager with Derby County but the poorest manager Colin played under – before he was back in Scotland for spells with Hamilton Academical, St Johnstone, Hearts, Dunfermline Athletic and Ayr United. During his year-long stint with Hearts he played, and scored, against Rangers in a Scottish Cup tie at Tynecastle, drawing praise too for nullifying the threat posed by Brian Laudrup.

'When I played at Celtic Park I got booed, even during the warm-up,' remembered Miller. 'They would call me an orange bastard. When I played against Rangers I had to be professional. But one day when I was at Dunfermline we were getting beaten 5-0 at Ibrox and the fans were singing and I ended up joining in! Andy Tod, our centre-half, asked me what I was doing and I said, "Toddy, it's f*****g 5-0 I'm joining in."'

He continued, 'I loved my time at Hearts too. For me they're the third biggest team in Scotland. We had some former Rangers players in the team like big Slim [Dave McPherson] and David Hagen. We beat Rangers 4-2 in the cup tie and when we came in afterwards the likes of John Robertson were telling the manager to fine me as I didn't celebrate my goal! In terms of Laudrup, whatever club I played for I had to man-mark either Rangers or Celtic's top player. I didn't realise how big he was – I'm 5ft 7in and he must have been about 6ft 2in – so it was quite a challenge. At that time he must have been involved in about 75-80% of Rangers' goals. He was a frightening proposition. I was an aggressive but fair player and used to give him a couple of whacks. In one game at Ibrox, one of my best pals called me a "dirty wee bastard" after one of the challenges.'

After finishing his playing career back in Canada with Abbotsford Mariners, Miller moved into coaching. It had always been his intention to do this after the cessation of his time as a player and he enjoyed several successful stints on the coaching staff at clubs like Hamilton Academical, Derby County and also for the Canadian national team.

'I did my first coaching qualification when I was at Doncaster when I was 21,' said Miller. 'By the time I was 27 or 28 I had all my UEFA A Licence badges. I was still playing so everyone, including the referees, used to call me "coach".'

Colin Miller played seven first-team games for Rangers. He won the Glasgow Cup in 1985/86 and picked up a Premier Reserve League Championship winners' medal that season too. Today he works in grassroots football back in Canada but his heart will always be at Ibrox.

He concluded, 'The Rangers result was the first result I looked for when I was playing. I played with a lot of great players and special people like Terry Butcher, Ally McCoist and Davie Cooper. Coop and I used to spend a lot of time together and would go out for dinner. [Journalist] Doug Baillie once said to me that he knew how much the club meant to me and how I was disappointed that things didn't work out. However, he assured me that every article anyone wrote about me would always refer to me as "Colin Miller, ex-Rangers" and that was the case. Once you're a bluenose, you're a bluenose forever.'

Goughie
Richard Gough (1987–1998)

The pantheon of great Rangers captains is festooned with legendary figures from the illustrious history of this wonderful football club. In there you would find the likes of Jock Drummond, Davie Meiklejohn, Jock 'Tiger' Shaw, Bobby Shearer, John Greig and Barry Ferguson. But for Rangers supporters who followed the club in the 1980s and 1990s, there is one skipper who stands tall above the rest: Charles Richard Gough.

Born in Stockholm on 5 April 1962, Gough's route to Ibrox was a circuitous one. Deemed not good enough to play for Rangers in the early 1980s, he established himself as one of Scotland's finest defenders whilst at Dundee United. Courted by Graeme Souness in 1986 to form part of the Rangers revolution, he went to Tottenham Hotspur when it became clear that United manager, Jim McLean, did not want to sell him to a rival club. But in October 1987 Souness finally got his man. It may have cost him over £1 million but Souness would later rate Gough as, pound for pound, the best signing he ever made.

'My mum was Swedish and my dad, who was from Hillington, was a paratrooper in the British Army,' recalled Gough, who even at the age of 57 still looks as if he could do a job at the heart of the Rangers defence. 'My dad captained the British Army team but was bought out the army by Charlton Athletic. When I was born, he was serving with the parachute regiment in Bahrain and my mother was in Aldershot. He didn't want me born in England so my mum asked to go back to Sweden which is why I was born there. My dad then emigrated to South Africa to play football in 1965.

'I started playing football there and got a trial with my dad's old club, Charlton, when I was 15. They signed me as an apprentice but I got homesick so I went back and played in the South African league for a bit. In February 1980 I came over to Scotland and Joe Gilroy, who had played with my dad and been manager at Queen's Park, had trials set up for me with Rangers, Dundee United and Aberdeen. The Rangers first team were in Saudi Arabia then so I went with the reserves and the youngsters to play in a game at Lesser Hampden against Queen's Park. Joe told me after the game that I had played really well and expected that I would get signed. After about a week John Greig was back so I told him I needed an answer as I had the other trials to go to. He told me that he had enough boys in my position so wouldn't be signing me. I was gutted. I was a Rangers supporter and wanted to sign for them. But I don't think my career would have worked out the way it did had I signed for Rangers then.'

As a matter of courtesy Gough decided to travel to Dundee for the trial with Dundee United. He went with the intention of going through the motions before returning to South Africa to look for employment. But it did not quite turn out that way.

'I played in the trial at Gayfield against Arbroath,' said Gough. 'I played centre-back and Walter Smith was at left-back. I didn't play very well so I said I would just move on and go to the trial at Aberdeen. But Jim McLean offered me a contract and I signed for Dundee United. I got homesick again so I went home at Christmas in 1981. I was home for about six weeks but didn't miss a game as it was a really bad winter. Jim McLean then phoned my father and told him that, in his opinion, I'd play for Scotland before I was 21. My dad persuaded me to go back and give it one more shot, which was good advice. When I came back I was never out the first team, playing midfield, right-back or left-back. It turned out to be a very good Dundee United team and I had great experiences during that period.'

Despite those great experiences and the success he had, Gough and United did not enjoy the best of fortunes against Rangers. The season after they were crowned champions and in the campaign that saw them reach the semi-finals of the European Cup, season 1983/84, United were eliminated from the League Cup by Rangers and they often struggled for results in the Premier Division too.

'We had a far better record against Celtic than we did against Rangers and Celtic were a much better team at the time,' remembered Richard. 'We had a good record against Aberdeen too and I remember scoring five or six goals against them and three or four against Celtic. Rangers always seemed to beat us, though, and even in the season after we won the league, they beat us a couple of times at Tannadice. They had a few good players, like Davie Cooper, but nowhere near enough.'

If the Rangers star was waning then Gough's was most definitely on the rise. His yearning for a return to South Africa was now a distant memory and he was an integral part of the Dundee United side that were so successful on all fronts in the early 80s.

Gough said, 'By the time I was 19 I was a regular for United at full-back. I was lucky enough to win the League Championship [in season 1982/83] and we were a good team in Europe too. There was interest from English clubs in me but United managed to stave them off before the Rangers interest came about. Graeme Souness was my captain for Scotland and I think he wanted me to be his first signing.'

Given Jim McLean had been reticent to the idea of selling Gough to an English club, it will come as no surprise that he was even more resistant when Rangers came calling with an offer of £650,000.

'Jim McLean and Dundee United didn't want to sell to a rival, which is fair enough, but when they couldn't get me, Rangers went and got big Terry [Butcher],' said Gough. 'I then went to Tottenham and everyone said to me that I was only going there for a year then I would come back to Rangers. That wasn't the case. I became captain down there and had signed a five-year contract at the start of season 1987/88. In October Rangers came back in for me but I don't think they thought Tottenham would accept the offer. They put in a ridiculous offer, something like £1.5 million [a British record fee for a defender] which was a lot of money then. Terry, who was probably the best central defender in Britain then, had cost £750,000 the year before but the offer for me was accepted. I was having some problems off the field at the time and my wife had moved back up to Scotland so everything just fell into place. I came up to speak to Rangers and signed on 3 October 1987.'

He continued, 'I was an experienced player when I came up here. I was 25 years old and had played for Scotland 35 times but the press questioned the size of the fee for me. But Graeme took a lot of pressure off me by saying that I would play for the club for ten years which worked out at £150,000 per year. On the same day I signed for Rangers, Celtic signed Frank McAvennie. I was captain of Tottenham and he was the top scorer in the English First Division. Can you imagine that happening today? That's like Harry Kane coming up to play in Scotland.'

Gough joined a team laden with international players like Butcher, Woods, Nicholl, McCoist, Durrant and Cooper, but the team ended up in a state of flux in what was Souness's second season in charge.

He noted, 'There was a big turnover of players. Graeme brought a lot of players in but when he realised he had made a mistake and that a player wasn't good enough for the club, he moved them on very quickly. That turnover wasn't good for the team, though, and we struggled that season, especially after Terry broke his leg.'

Gough enjoyed a whirlwind start to his Rangers career. He made his debut, ironically, against Dundee United at Tannadice and before his first month at the club had ended, he had pocketed a winners' medal and scored a last-gasp goal in a tempestuous Old Firm game.

'Iain Ferguson, the former Rangers player, scored the winning goal for United on my debut and the following week I made my home debut against Celtic,' said Gough. 'We were down to nine men – Woods and Butcher were sent off – but I scored the equaliser in the last minute. We then played Aberdeen in the League Cup Final and I can remember that as being Durrant's cup final. He was fantastic that day and I thought he was going to be some player. Aberdeen were a very strong, powerful team at that time, with players like Bett, McLeish, McKimmie and Leighton. If you watch the match back it was some game of football and we showed our spirit that day by winning on penalties. Our togetherness was starting to grow and we were learning how to win.'

The next time Rangers faced Aberdeen was not so memorable. In addition to losing 1-0, Terry Butcher broke his leg and that injury would eventually rule him out for the remainder of the season. The loss of Butcher, who had been colossal since he had signed for the club, was massive and many felt that any hopes of retaining the Premier Division title ended that fateful evening. Butcher's prolonged absence meant a defensive reshuffle, with Gough moving from right-back to his more favoured position of centre-back. His partner at the heart of the Rangers defence, Graham Roberts, had also come from Tottenham and was a cult hero amongst the Rangers support.

'I had played centre-back for the whole of the previous season at Tottenham but initially at Rangers, Graeme played me at right-back,' said Richard. 'But when Terry got injured I moved to centre-back which suited me. Graham Roberts was a terrific player and had had a good season the year before. But I think he was getting towards the end of his time and then he had a falling out with Graeme. No one wins after falling out with Graeme.'

He continued, 'The following season it really started to kick off for me. I got a good pre-season, Terry was back and Gary Stevens came in [at right-back] and made a big difference. I was playing in my favoured position – although Andy Roxburgh was still playing me at right-back for Scotland – and it all started to fall into place at Rangers.'

In season 1988/89 Gough missed just one of the 36 Premier Division matches and the returning Butcher was absent from duty just twice. That consistency of selection was the foundation upon which the title challenge was built and Rangers won what would prove to be the first of nine successive league titles when Hearts were beaten 4-0 at Ibrox in April 1989.

'That was a very strong Rangers team,' said Gough. 'That team and the one in 1992/93 were resilient whereas in 1995/96 when we had Gascoigne and Laudrup, we were much more flamboyant. But in 1988/89 we had guys like Stevens, myself, Butcher, John Brown or Stuart Munro, Wilkins, Durrant, Cooper, Walters and Ferguson in the middle of the park and McCoist and Drinkell up front. That was probably the strongest and most physical Rangers team that I played in. Souness realised very quickly that teams were going to try and kick us off the park so he brought in players that weren't going to be intimidated and could also fight as well as play. Celtic had a strong team too but we battered them 5-1 and 4-1 that season.'

With Mark Walters laying claim to the number 11 jersey more often than not, it meant less game time for Davie Cooper, a player Gough had been a direct opponent of during his time at Dundee United. At the start of the season Cooper's service to Rangers was recognised with a testimonial against Bordeaux and Gough has fond memories of a world-class player.

'Davie didn't really talk to too many people but I knew him through the Scotland team,' recalled Richard. 'I always liked him a lot as a man. He had a sharp sense of humour too. He said something interesting to me one day. He said he wished guys like myself had been at the club five years earlier. He was the diamond in the teams of the early 80s but couldn't shine as much as he did after we arrived. He was now playing with better players and was getting more of the ball. I look at the Rangers team now and look at [Andy] Halliday. He did alright but he's now doing really well, because he's playing with better players. By playing with better players your game elevates itself and that's why it's always good to refresh your team.'

Another enthralling League Cup Final win over Aberdeen – a double from McCoist and a spectacular strike from Ian Ferguson gave Rangers a 3-2 win – coupled with the title win, set Rangers up for a shot at winning the domestic Treble for the first time since season 1977/78. It was not to be, though, as a freak Joe Miller goal gave Celtic a 1-0 win.

'I remember it well,' said Gough. 'It was a typical Old Firm final, a tousy affair. Gary Stevens was short with a pass back after Roy Aitken took a throw-in that wasn't theirs. But we didn't play well enough on the day to get the win. I always remember Souness coming into the dressing room at the end of the game and he threw his medal right down the dressing room. He said he didn't collect second prizes. All the young boys were diving to get it and one of them did and put it in his pocket.'

Season 1988/89 was also memorable for Gough on a personal level as he picked up the Scottish Football Writers' Player of the Year award. He was the first Rangers player to win the award since Derek Johnstone 11 years earlier and it added to his own collection too as he had been voted PFA Scotland Player of the Year by his fellow professionals in season 1985/86.

Another stalwart for Rangers at that time was Ray Wilkins. Brought to Ibrox a matter of weeks after Gough had arrived, he added a touch of class and experience to the Rangers midfield. He also brought with him sage advice following spells in Italy with AC Milan and France with Monaco.

'Ray was brilliant,' recalled Gough. 'At half-time in one game Butcher and I weren't happy with each other and we were arguing in the dressing room. Wilkins stood up between us and separated us and told us we were better than that. He stopped an incident that could have caused a big problem between me and Terry. Souness wrote a piece on him recently in the *Sunday Times* after Wilkins had died. He wrote that at that time we didn't have any shrinking violets in the dressing room but because of his experience, Ray, who wasn't a shouter and a bawler, could cut between us and we would listen to him.'

Gough added, 'He was a great friend of mine and a very important part of the football club for just over two years. I was sorry to see him go. He lived next door to me in Bothwell and I used to go to his house to watch AC Milan, who were the best team in Europe at that time. He told me that my body was my bank and once my body didn't work any more, I wasn't going to get any money any more. He said we would both play until we were 40. He said he could do it as he had no pace and that would mean people wouldn't say he was finished as he had lost his pace. It was different for me as I was a defender but he said as I was such a good athlete, if I looked after myself I'd be fine. That advice got me playing until I was 39 in the English Premiership, becoming Everton's oldest outfield player of all time.'

It was clear even in the early days of his Rangers career that Gough was heeding the advice of Wilkins. Of the 94 matches Rangers had played since his arrival, the lionhearted defender had missed just five. But in season 1989/90 injury eventually caught up with him.

'I picked up a foot injury,' recalled Gough. 'We thought it was a metatarsal at first but I went in for an operation and got an infection. It eventually trailed on until the World Cup in Italy and I tried to play on through it. I ultimately went down to Harley Street and got it all fixed up but it could have been sorted a lot earlier than what it was.'

When he played he did so alongside arguably the most controversial signing in Rangers' history, one Maurice John Giblin Johnston. He was the first high-profile Roman Catholic to sign for the club and his arrival split the Rangers support. For the players, though, the arrival of Johnston fortified an already formidable first-team squad.

'I just felt we had signed a good striker,' said Gough. 'For the first six months of his career here, he was as good as any striker I've ever played with at the club. On his game he was one of the best Scottish strikers of all time. What he did at that time was very brave.'

With Johnston forging a fine attacking spearhead with McCoist – Mo scored 15 league goals and Ally notched 14 – and Gough part of a defence that shipped a mere 19 goals in the 36-game Premier Division, Rangers retained the league title for the first time since 1976.

'You obviously need your strikers to score – it's the hardest thing to do – but I always say that at big clubs, your centre-backs need to be your two best players,' noted Gough. 'Along with the goalkeeper they need to be really solid. The two full-backs will push forward, attacking, so you could get hit on the break, meaning the boys at the back need to be really sharp. From then onwards that's how we were built.'

Now injury-free, Gough was back alongside Butcher to give Rangers defensive solidity at the outset of season 1990/91. However, by the end of September the partnership was broken up when Butcher was dropped then sold to Coventry City. Although his departure saw Gough take the captain's armband, Richard did not want his sidekick to leave.

He recalled, 'I was disappointed to see him leave, because he was a good player. But I think he had gone to the World Cup with an injury. Souness didn't want him to play but Terry was a true Englishman and wanted to play. He had a marvellous World Cup but when he came back he was struggling with his knee. He scored a couple of own goals and fell out with Graeme, which is never a good thing to do. It was a sad way for him to go. We never really got a chance to say a proper goodbye. He was the catalyst for the success we had and he was the best central defender I played with. He was a good leader.'

He continued, 'Graeme came to me and said that Terry was leaving and he wanted me to be captain of the football club. I was captain of Everton and Tottenham and Dundee United sometimes as well. But the best honour for me was being captain of Rangers Football Club. I was a different personality as captain than Terry. I wasn't a screamer in the dressing room – I was maybe a bit quieter than Terry – but I was going to do it my own way. I've said the same to [James] Tavernier, don't change your character. You're made captain because of the way you play and the way you are.'

Gough was fortunate that the team he led was full of natural leaders. The Rangers players were competitive and did not like losing and this was demonstrated in Gough's first cup final as skipper, the 1990 League Cup Final against Celtic. Trailing 1-0, Mark Walters equalised to force extra time, wherein the new captain played his part.

'I still had a problem with my foot at the time so I wasn't going up for many set-pieces,' remembered Gough. 'It was painful to run and I was taking painkillers and injections before games so I could play. But on this occasion I decided to go up and managed to get between Bonner and Morris and knock it in.'

That trophy would be the first of 14 Gough would lead Rangers to. But when they clinched a third successive title on a memorable final-day showdown with Aberdeen at Ibrox in May 1991, Gough was laid up in a hospital bed.

'I was living by myself at the time and I had been in bed for two days, sweating like mad,' recalled Gough. 'I was drinking Lucozade to try and make myself feel a bit better. I was supposed to go away with Scotland, who I was having a few problems with at the time. Graeme didn't like us going away for friendlies but I phoned Doctor Cruickshanks. He came over and took one look at me and said I needed to go to hospital. I had picked up hepatitis from food poisoning. At that time we had just lost our manager [Souness had left to take over at Liverpool] and I missed the last two games as I was in hospital for two weeks. We went to Motherwell and lost 3-0 which meant we now had to beat Aberdeen at home. That was a crucial time but we managed to get over the line and that was one of the most crucial games in that period.'

The departure of Souness had not exactly come at an optimum time. Rangers had built up a decent lead in the title race but defeats at Pittodrie and Parkhead kept Aberdeen in the hunt. Walter Smith moved from assistant manager to the man in charge and he would go on to establish himself as one of the greatest managers in Rangers' history. But the significance of that last-gasp, resilient triumph cannot be overestimated.

In their first season as captain and manager Smith named Gough in his starting XI in all but 11 of the 44 Premier Division matches. Rangers ended the season nine points ahead of runners-up Hearts to make it four-in-a-row and Gough became the first Rangers captain to get his hands on the Scottish Cup since Ally Dawson 11 years earlier.

'In the League Cup we were fine but we had a wee problem in the Scottish Cup,' stated Gough. 'Even with the good team we had we were still vulnerable on any given day. But that win over Airdrie was an important game for us.'

The winning goal at Hampden was scored by Ally McCoist, his 39th strike of the season. The following season he almost hit the half century, netting 49 goals in 52 appearances, as Rangers won the domestic Treble.

'I had a great relationship with him and he's a great friend of mine,' said Gough. 'Coisty and I knew each other since we were kids, playing against each other when I was at Dundee United. He had a good record against United but I used to joke with him that that was against Hegarty and Narey as I was playing right-back. He's a loveable boy who likes a laugh and a joke and kept the dressing room lively and bubbly. But he also has a very competitive edge running through him that a lot of people don't see. He wants to win very badly and he was one of the crucial factors in our team through nine-in-a-row. To score 355 goals for the football club is amazing and he was a big-game player.'

He added, 'When I was out injured he would be the captain most of the time. I think he had an unbeaten record [as captain] and he was very proud of that. He was a great team-mate but we had a few altercations in training over the years. But that was because we were both very similar, very competitive and wanted to win badly. That was good for the younger players to see us training really hard and being competitive. It showed what the club meant to people.'

McCoist was one of the senior professionals in a dressing room full of potential leaders. With others like Goram, Brown, McCall, Ferguson, McPherson and Durrant, it was no wonder that Rangers enjoyed so much success at this time.

'The senior players run the dressing room at any club,' stated Gough. 'The younger players should look up to them and I always told them at Rangers to pick a player to use as an example. We just tried to keep a happy dressing room and although there were lots of arguments in training, it was over with fairly quickly. Nothing was left to linger. We used to go out when we got beaten – which didn't happen too many times – and it became a ritual. I would speak to Walter and tell him the boys needed a bit of a blowout. He would usually give us the day off the next day and him and Archie [Knox] would come and leave after the meal. We used to go to La Parmigiana in Great Western Road and blow off some steam. We were a very close bunch of boys but we didn't go out nearly as often as people said we did.'

Season 1992/93, Gough's fifth full season as a Rangers player, proved to be an exceptional campaign on all fronts. Gough led the team to the domestic Treble and they went ten games unbeaten in the Champions League. With a bit of luck they may well have made the final against AC Milan but they were pipped at the post by French champions, Marseille, who went on to win the competition.

'Marseille were the best club team I played against,' said Gough. 'They had Barthez, Angloma, Boli, Sauzee, Deschamps, Voller and Boksic, a team full of superstars. In our team we had to put

Scottish players in [because of the three-foreigner rule] and sell a lot of the English players which weakened us. We had brought in David Robertson and Andy Goram but they were still fitting into the team. We came very close to going through. Had we won in Marseille we would have gone through to the final. But they were a very good side. I wouldn't say we were unlucky but Hateley was suspended for the Marseille game. I'd have liked to see him play there but we went there and put up a good performance in a hostile atmosphere.'

Gough played in seven of the ten European games and 32 of the 54 domestic matches. He had been hampered throughout the season by a groin injury but he went through the pain barrier when it mattered. Aberdeen were runners-up in all three domestic competitions, with the Treble clinched at Parkhead in front of the famous 'Jungle' in May.

The league triumph was the fifth in succession. Ibrox was a fortress – Rangers were unbeaten there and dropped points in just two of the 22 home fixtures and this must have pleased Gough as he had intimated pre-season that the club had to endeavour to drop less points on their own turf. Away from Ibrox they were imperious too and despite losing two of their last four matches, Smith's side still finished nine points ahead of Aberdeen.

An unprecedented back-to-back Treble was denied in season 1993/94 but the focus was now turning to a record set by Jock Stein's Celtic in the late 60s and early 70s. Walter Smith's side were now just three titles away from the coveted nine-in-a-row.

'Celtic were in a bit of disarray so after we got to six I thought we had a wee chance of getting nine,' recalled Richard. 'However, by 1995 Celtic had started to get their act together and were getting a better quality of player. We knew after that it would be tough.'

Recognising Celtic's intent to topple them from their lofty perch, Rangers bolstered their squad. In the summer of 1994 Brian Laudrup and Basile Boli arrived and 12 months later, the mercurial Paul Gascoigne signed for £4 million.

'I thought Basile was a wee bit unlucky,' opined Gough. 'He was a great guy, good in the dressing room. He came in on the first day with a tracksuit on so I had to tell him we were the only club in

Britain where you had to come in with a collar and tie every day. The next day he came in, still in his tracksuit but wearing a collar and tie! It was brilliant and the boys gave him a standing ovation. From that day onwards he was the best dressed guy at the club. But Basile was a man-marker and at that time we played in a zonal four. He was all over the place so I felt a wee bit for him. You get signings like that that don't work out, while you get others that do.'

He added, 'In 1994/95 we lost three times at home in a week which was a disaster. All of a sudden Walter was useless and, at 32, I was too old. McCoist was supposedly done too. This was a typical reaction to losing three games in a row. But then we buckled down, got on a good run and eventually won the title.'

The gap between Rangers and runners-up Motherwell was a mammoth 15 points. After initial misgivings, Laudrup eventually settled and won the Player of the Year award.

'He was very special,' recalled Richard. 'He was a quality player but he had been playing with a cloud over his head in Italy. Walter gave him freedom and he enjoyed the environment around here. He spoke perfect English and he enjoyed his time here.'

What Laudrup did in season 1994/95, Gascoigne replicated the following season. With breathtaking regularity he was at his world-class best, never more so than in the penultimate league match when his hat-trick secured victory over Aberdeen and staved off a resurgent Celtic to secure eight-in-a-row.

'I always get asked who the best player was I played with but if I had to choose one player to win me a game it would be Gascoigne,' said Gough. 'He was at the club for two-and-a-half years and gave us all marvellous memories. However, as captain I also remember some of the not so good things he did like getting sent off in Dortmund and also against Ajax. He was difficult for the manager to handle but overall he was brilliant for us. That game against Aberdeen, everything was on the line. We went 1-0 down but Paul took the game by the scruff of the neck. In situations like that he was sensational.'

He added, 'We changed our system that season and went to three at the back. Folk said that was because I was getting older but it was to let Gascoigne and Laudrup be free when we got the ball back. I could make it a five quite quickly and had Ferguson and McCall in front so we actually became more like a counter-attacking team. We were very good at that.'

Gough and Rangers were now on the cusp of greatness. Season 1996/97 would present the opportunity to make it nine successive Premier Division titles. For Gough it appeared it would be his last in a Rangers jersey too.

'I said before the season started the league would be 36 cup finals,' recalled Gough. 'After the Aberdeen game at the end of the previous season I went to a function and a supporter said, "Great result today but whatever you do don't f**k it up next year." The pressure was on straight away.

'We started the season really well but coming down the home stretch I picked up an injury and we dropped points against Aberdeen and Dundee United. I came back for the game at Parkhead that we needed to win. I shouldn't really have played but I did and we got the result.'

Gough missed seven of the last nine league matches but when the title was eventually sealed with a game to spare following a 1-0 win over Dundee United at Tannadice, an emotional skipper was there to lift the trophy. It looked like it was his last act as Rangers captain as he left in the summer to join Kansas City Wizard in the USA.

'I wanted to be honest with the supporters so I announced in October that I'd be leaving at the end of the season,' stated Gough. 'I wanted to go off into the sunset so I played about ten games for Kansas before I got a phone call from Walter asking me to come back. Amoruso was out for the season and Alan McLaren was struggling with injury. We had been knocked out of Europe and the League Cup and were struggling in the league.'

Richard the Lionheart returned and made an immediate impact, scoring the only goal of the season's first Old Firm game at Ibrox. But any notion of a romantic return galvanising Rangers to a then unprecedented tenth title on the trot soon petered out.

Richard recalled, 'The bookends of my 11 years at Rangers – 1987/88 and 1997/98 – were the only two years that we didn't win the championship. That season I had no injuries and was virtually ever-present [Gough missed only five league matches] so I played another 30 games for the club. We only lost to Celtic at New Year and beat them in the Scottish Cup semi-final when Coisty scored. We were pretty comfortable but then drew at home against Dunfermline – they scored in the last minute – and then lost to Kilmarnock at home. That cost us five points and that was what done us.'

He added, 'We lost the cup final that year too, so having won so much it was a strange way to end my Rangers career. But I was at a presentation a few months back to mark John Greig's 60 years at Rangers. It was a very private affair – there were only six of us in the room – but Walter said the biggest thing he remembered about John Greig was that he played for our club at a time when Celtic were dominant. He said that the way John handled losing with such dignity [Rangers went 11 years without winning the league] was what made him stand out. So, to be fair to myself, I played for Rangers for 11 years and only didn't win the title in two of those years which was pretty decent.'

Although Gough had penned a two-year contract on his return and the new manager, Dick Advocaat, wanted him to stay, he thought it was time for change for himself and the club.

'I felt at that time we shouldn't have had players of 36 or 37 playing for our team,' said Gough. 'Advocaat wanted me to stay but I thought it was time for the new manager to come in and put his own stamp on the team. Of the senior players I think only Ferguson and Durie stayed.'

Rather than take the easy road to retirement, Gough was soon plying his trade in the self-styled best league in the world. After a brief stint with San Jose Earthquake, he had a spell on loan under Ron Atkinson at Nottingham Forest before signing for Everton in the summer of 1999. He had also been courted by Harry Redknapp, who was in charge at West Ham. Redknapp wanted Gough to work with the emerging talent of Rio Ferdinand but the fact Walter Smith was in charge at Everton was the decisive factor. It would mean that Gough and Smith would be working together in all but one of Richard's 25 years as a professional. After two seasons on Merseyside Gough finally called it a day and returned to America where he still resides today. Despite living stateside, Richard is still a frequent visitor to Ibrox. Inducted into the Hall of Fame in 2002, he was appointed as a global ambassador in 2015.

'In my eyes I've always been an ambassador for the football club,' stated Gough proudly. 'When I come back to Glasgow there's still huge respect for me because of what happened when I played here. Dave King asked me to come on board and help him take control of the football club, which was in a bad way at the time with people running the club who didn't have the best interests of the club at heart. Supporters weren't buying season tickets until these people were out, which was a huge concern for me. Everyone has a story about how they were going to save Rangers but we must remember that Dave King saved Rangers. How he's managed to get Steven Gerrard I don't know. The change in the club in three years has been unbelievable.'

He continued, 'In America they don't know the ins and outs of it but when Rangers were put down to the bottom tier I'd often be asked why Scottish Football were putting their biggest franchise down to the minors. I would say that only in Scotland would they cut off their nose to spite their face and destroy Scottish Football. We lost players to the value of about £50 million for nothing as they weren't going to play in the bottom tier. I've been asked what I would've done as I'm a Rangers man through and through. If I was 24 years old I would have gone to the Premiership but if I was 37 I would have stayed.'

Like his fellow supporters, Gough is delighted to be witnessing an upturn in Rangers' on-field fortunes since the arrival of Steven Gerrard. However, he is loath to compare the start of the era under this Liverpool legend to the one that he was part of some 30 years earlier.

'Different times now,' was his assessment. 'Steven is buying £2 million players but Graeme was buying players who were worth the equivalent of £75 million today. That's the big difference. Rangers need good football players and this year we have done a bit better. Getting McGregor back has been good and the centre-backs look alright but there's still a long way to go. I think we're still a wee bit short [in terms of winning the league] but Gerrard is getting there and it's so much better than it was in previous years. He has brought the right professional attitude to everything and the players he has brought in have been an upgrade on what the previous two managers bought.'

He concluded, 'Steven has been great with me. The first time I met him he asked what I thought about the two centre-backs [Goldson and Katic] and I told him my opinion. None of the previous managers had done that. Gerrard has brought in his own team so he doesn't need me to tell him what's needed here. I've had lunch with him and he's invited me up to the training ground and I've told him I'm available any time he needs to ask me anything. [Ibrox] is not an easy place to play. I've got some players' numbers so if I can pass on any tips to Goldson or Katic or Tavernier, I'll send them a message so it's all good. I did that as a captain. I never went and told young players what to do or how to behave but if they had a problem and came to ask me about it then I'd be there.'

Richard Gough made 466 appearances for Rangers and scored 36 goals. He won nine Premier Division titles (1988/89, 1989/90, 1990/91, 1991/92, 1992/93, 1993/94, 1994/95, 1995/96 and 1996/97), three Scottish Cups (1991/92, 1992/93 and 1995/96) and six League Cups (1987/88, 1988/89, 1990/91, 1992/93, 1993/94 and 1996/97). He was captain of the club for all but four of those trophy successes.

Slim

Dave McPherson
(1977–1987, 1992–1994)

Born in Paisley in January 1964, David McPherson was not your stereotypical 1980s Scottish centre-half. He was not the rough and ready giant that battered and barged centre-forwards from pillar to post. McPherson was more cultured and when he signed for his boyhood heroes, they were getting a player who modelled himself on the great Dutch defender, Ruud Krol.

'I was very good at reading the game and, for a tall guy, I was very skilful, a different breed to the players playing at the time,' said McPherson, who signed for Rangers in season 1977/78 as a schoolboy. 'I was playing in the school team and also with the youth team, Pollock United, when I signed an 'S' form, which was similar to the Academies now.

'When I left school at 16, rather than go straight into the reserves, I was farmed out to Gartcosh United for a short spell. Gartcosh were a very good team and other scouts would go and watch their matches. Celtic were interested in signing me at that point but didn't realise I'd already signed for Rangers.'

On his return from Gartcosh, McPherson made his way into the Rangers reserve team and played in the prestigious Croix tournament for three successive years between 1979 and 1981. He picked up two winners' medals and in 1981, he and Billy Davies were both shortlisted for the Player of the Tournament award. Indeed,

McPherson performed to such a high standard that one of Europe's leading clubs expressed an interest in signing him.

'The Croix tournament was fantastic because of the calibre of teams and players that were taking part,' recalled McPherson. 'It gave me an indication of the fitness level and skill level you needed to be at and these were all invaluable for young Rangers players. It was a tough competition but one we seemed to do very well in.'

He continued, 'After the tournament in 1981 the Ajax head coach tried to sign me. Ajax were one of my favourite teams growing up because of the players they had and I always loved and admired Dutch football. Willie Thornton used to go to all the Croix tournaments and he told me afterwards about it. He told me he had said no as I was staying with Rangers.'

The timing of McPherson's showing prominence in the reserve team was impeccable. At the start of the 1980s a number of experienced players were heading towards retirement or pastures new as John Greig tried to mould a team of his own after taking over from Jock Wallace. This afforded young McPherson the opportunity to play alongside players he had watched and idolised from the slopes of Ibrox Stadium when growing up.

'The reserves was probably the biggest learning curve,' recalled McPherson. 'You were playing alongside and against very experienced players so, from my perspective as a young boy, there was nothing better than that. There were people like Colin Jackson, Tam Forsyth, Alex Miller and Tommy McLean in our team, guys who had won Trebles at Rangers and my heroes growing up. It taught you a lot about the level you need to play at and the pressure as well. In one reserve match against Celtic at Ibrox about 30,000 turned up which, for a young boy of 16/17, was a fantastic experience.'

McPherson's composed displays in the second team eventually earned him a place in the first team. He made his competitive debut in a League Cup tie against Brechin City at Ibrox on 23 September 1981 in front of just 5,000 paying patrons. He was aged 17 years and 238 days.

'At training the day before the game John Greig told me that I would be getting my first start,' remembered McPherson. 'I'd been training on and off with the first team and, when that became more frequent, I had a rough idea that I would be making my debut sooner rather than later. It was still a big thrill though when it happened, to play for the team you've supported all your days. It was a great night. Making your first-team debut is one of the biggest hurdles as a young player as you don't know how you're going to cope regarding the nerves. But playing in front of big crowds and with experienced players in the reserves helped. The small crowd that night was like playing in a minor reserve game so it was easier to cope with.'

Further growth in the reserves continued afterwards but there would be another appearance in a cup tie before the season had ended. And this one, on 6 February 1982 against Albion Rovers in the Scottish Cup, was marked with his first goal for Rangers. He ended up with a good goalscoring ratio for a centre-back – about one goal in every ten appearances – but this would be the only one he would net from the penalty spot.

'It was a mis-hit, I sclaffed it,' admitted McPherson honestly. 'I don't know how it went into the back of the net but it did.'

McPherson was again drip fed into the first team in season 1982/83. He made his Premier Division debut on 9 September 1982 when he came on as substitute for Robert Prytz in a 0-0 draw against Morton at Cappielow and ended up playing in 14 of the last 15 league matches. He partnered Craig Paterson at centre-half and was alongside the future club captain again in May when Rangers faced Aberdeen in the Scottish Cup Final. This was an Aberdeen team fresh from beating Real Madrid to win the European Cup Winners' Cup and, in the lead-up to the game, McPherson had expressed his excitement ahead of his first major cup final. However, he and his Rangers team-mates left empty-handed as a single goal four minutes from the end of extra time was sufficient to take the trophy back to the north-east.

'It was a sore one to take as I felt we should have won the match,' recalled McPherson. 'Aberdeen sneaked a goal – Eric Black scored – which was a body blow. It was also a blow for me personally for a couple of reasons. Firstly, we had lost in my first Scottish Cup Final, which was disappointing, but secondly, straight after the match I was flying to Mexico City with the Scotland U19s for the World Cup and I was sharing a room with Eric Black! He was a good friend but it took me a couple of days before I could speak to him.'

The Scotland squad that travelled to South America was packed with emerging talents in the game. In addition to McPherson and Black, Celtic's Paul McStay, Neale Cooper of Aberdeen, Brian McClair, who had just joined Celtic for £100,000, and Pat Nevin, who would sign for Chelsea a few months later, were in the travelling party. The Scots were drawn in Group A alongside South Korea, Australia and the hosts, Mexico. Wins over the Koreans (2-0) and the Mexicans (current Kilmarnock manager, Steve Clarke, scoring the only goal of the game) took the Scots through to the quarter-final but they were eliminated by Poland at that stage.

'It was a great experience but the biggest test for the Scotland players was the altitude,' admitted McPherson. 'Our first two games were played in Toluca [8,793ft above sea level] and before there we went to Colorado Springs to do altitude training. I kept getting nosebleeds every day as I couldn't handle the altitude.'

Imbued by the confidence garnered from his late-season run in the team and the trip to Mexico with the national team, McPherson was firmly in the first-team picture in the prelude to season 1983/84. He played in nine of the friendlies arranged and picked up his first winners' medal when Celtic were beaten 1-0 at Hampden in the final of the Glasgow Cup.

'That medal means a lot to me,' said McPherson. 'It was the last game we played before the first league match and it was an unbelievable experience for me. We played for pride in the Glasgow Cup – there was no bonus – but that match meant as much to me as a Scottish Cup Final or a League Cup Final, because you're a Rangers player playing against Celtic.'

That campaign proved to be the one when the name 'McPherson' became an almost permanent fixture on the team sheet that would be pinned on the noticeboard every week. He was one of only two players to appear in all 36 Premier Division matches and the only first-team game he missed was a 2-0 win over Hearts in the League Cup at Ibrox in October. He also debuted on the European stage, making an historic contribution to the 8-0 win over the Maltese side, Valletta, in the European Cup Winners' Cup.

'I always said to myself that once I got in the first team I was going to stay there,' said McPherson. 'When you're younger, you're still growing so you don't have that strength to play that many games back-to-back but in 83/84 once I was in, I was going to do my best to make sure I was never going to be left out.'

He continued, 'Valletta was my European debut so to score four goals made it a great night for me. However, I didn't even get to keep the match ball! To score one goal in Europe is great, but to score four, irrespective of the opposition, is not easy. And I don't think there will be many centre-backs in Europe that have managed it either.'

Although the league challenge continued to follow the depressing trend of petering out and Dundee ended a run of eight successive Scottish Cup finals, the season did not end with an empty trophy cabinet. The League Cup was won in March 1984 and McPherson was part of the XI that overcame a Celtic side that ended the season trophy-less.

'One thing that struck me was, after the 1983 cup final against Aberdeen, we went back to Ibrox but everything was muted,' recalled McPherson. 'I remember leaving after the dinner and not one person said "good luck in Mexico" to me. I basically walked out with my boots and had to go. That just showed what losing in a cup final meant to the staff and players at Ibrox.'

He added, 'For me, getting across the line and winning a [national] cup final was so important. It proves to yourself and everybody else that you've got the winning mentality. I played left-midfield that day and was asked to mark Paul McStay and, even though I was a centre-back, I managed to keep him quiet. It wasn't a problem moving in to midfield as it was more a man-to-man marking role.'

The man in charge that day was Jock Wallace. He had replaced John Grieg in October 1983 after Alex Ferguson and Jim McLean had rejected the overtures of the Rangers board. McPherson, who had been nurtured by Greig and handed his first-team debut by the legendary figure, was understandably sad to see him leave.

'Greigy was a hero of mine as a player and he signed me both as a schoolboy and on professional forms so I loved him,' recalled

McPherson fondly. 'He also gave me my chance in the first team so I was devastated when he left. I was in tears as it was the first time I had experienced a manager leaving the club. It was a big blow for me and I found it hard to take at the time.'

He added, 'Jock came in and he had a reputation of being a great man-manager and you knew with him if you worked hard, you would get his full support and backing. He was tough but if you're the manager of Rangers you have to be tough. He did have a softer side and he would respect you if you gave your all for the jersey. I loved him too and he was great for me.'

Wallace elected to end the season with a round-the-world tour. He had implemented a similar strategy in 1975 and the net result was a domestic Treble in season 1975/76. A similar outcome would have been welcomed by the Rangers faithful this time around and McPherson has fond memories of a trip that stopped off in Melbourne, Sydney, Toronto and Auckland.

'Being so young and being told you were going on a world tour was difficult to get your head around,' remembered McPherson. 'We were given the itinerary and it was basically a book as there was that much involved. We had nine games over four weeks but the journey was horrendous. We arrived about 6am in Melbourne and Jock immediately took us out on to the pitch for training! It was crazy but it was an unbelievable trip for a young boy.'

In the summer of 1984, the feel-good factor appeared to be back at Ibrox. Jock Wallace's return had boosted morale and prompted a fine unbeaten run in the Premier Division. The general consensus was that should the team be able to string together a similar sequence in season 1984/85, then the league title would be making its way back to Ibrox. This would be McPherson's first experience of pre-season training Wallace-style but unlike many of his team-mates, he already had experience of the place that still has Rangers players of that era quivering at the mere mention of its name.

'Jock loved Gullane but I first went there for my first pre-season with John Greig when I was 16,' said McPherson. 'At 16 your body hasn't developed and you wouldn't put a 16-year-old through that nowadays, because you're not ready for it. After doing it I couldn't walk the next day but I still had to go in and do another day of pre-season training. However, Jock was on a different level, a real sergeant major on the sand dunes. It was mad, physical punishment. And it didn't matter what the weather was like, we trained there whether it was a good day or a bad day.'

The training stood McPherson, in particular, in good stead. He was now a mainstay in the team and any games he missed – such as the five in the 1984/85 Premier Division – were as a result of accruing too many penalty points rather than through injury.

He noted, 'Very rarely did I get injured. Throughout my career I never had any major injuries, mainly wear and tear. So, any games I missed were down to suspension.'

Although the expected title tilt failed to materialise, the League Cup was retained – new boy Iain Ferguson getting the winner against Dundee United – but Dundee ended hopes of a cup double with a 1-0 win at Ibrox in the fourth round. In the previous round Rangers had squeezed past Morton in a replay. The first match – a 3-3 draw at a snow-bound Cappielow – was a memorable day for Dave in more ways than one.

He remembered, 'I elbowed somebody in the nose and the *Daily Record* used to do cartoons at that time. They did one of me and the Morton player – I can't remember his name – but the Morton player was a snowman with his head chopped off! The game should never have been on but I scored and earned the nickname "Bambi" too. That was due to my height and long legs and playing in those conditions.'

The early exit from the Scottish Cup freed up a weekend for Rangers and rather than give his players time off, Jock Wallace decided to take his players to the Middle East to play a couple of games. It was an eventful and eye-opening trip.

'That was a challenge,' was Dave's rueful recollection. 'We went to Jordan for a match and then we flew on to Baghdad to play the Iraqi national team. I enjoyed Jordan but we had to do an internal flight. I was sitting next to Derek Johnstone and the aircraft dropped about 1,000 feet and everyone was screaming as we thought our number was up. We then came in to Baghdad airport and the runway lights were off. Basically they turned them on just as you were touching down then turned them back off. There was a civil war at the time so we had to go through all these checkpoints before we got to the hotel. When we got there it was dark and all the curtains were shut but when we woke up in the morning, all we could see were anti-aircraft guns on the roofs.'

He continued, 'There were a lot of ex-pats living there, working in the oil industry so Jock took us to the St Andrews Club for a team bonding session. In the match itself, Ally McCoist scored one of the best goals I've ever seen, a strike from about 35 or 40 yards. The stadium was full of Republican Guards and there were machine guns everywhere. We met Saddam Hussein too and I look back now and ask myself if it actually happened. In those days, though, big Jock would have travelled anywhere; if it was the Vietnam War, he'd have taken us there. He saw it as character-building which it certainly was!'

Ultimately Wallace's side had not lived up to the heightened expectations at the start of the campaign. They had once again meekly surrendered in the race for the title and all the season served to confirm was that Rangers were now a cup team rather than contenders for the league.

'There were a lot of changes, with older players getting towards the end of their career,' reflected McPherson. 'You always get that, the transition, when you get young boys like myself coming in, players getting signed and the older players moving on. That's where the inconsistency comes from as it takes a bit of time. But at Rangers the fans don't have that patience. Greigy was in an impossible position, because as manager he had played with a lot of the boys then all of a sudden he was their manager. He then had to decide if he had to leave them out or move them on and he had to make unpopular decisions.'

One thing that was consistent at that time was the presence of Dave McPherson at the heart of the Rangers defence. In season 1985/86 he missed only two Premier Division matches – successive 2-1 defeats against Hibernian and St Mirren in October 1985 – both through suspension. He netted five goals, the last of which was of huge significance. It was the opening goal against Motherwell on the final day of the season which set Rangers on the way to a

2-0 win that clinched fifth place and a UEFA Cup place for season 1986/87.

'I just happened to be in the right place at the right time,' said McPherson modestly. 'I had the finishing boots on that day – it was another strike with my right foot rather than a header – and a lot of people think most of my goals were headers. But I actually scored less headers than what you would think.'

As one would suspect, a fifth-place finish in the title race was catastrophic for Rangers. Adding to that a defeat in the opening round of the Scottish Cup against Hearts and a semi-final loss to Hibernian in the League Cup signalled that it was time for change at Ibrox.

'I loved Jock,' said McPherson. 'He was a diamond, a father figure. If you worked hard and did your bit on the park, he made sure you were well looked after. I loved his man-management style. But there was movement in the boardroom and when that happens, for a manager, it's 50/50 whether you stay or go. When David Holmes came in he was talking up Rangers as challenging for league titles so you felt that something was going to happen at some point.'

He continued, 'Graeme Souness came in and obviously had experience of playing at Liverpool, playing in Italy and playing for Scotland in World Cups. He had a different mindset, a different way of approaching the games. Where Jock was all about man-management and battle, battle, battle, Graeme came in and tried to be a bit more cultured. He talked a bit more of about how he lived off the pitch, like diets and drinking habits.'

Despite being first choice in the first team for three seasons, the change at the Ibrox helm could have understandably sown seeds of doubt in McPherson's head. But a chat with new assistant manager, Walter Smith, had put his mind at rest.

'There was a game at Clydebank that we lost,' recalled McPherson. 'Mike Conroy scored and I later played with him in Australia. I spoke to Walter after the game and he told me I was in Graeme's plans so that gave me a level of confidence that, if I got a good pre-season, I'd be in the starting line-up.'

Alongside McPherson in central defence in season 1986/87 would be the England captain, Terry Butcher. Behind him in goal would be the understudy to Peter Shilton, Chris Woods. Rangers were flexing their muscles in the transfer market and making it clear to all and sundry that they were intent on restoring themselves at the summit of the Scottish game sooner rather than later.

'I had watched Terry play a number of times and had a great deal of respect for him,' said McPherson. 'Apart from the fact he was English, of course! He had a great left foot and was a cultured player but was very good in the air and loved a tackle. I learned so much from him in a short space of time. The experience he had meant he was great to play alongside. I think our styles complemented each other. I was a good reader of the game so if Terry went for a tackle or a header – not that he missed many – I would do a lot of covering for him. We got on well off the park too.'

In common with previous seasons, Dave McPherson was rarely missing from the team sheet for the first team. Indeed, the defence was the cornerstone for the Championship-winning season. Chris Woods missed just two of the 44 league matches, left-back Stuart Munro made 43 appearances as did Butcher. McPherson was only absent for two matches, a 0-0 draw at Tannadice against Dundee United in late October and a 3-0 home win over Hearts in November. Once again it was suspension that counted him out but this time it also cost him another medal.

'I missed the League Cup Final after I got booked in the first match of the season against Hibs,' recalled McPherson. 'I was booked in that match but afterwards the SFA decided that every Rangers player that played that day would be given another yellow card [due to the ruckus that followed Graeme Souness's red card]. That took me over the points threshold so I missed the cup final. I wasn't very happy with the governing body but I had to take it on the chin.'

He added, 'I got sent off against Aberdeen at Pittodrie [in a 1-0 defeat on 22 November 1986] and I couldn't really complain about it. It was another elbow and I didn't mean to catch him in the face but it was Davie Dodds so it didn't really make any difference!'

Despite being nine points adrift of leaders Celtic in December, albeit having played a game less, Rangers were rampant over the festive period. A 2-0 win in the New Year Old Firm game was pivotal and by the end of January, Souness's side were top of the table. Their form was formidable thereafter and following a 1-1 draw against Aberdeen at Pittodrie in the penultimate game of the season, they were crowned champions.

'We were on such a good run that we felt as if we were unbeatable,' said McPherson. 'We won away games back-to-back against Dundee and Dundee United and I scored in both games. They were two tough games and Dens Park and Tannadice are never easy places to go to. These victories were key to give us that determination and push us on and show us that we could win away from home at these difficult venues.'

He added with a smile, 'There was no singing or dancing at all on the bus journey back from Aberdeen and no champagne! There was definitely a bit of relief. At a club like Rangers you have to be challenging for the league. We had fallen short for a few seasons before that but it's like winning your first cup medal, it's about getting across the finishing line. Winning the league takes you to another level in terms of belief.'

The only blot on the Souness copybook was a shock defeat against Hamilton in the third round of the Scottish Cup. With Chris Woods and his back four closing in on a British record of time without conceding a goal and McCoist and Fleck scoring goals with breathtaking regularity, no one expected John Lambie's Hamilton to have a chance. But an inspired display from their goalkeeper, Dave McKellar, and a goal from Adrian Sprott dramatically extinguished Rangers' hopes of a domestic Treble.

'That was particularly disappointing,' reflected McPherson ruefully. 'There was miscommunication between myself and Graham Roberts. I thought he was going to header it but he didn't and the ball bounced beyond me and Adrian Sprott ran through and scored. We had about 30 chances to score, though, and it was one of those days when nothing went for us at all. One wee bit of bad luck meant we lost the game.'

As McPherson left to go on holiday at the end of season 1986/87 he had no reason to think he would be plying his trade anywhere other than Ibrox for the foreseeable future. His partnership with

Terry Butcher had been solid and the addition of Graham Roberts in December 1986 had further fortified a formidable back-line. But one phone call was about to change all that. McPherson takes up the story.

'I had gone on holiday with Terry and Chris Woods but when I got back, I got a phone call from Graeme at home to tell me he had had an offer from Hearts that had been accepted. He pretty much made it clear that I was going. I went to meet Walter at Ibrox as I wasn't sure what was happening. I had played almost every game when we had won the league, yet now I was leaving. When I spoke to Walter I made the decision that I wasn't going to stay if I wasn't wanted. I spoke to Alex MacDonald and Sandy Jardine, the managers at Hearts, and [chairman] Wallace Mercer and they sold the club and what they were looking to do to me. I didn't look upon the move as a step back, more of a step to the side. In pre-season I was made captain and I never looked back.'

He added, 'I didn't want to leave Rangers. I was still under contract but if you're going to stay at a football club, you want to play. I was going to a club that wanted me and I felt I would become a better player by being there. It was ironic because Terry broke his leg [in November 1987] which left Rangers short of a centre-back. I knew deep down that Graeme had made the wrong decision in selling me but I think it was down to the fact he didn't want me there. He could be impulsive and the way he came across was that he didn't want any of the Scottish boys there, he wanted to change the whole team. He had been fortunate to go to Italy to learn about things like diets but we were still learning about that in Scotland.'

The fee for the cultured McPherson, a pivotal player at the heart of the Rangers defence and on the fringes of the Scottish national team, was a paltry £440,000. However, instead of regressing, Dave's time at Hearts saw him improve and gain international recognition.

'I went to Hearts looking to ensure we challenged for the league and we ended up finishing second in my first season there,' recalled McPherson proudly. 'I ended up scoring against Rangers at Ibrox [a 66th-minute equaliser in a 2-1 win in March 1988 that resulted in the phrase "AW NAW" being flashed up on the Ibrox scoreboard] and in many ways I had a point to prove that Graeme made the wrong decision. I'd like to think he sees that now.'

He continued, 'Because of my consistency at Hearts and fitness – Alex was a fitness fanatic so there was no team in the league fitter than us – it gave me belief and before I knew it, I was getting a Scotland cap.'

That first cap, one of 27 McPherson would earn between 1989 and 1993, was won in a 2-1 victory over Cyprus in a World Cup qualifier at Hampden in April 1989. Among his appearances for the national side were three at the Italia 90 World Cup and another three at the European Championships in 1992.

Similar to his time at Rangers, McPherson rarely missed a match for Hearts. In five seasons he was absent for just seven Premier Division matches, making 189 appearances and scoring 16 goals. But in the summer of 1992 the chance arose to return to his boyhood heroes.

'There were a number of clubs trying to buy me as I was an international player doing well,' said McPherson. 'Southampton, Tottenham, Borussia Dortmund and Seville were keen to speak to me but it was pre-Bosman and even though I was out of contract, I couldn't make the decision to leave and pick the club I wanted to go to.'

He added, 'Scotland played Norway in Oslo [in June 1992] and I met Walter [Smith] and he told me he was going to put in an offer for me. He asked if I wanted to come back to Rangers and I told him that as I was a Rangers fan, of course I did. From there an offer of £1.4 million was put in and I was on my way back to Ibrox.'

The first season of McPherson's second spell proved to be one of the most successful in Rangers' history. Walter Smith's side won the domestic Treble, went 44 games unbeaten (including ten in Europe), beat Leeds United home and away and came within a goal of reaching the inaugural Champions League Final.

'Everything just seemed to go right for us that season,' recalled McPherson. 'We had a really good team. Although I was brought back as a centre-back, I ended up playing right-back as Gary Stevens got injured. It wasn't ideal from my point of view as it wasn't my favourite position but when Walter asked if I was okay with it, I told him that I was playing for Rangers so I wasn't going to complain. We just went from strength to strength and it was a fantastic season.'

As always Dave McPherson was the model of consistency in that campaign, making 53 appearances, but like most of his team-mates the rigours of fighting on four fronts took its toll in season 1993/94.

'I very rarely missed a game but, with the benefit of hindsight, there are games I should never have played in,' said McPherson. 'I was perhaps carrying an injury but would play rather than take time out to recover. In those days you just wanted to play football but nowadays with sports science and how players are monitored, you'd have been told not to play. At that time I had a hernia operation but was back playing within five weeks which is unheard of. I played against Celtic and got Man of the Match but the next day I couldn't walk as I had torn my hernia again. While it was great to play against Celtic, decisions like that meant I was out for another five or six weeks.'

Walter's walking wounded managed to summon up enough resolve to win a sixth successive title. The League Cup was won in October in dramatic fashion thanks to a stunning overhead kick from the irrepressible Ally McCoist which left Rangers on the verge of a then unprecedented back-to-back domestic Treble.

'In the League Cup Final I scored an own goal but nobody knew it at that time,' remembered McPherson. 'It wasn't seen until the camera got the right angle but the ball just grazed my hair and ended up in the back of the net. I thought we should have beaten Dundee United in the Scottish Cup Final but they defended really deeply. Our goalkeeper [Ally Maxwell] then made a mistake [hitting a McPherson back pass against Christian Dailly, and when his shot hit the post, Craig Brewster rolled in the rebound] and tried to blame me. I didn't think there was anything wrong with the back pass and after the game Walter agreed and made it pretty clear who was to blame for it.'

Season 1994/95 would prove to be Dave McPherson's last in a Rangers jersey. He started the season as part of a back three alongside

Richard Gough and Basile Boli but in late October, he was heading back along the M8 to Tynecastle.

'I was carrying niggly injuries and Walter knew that,' said McPherson. 'I knew I wasn't going to be a regular and Walter made the right decision as a manager. He had the chance to bring a fresh face in, Alan McLaren, and there was a chance for me to go back to Hearts. It wasn't an easy decision but sometimes you've got to make them in football.'

The highlight of McPherson's second stint at Hearts was a Scottish Cup win over Rangers in 1998. He played a further season at Tynecastle before enjoying a year in Australia with Carlton Soccer Club. He spent season 2001/02 with Greenock Morton where he became assistant manager to Peter Cormack. He replaced Cormack in March 2002 for his one and only managerial role but just 13 games into season 2002/03, he was sacked. Today he is a director with Global Sports Recruitment, who provide amateur sportspeople in the UK with a chance to undertake scholarships in the USA.

A member of both the Rangers and Hearts halls of fame, Dave McPherson made 393 appearances for Rangers and scored 53 goals. He won three Premier Division championships (1986/87, 1992/93 and 1993/94), the Scottish Cup once (1992/93), the League Cup on four occasions (1983/84, 1984/85, 1992/93 and 1993/94) and the Glasgow Cup twice (1983/84 and 1985/86).

Reflecting on his Rangers career, McPherson concluded, 'We had a great dressing room which was part of the joy of being at Rangers. There were very few players that nobody got on with and if a player was a bad egg, he didn't last long. The best players I played alongside have to be Terry [Butcher] and Richard Gough. I played well when I played with either and we seemed to complement each other. We understood each other and communicated well. The highlight was winning the Treble, it was the pinnacle, an unbelievable achievement. Regrets? If anything it would be decision-making when playing in matches that I shouldn't have. But that's not really a regret as I just wanted to play for Rangers.'

THE ENGINE ROOM
THE MIDFIELDERS

Rusty
Bobby Russell (1977–1987)

Robert Russell had just turned 20 when he arrived at Ibrox as one third of a trio of new signings at the start of season 1977/78. He was a skilful, attacking midfielder with an eye for a killer pass and the injection of youth he and fellow acquisitions, Davie Cooper and Gordon Smith, provided was expected to reinvigorate a Rangers side that had stagnated badly in 1976/77, just one season after securing the domestic Treble.

'I signed a provisional contract for Rangers in 1976 which meant that I stayed with Shettleston until we were knocked out the Scottish Junior Cup,' explained Russell. 'I then made my debut for Rangers in a pre-season friendly against Nairn County [Russell scored in a 3-2 win] before we went back to Glasgow and I made my home debut against Southampton.'

Russell made his competitive debut – and continued his scoring streak – against Aberdeen at Pittodrie in the opening Premier Division fixture of season 1977/78. His goal on this occasion – a fine right-foot strike after 31 minutes, after latching on to a flick from Davie Cooper – brought Rangers level at 1-1 but two second-half goals gave the home side the points. However, despite that early setback, the Light Blues soon recovered, and aided by the promptings of Russell and Cooper and the goals of Derek Johnstone, they emerged from the pack to secure the Premier Division title.

Russell missed just three of the 36 league fixtures, and added to his goal against Aberdeen on the opening day of the season with further strikes in a 4-0 win over Partick Thistle at Firhill and a 1-0 win over Dundee United at Tannadice.

Although slender in build, Russell had in his repertoire a wide range of passing. He was compared to a fellow Scot, the late John White. White, nicknamed the Ghost, was the beating heart of the Tottenham Hotspur team that won the Double in 1961, and Russell was showing signs that he could play a similar role at Ibrox.

Russell was also outstanding as Rangers secured legs two and three of the domestic Treble. His chip into the penalty area created the opening goal of the Scottish Cup Final for Alex MacDonald, and although he missed the League Cup Final against Celtic, he wore the number eight jersey in each of the previous seven ties that Rangers had played in the tournament.

'I had a virus of some sort so missed out on the League Cup Final,' said Russell. 'In those days you were only allowed one sub and although I was in the squad, on the day of the final big Jock didn't want to take a chance as I wasn't 100% fit. But Sandy Jardine gave me his medal at the end of the game which was a nice gesture.'

In his second season at Ibrox, Russell was an ever-present, playing in each of the 61 matches that Rangers contested at home and abroad. He added Scottish Cup and League Cup winners' medals to his collection, although a second successive Treble was snatched from Rangers' grasp when the Light Blues lost out to Celtic by three points.

'You're talking about seven minutes away from doing back-to-back Trebles but it wasn't meant to be,' recalled Russell ruefully. 'I had scored a hat-trick – including two headers I might add – a few weeks earlier against Hearts and scored our second goal against Celtic. If we had got a draw [at Parkhead] that would probably have been enough but it was one of these unfortunate things.'

It was in the European arena that Rangers and Bobby truly shone, particularly in the second round of the European Cup when the Light Blues became the first team to win a European tie at the home of PSV Eindhoven. After a goalless draw at Ibrox, few gave the Light Blues much hope of progressing to the last eight of the competition. However, in a spirited display the visitors came back twice to restore parity at 2-2. Rangers were through at this stage on the 'away goals' rule but the progression was confirmed in the dying moments. A PSV attack was repelled by a clearing header from Derek Johnstone and the ball broke to Tommy McLean. Suddenly Rangers were on the front foot and McLean's perfectly-weighted pass released Russell who scampered down the right flank. Although he was being closed down by PSV defenders, he remained cool, drawing the goalkeeper from his line before curling a sumptuous shot into the net.

Russell recalled, 'We went on a great run in the European Cup [Rangers eventually exited at the hands of Cologne in the last eight] and that's possibly why we missed out on the Treble. In Europe we were up against different styles, more movement and interchanging whereas in Scottish football you played in straight lines.'

The 1979/80 season was one of disappointment in Govan, with Rangers slumping to a fifth-place finish in the Premier Division and losing to Celtic in the Scottish Cup Final. Russell endured a stop-start season, missing 13 league matches through injury. He did add another goal against Celtic, netting in a 2-2 draw at Ibrox and he also played in the infamous Drybrough Cup Final, a match indelibly inked into Rangers folklore thanks to a magnificent goal from Davie Cooper.

'Coop was a great player to play with because his control and technique were superb,' said Russell, who developed an almost telepathic understanding with the mercurial winger. 'I knew when to make a run and he would find me. He was very gifted that way. Ian Durrant and Jimmy Bett would play off him as well and, when he went to Motherwell, so would Phil O'Donnell and Tommy Boyd. He was just a great player to play alongside because he was so talented.'

Post season Rangers went on tour to Canada and Bobby played in all four matches in the Red Leaf Cup.

'We went to Niagara Falls and did a bit of the tourist stuff and played in a wee tournament,' said Russell. 'In one of the games we played on Astroturf and it was the first time I'd played on it. It was scorching and I hadn't experienced playing in that kind of heat before. At half-time you were dipping your head in buckets of ice to try and cool down. It was horrendous.'

Having already collected five winners' medals during his first three years with Rangers, Bobby Russell supplemented his collection of honours in the 1980/81 season when he added another Scottish Cup winners' medal. Having had his 1979/80 season blighted by a knee injury, he returned to form in the first full campaign of the 1980s and was instrumental in Rangers' Scottish Cup success. It was Russell's goal that secured a 2-1 win over Morton in the last four, and he was on the scoresheet in the final replay too, ghosting in at the back post to rifle a cross from Davie Cooper into the net with his right foot.

'Everything [in the final] was overshadowed by the performance of Davie Cooper,' said Russell. 'There were a lot of good performances in the replay but Coop and wee John MacDonald were outstanding. It was a team performance and we all gelled that night.'

Jim McLean's Dundee United were the beaten opponents in the final and the Tangerines were put to the sword again in season 1981/82 when Rangers claimed the League Cup. Russell was once again a prominent figure in the team that negotiated its way to the final, playing nine matches and scoring twice in an emphatic 8-1 win over Raith Rovers. However, although he missed only four league matches and scored six goals, Rangers finished third in the title race, 12 points adrift of champions Celtic. The club's slide towards mediocrity was confirmed when a seventh successive Scottish Cup Final resulted in a 4-1 defeat at the hands of Aberdeen.

'I played in six consecutive cup finals,' explained Russell. 'We weren't winning consistently in the league but, on our day, we could beat anybody which was proven by the fact we got to so many cup finals.'

Season 1981/82 was significant for the completion of the next phase of the redevelopment of Ibrox. The old Centenary Stand was replaced by the Govan Stand and the new stadium was officially opened when European Cup holders Liverpool came to the stadium in August 1981.

'I didn't last very long in that game,' recalled Russell. 'I hurt my knee so I only lasted about ten or 15 minutes of the first half. I think it was a wee bit of a blessing in disguise as they gave us a bit of a run-around that night. They proved what a good side they were and they toyed with us a wee bit. Although I didn't play for long it was still a good experience playing on the same pitch as Souness and Dalglish. Before each game John Greig would usually go over each opposition player and talk about their strengths and weaknesses. He said there wasn't really a weakness in the Liverpool side apart from a young 17-year-old called Ronnie Whelan. He then went and scored with a chip over Jim Stewart from about 40 yards, so if he was the weak link we knew we were in trouble.'

Rangers' spell in the doldrums was showing no sign of ending in the early 80s but Bobby Russell was a shining light amidst the gloom. However, in season 1982/83 he began to be hampered by a knee injury.

'That happened against Fortuna Dusseldorf in 1979,' said Russell. 'I tore my cruciate ligament which was a career-threatening injury at the time. It wasn't broadcast in the papers and I was out for about nine weeks. The day after the Fortuna match I was taken in for an exploratory operation and they took the offending piece out and stitched me up and that was it. I had to do a bit of recuperation but I shouldn't have played again as quickly as I did. It definitely affected me in a big way and over the next few years I ended up getting five operations on it. As people didn't know about the injury folk started to say I was injury-prone but my knee was buggered.'

Russell made just 29 appearances as Rangers finished fourth in the league in 1982/83 and they also lost out in both domestic cup finals. Bobby was back, firing on all cylinders the following season though. Buoyed by the return of his former mentor Jock Wallace to the Ibrox helm, Russell delivered a Man-of-the-Match display in the League Cup Final against Celtic, winning the first-half penalty, which was converted by Ally McCoist and constantly probing and prompting from midfield.

He said, 'I felt good that day and my knee wasn't giving me a lot of trouble. Jock had us all built up, talking about the battle fever, and although we knew we were up against a good side, we knew that on our day we could beat anybody. We showed a lot of character because we had them beat at 2-0 then they came back and took it into extra time. We could have been deflated and thought we were going to get beat but we went on to win it. McCoist was magnificent that day, scoring a hat-trick, and he is well remembered for that.'

A poor start to the league campaign saw John Greig tender his resignation and also meant that the 1983/84 Premier Division title would not be joining the League Cup on the Ibrox sideboard. Aberdeen won the Championship and Rangers' interest in the Scottish Cup was ended at the quarter-final stage by Dundee.

'For Greigy there were a lot of things happening like the reconstruction of Ibrox and the team he inherited from Jock was ageing,' recalled Russell. 'It was a transition period but he was unlucky that we missed out on winning the Treble back-to-back. Losing the match against Celtic at Parkhead was a sore one for John Greig. Not being in contention for the league put a lot of pressure on him. He did well in Europe but you could see that he wasn't happy and players were letting him down. Big Jock came back in and got us going again. He was a great man, a great inspiration.'

At the conclusion of the campaign Wallace took his players on a world tour, stopping off for games in Australia, Canada, New Zealand and the USA. Ostensibly the plan was to foster team spirit ahead of another attempt to bring the league title back to Ibrox and Russell was among the 18-man squad that embarked on the journey.

'We played a lot of games, including the Australia B side three times, the New Zealand national side and Minnesota Strikers in Los Angeles on Astroturf,' said Russell. 'I missed the games played on Astroturf, though, because of my knee. About a year later we went to the Middle East and played Iraq but that was a money-making venture. I didn't really want to go and play over there as I needed to rest my knee. It gave Jock a chance to try out a couple of players but I didn't really enjoy the trip.'

Still beset with trouble from his knee, Russell endured a nightmare campaign in season 1984/85, appearing in just half of Rangers' 36 league fixtures. It was a similar story in season 1985/86 too. Although he missed just one of Rangers' first 24 league fixtures, the injury flared up again and Bobby made just four more appearances in the first team before the end of a doleful campaign in Govan. Rangers ended the season without a trophy and plummeted to a fifth-place finish in the Premier Division.

Russell's injury issues also had a detrimental effect on his international prospects. He had played three times for the Under 21s but his chances of playing for the full squad were curtailed.

'It bugs me now that I'm tagged as one of the best players never to be capped,' explained Russell. 'Basically, I was fit enough to play club football but in international football you're stepping up a couple of levels and I wasn't fit enough to do that.'

After such a cataclysmic season the winds of change gusted through Ibrox in the summer of 1986, and the arrival of Graeme Souness was expected to kick-start Bobby's career again. Alas, another injury sustained in a UEFA Cup tie against Ilves Tampere meant he made just two appearances in the 1986/87 season.

'I don't think anybody knew about the extent of how it was going to change,' said Russell. 'We were going to play Clydebank in a reserve game at Ibrox and the rumour was that Souness was upstairs in the Blue Room. We didn't believe it but it was a major coup for Rangers to get him. It transformed Rangers and Scottish football.'

Pre-season in 1986 saw Russell included in the first-team squad that travelled to West Germany and he played in three of the four matches. However, on their return to Scotland, despite coming on as substitute in the home friendly against Bayern Munich, he was with the reserves, playing in a 3-1 win over Falkirk and scoring with a shot from 20 yards in a 2-1 defeat at the hands of Raith Rovers. He returned to the first-team fold, playing alongside his new gaffer in midfield in what proved to be a fiery opening Premier Division encounter against Hibernian at Easter Road. However, that would prove to be his only league appearance of the season. The following weekend he played, and scored, in a 7-0 win over Dundee United Reserves at Tannadice and he scored again in a 1-1 draw against the Motherwell second string in September.

'All of a sudden we were getting big players from England coming up but initially I was one of the ones Souness wanted to keep,' said Russell. 'Maybe there was a question mark against me as Souness played in the position I played in so I ended up getting played wide-right. I regret it now as I probably rebelled against it. I could have played for another two or three seasons at Rangers, as I proved when I went to Motherwell that there was still a bit of life left in me.'

He continued, 'After the Hibs game I played in Finland [in the UEFA Cup against Ilves Tampere]. The tie was over as we had won 4-0 at Ibrox. It was a wet night and the pitch was muddy and I was stuck out on the right. I didn't play well and they weren't slow in letting me know it wasn't what they were expecting from me. I knew then it was time to go to pastures new.'

After the game in Finland, Russell endured a spell on the sidelines. This time it was not the perennial knee problem but an issue with his pelvis. He was out of the picture until Valentine's Day in 1987 when he returned to the fold with a fine performance against Hamilton Accies Reserves at Ibrox. But any hopes of a return to the first team were quickly scuppered. Despite playing a starring role in a 4-2 win over Falkirk Reserves, capped off by a superb solo goal, the return of his old knee problem meant his campaign, and Rangers career, was over.

'I played in a game against Troon Juniors but ended up injuring my knee again,' recalled Russell. 'I was taken in not long after that and told my contract was up at the end of the season and they were letting me go. It left a bit of a bitter taste but at the end of the day they had a job to do. But it made me more determined. I ended up going to Motherwell and proved there was still a wee bit of life left in the old dog!'

Russell signed for Motherwell, managed by former Rangers team-mate Tommy McLean, on 8 July 1987 and scored on his league debut, a 2-1 win over St Mirren at Fir Park. He made a total of 32 league appearances in season 1987/88, adding further goals against Dunfermline Athletic and Morton as Motherwell finished eighth in the Premier Division. He also netted a double in the third round of the Skol League Cup against Albion Rovers as Motherwell progressed to the semi-final, where they were eliminated by Rangers. In season 1988/89 his five-goal haul included a memorable strike at Ibrox against Rangers and in season 1989/90 he netted the winner in a 1-0 win over Souness's side at Fir Park. However, the pinnacle of his time at Motherwell was playing a part in the run to the Scottish Cup Final in 1991. He was part of a squad that included former Rangers team-mates Iain Ferguson, Craig Paterson and Davie Cooper and although injury counted him out of the showpiece match against Dundee United – Motherwell won an enthralling match 4-3 after extra time – he was an integral part of that team.

After just 16 appearances in season 1991/92 Russell left Motherwell and signed for Ayr United. Thereafter he had spells at Arbroath, Cowdenbeath and Albion Rovers before he called time on his career in 1997.

Reflecting back on his time with Rangers, where he worked under three managers, Russell has good memories.

'The highlight of my time at Rangers was winning the Treble and doing well in Europe,' said Russell. 'My biggest regret was not buckling down when Souness came in and accepting that I was going to be played in a certain position. It worked out okay as I had five good seasons under Tommy McLean at Motherwell. At the end of the day you make decisions then that you think are right but I have a lot of good memories of playing for Rangers.'

Bobby Russell made a total of 457 appearances for Rangers and scored 44 goals. He won one Premier Division title (1977/78), the Scottish Cup three times (1977/78, 1978/79 and 1980/81) and the League Cup on five occasions (1977/78, 1978/79, 1981/82, 1983/84 and 1984/85). When asked who was the best player he played with at Rangers, for Bobby Russell there is only one answer.

'It's got to be Coop,' he said. 'There were a lot of good players like Jimmy Bett, who was an all-round midfield player, wee Alex MacDonald, Tommy McLean, and at the back, Greigy. I was able to go from Shettleston Juniors straight into the Rangers team because there were international players who had been over the course and won Trebles. But to point one player out, it's Coop simply because of the good understanding we had.'

Fergie (1)
Derek Ferguson (1982–1990)

He was the heir apparent at the age of just 20, the protégé who had been earmarked to be at the heart of the Rangers and Scotland midfield for years to come. Derek Ferguson, who had debuted in a Rangers jersey 126 days before his 16th birthday and had been voted Man of the Match in a national cup final, aged 19, seemingly had the footballing world at his feet. However, a fractious relationship with Graeme Souness signalled a premature end to his Rangers career just when he should have been establishing himself as a mainstay in the first team.

'It was a totally different format than what it is just now,' said Ferguson of the start to his Rangers career. 'We were only in once a week – a Tuesday night – for training and during summer and Easter holidays for extra training. We trained on the red ash over at The Albion under the floodlights. What I remember about that was at night time in the winter we weren't allowed tracksuit bottoms, gloves or a hat. We got a T-shirt, a cotton top, shorts and socks that had to be rolled up. We didn't moan, though, it was all part of the discipline. We also each got a ball and you had to go back with that ball; if it went over the wall you had to chase it and go and get it.'

He continued, 'Unlike boys today I wasn't getting lifted and laid. I stayed in Hamilton at that time. It was a mad sprint from Earnock High School to get home and changed before getting the bus about twenty past four. It was the number 62 bus from Little Earnock to Hamilton Central and from there into Glasgow and then out to Ibrox on the subway. We got a fiver for expenses, which was actually a lot of money at that time.'

Rangers were not the only club who showed an interest in young Ferguson. He spent time at Old Trafford with Manchester United and trained with Celtic too. It was the camaraderie at Ibrox and the fact he was a Rangers supporter that made up Derek's mind.

'It was really quiet at Celtic, totally different to the atmosphere among the boys at Rangers,' recalled Ferguson. 'There was real buzz at Ibrox and I loved it.'

In addition to training with Rangers, Ferguson got game time with Burnbank – with whom he won the U13 Scottish Cup – and Gartcosh United. However, he was soon earmarked by John Greig for a place in the Rangers reserve team.

'Greigy reckoned I was getting into bad habits at Gartcosh,' said Ferguson. 'His idea of bad habits was me beating five or six players then sticking one in the top corner! They took me out of that and into the reserves to learn the game. Physically I wasn't strong enough at that age to do what I had been doing at Gartcosh. I was coming up against men so I had to change my game. I had to release the ball quicker but when I think back, it was too much of a switch. Maybe I could have been given a bit more time to develop [at boys' club level] but I wasn't going to grumble as, at 15, I was mixing it with the likes of John MacDonald and Bobby Russell. I was going to watch these guys from the Centenary Stand and now I was playing with them.'

Ferguson signed full-time with Rangers on 23 August 1983, two months after his 16th birthday. By then, however, he had already played in the first team.

'It was big Tam Forsyth's testimonial against Swansea City and I thought I was going along to help out with the kit and if the first team boys needed anything like a cup of tea or a paper,' said Derek. 'Then Greigy said he was going to strip me for the experience so I thought I would maybe get on at half-time and get a wee kickabout with the other boys that were substitutes. I loved that but didn't think for a minute I would go on. With about 25 minutes to go I was asked to go and warm up and when I came back I was told I was going on. I was told to just go on and enjoy it and get on the ball. I hadn't even signed as a professional at the club by then. I knew I was going to get a contract but you had to wait until you were 16 to sign it.'

Derek was handed the number 17 jersey. In his Rangers career his blue jersey would be replete with all manner of outfield shirt numbers, all bar the number three.

'Barry was synonymous with number six but I played in a host of different positions, including sweeper,' recalled Ferguson. 'The number never really bothered me; I was just delighted to get a jersey.'

Although still changing in the away dressing room with the second team, Ferguson was now training with the first-team squad alongside the likes of Cooper, McClelland and Russell. Although Derek did not figure in any of the pre-season friendly games, he was on the substitutes' bench when the competitive action got underway against Queen of the South at Ibrox in the League Cup. Sporting the number 12 jersey he replaced Craig Paterson for his Ibrox bow in front of a mere 8,000 supporters.

A month later Ferguson was on his travels as he was selected in the squad to face Maltese side Valletta in the opening round of the European Cup Winners' Cup. When he came off the bench in the September sunshine, he became the youngest player to represent Rangers in a European tie. For good measure that special spell also included a goal against Celtic in a 5-2 win for the reserves.

'We were in total control in Malta and knew we were going to win the game when we got a penalty,' explained Ferguson. 'Greigy wanted me to take it but I refused. I think he felt it would do me the world of good but it wouldn't have made any difference to me. I was quite strong minded and I was never about glory. I wasn't scared to take it: it just didn't feel it was my position to take it.'

Robert Prytz took the spot kick and scored, one of eight goals netted on the night by Greig's side. Ferguson featured again in the return leg, replacing Craig Paterson this time, but it was fellow 16-year-old Billy Davies that hogged the headlines, scoring one of Rangers' ten goals on the night.

'Billy Davies was my captain [in the reserve team] and was some player,' noted Ferguson. 'I looked up to Billy at that time. He was phenomenal and probably should have had a better career than he did. He was small in stature but had a big personality and had one of the best touches out of all the players at that time.'

A first start for the first team followed for Ferguson when Hearts visited Ibrox on 26 October – he set up a goal for Robert Prytz – but just when it seemed the youngster was set for a run in the team, he was given a rude awakening.

'We played St Mirren and Billy Abercrombie tried to break my leg,' said Ferguson. 'It was a wee eye-opener. I went in loose and learned quickly that you can't do that. Abercrombie was a good player but he was a hard man and he decided to lay a marker on me.'

Ferguson was replaced by Davie Cooper at half-time and that proved to be his last appearance for the top team until March. In the meantime, he returned to the reserves, featuring in 12 of the opening 18 Premier Reserve League matches. He was part of a side that won each of those 18 matches and would eventually win the title.

'We were a good side and the atmosphere in the dressing room was brilliant,' recalled Ferguson. 'When you went down to the first-team dressing room it was serious but in the away dressing room it was hilarious. The likes of big Andy Kennedy would come in and there was only one place in the dressing room where there was a mirror and that would be his place. He just loved himself but we used to get up to all sorts of daft stuff like boxing matches and we would play bowls too. I loved it that much I didn't want to leave and go to the first-team dressing room.'

During Ferguson's stint in the reserves Rangers had been reinvigorated by the arrival of Jock Wallace. He had taken over from John Greig and Rangers embarked on an unbeaten run in all three domestic competitions. That run ended on 17 March when Dundee won a Scottish Cup replay 3-2 at Ibrox and three days later Derek was back in the first-team picture. The following midweek he played the full 90 minutes of a friendly match against Linfield, scoring in a 4-0 win. With Prytz and Redford suspended for the League Cup Final against Celtic five days later, young Ferguson looked to have put himself in a strong position for a place in the squad.

'I wasn't picked but I wasn't disappointed,' said Ferguson. 'It was a fine line but I had a great lifestyle and was playing for the team I loved. I went to the hotel with the team and got to enjoy the build-up and going to watch the game as a fan.'

Ferguson had enjoyed a good debut season at Ibrox. Still only 16, he had made six appearances for the first team, played in Europe and also helped Rangers win the annual Tennent's Sixes. Coupled with that, he had played 39 times for the reserves, winning a Reserve League Championship medal. Ferguson had also been promoted at international level, moving from the U16s to the U18s. Alongside team-mate Hugh Burns, Derek had helped Scotland to qualify for the European Championships in Russia.

'I enjoyed it and always liked going away with Scotland,' said Ferguson. 'Andy Roxburgh and Craig Brown were in charge and I loved going and playing against different types of player. I roomed with Celtic's Peter Grant too and managed to get him to sing "yabba dabba doo, we support the boys in blue and it's Rangers"!'

Scotland, who had won the tournament in 1982, exited the competition at the group stages after finishing runners-up in Group A. The Scots lost 3-0 against the Republic of Ireland, drew 1-1 with Greece and defeated Portugal 3-1 but injury restricted Ferguson to just one appearance.

The mixture of first-team and reserve-team appearances continued for young Ferguson in season 1984/85. He featured three times in pre-season friendlies played in Switzerland and West Germany but it was December before he played in the first team, replacing Cammy Fraser 20 minutes from the end of a 1-1 home draw with Hearts. A run of seven successive starts followed, and included in this run was an Old Firm baptism and a rollicking from his manager.

'I turned up for the Celtic game with blond tips in my hair and Jock went through me,' recalled Ferguson. 'Ian Redford's wife had a salon in the West End and we got a discount up there. I had a mullet at the time and I got it dyed blond. My hair looked like straw! Jock said to me, "What the f**k is that all about? Get rid of it, that's not what a Rangers player should look like." I think he thought I was trying to be flash but I wasn't. I went and got it cut the following Monday!'

The match with Celtic at Parkhead ended 1-1. Brian McClair put the home side ahead after nine minutes and although Cammy Fraser missed a penalty six minutes into the second half, Davie Cooper earned Rangers a point when he capitalised on a Pat Bonner error in the 85th minute. Ferguson was lauded for his part in the second-half fightback, with the *Glasgow Herald* saying that he 'showed all the touches to suggest he is one of the best young Scottish players to emerge for years.'

'It was just what I expected, 90 miles per hour, tackles flying in,' said Ferguson who played the full 90 minutes. 'I was nervous and excited but just getting an opportunity to run out there against them, I had heard all the stories and it didn't disappoint me. The passion, the drive, the tackles, you just didn't want to let anybody down.'

Having played in the Old Firm reserve fixture on a number of occasions, the first-team equivalent was a different ball game. Derek continued, 'There are huge crowds and you see them as you're getting to the ground on the coach. You know you've got a responsibility to all the punters that are going to the game; you can make a difference to their weekend. If you get a result they can have a great weekend. In the reserves you don't feel that. As we got about 20 minutes from Parkhead, Jock would put a few wee songs on and you were pumped up as you were walking off the bus. You can't wait for kick-off but I was quite good at keeping a lid on it. My ritual was to play around with a ball in the shower room but guys like Bomber [John Brown], I thought his head was going to explode! He'd be blowing into a bag and the doctor would be with him trying to calm him down.'

Players would warm up differently too. 'I never wanted a touch of the ball,' said Ferguson. 'We would do a couple of widths of the park, jogging and heels up, then break away and do a few sprints. It was all about getting your mentality right. Jock was brilliant at that, because when we ran out there at five-to-three you could have taken on everybody.'

A common misconception is that in the heat of the battle there is no love lost between the two sides. However, on this occasion Ferguson drew praise for his performance from an unlikely source. He remembered, 'The older players in the Rangers team were a great help, guys like Prytzy, a Swedish internationalist, my captain, Ally Dawson, and Coop, who was cool as a cucumber. That day, though,

I was up against Tommy Burns and he actually praised me. I couldn't believe it. I knew what was coming, the physicality of the game, they were going to smash into me, I was going to smash into them but what Tommy did was a big surprise.'

Ferguson, by now captain of the Scotland U18 side, ended his spell in the first team when he was replaced by Ian Redford at half-time in a 5-1 defeat against Aberdeen in January. His season was concluded prematurely too, a twisted knee sustained whilst representing the youth team in the annual Dusseldorf Youth Tournament meaning a spell on the treatment table.

'I was still in the reserve-team dressing room at that time but there was no jealousy or resentment,' said Ferguson. 'It would have been so easy for that to happen but I never experienced it. I was the young pup getting games for the first team but that was the difference at that time, the lads were happy for you. They never treated me any differently and I loved that.'

Pre-season prominence ahead of season 1985/86 – Ferguson started all four friendly matches, scoring against Ross County and Ayr United – and a start in the opening Premier Division fixture against Dundee United suggested Derek was at the forefront of Jock Wallace's thoughts. However, he ended up yo-yoing between the first team and the reserves in the opening months of the campaign, notably scoring in a 7-2 win over Clydebank's second team in September and winning a Glasgow Cup medal as part of a strong side that beat Queen's Park 5-0 at Hampden.

A sustained run over the Christmas period – a run of eight consecutive starts – was ended 14 minutes from the end of a Scottish Cup third-round tie against Hearts at Tynecastle. Ferguson commented, 'I got sent off for giving Gary MacKay a "Glasgow Kiss"! I went on to play with Gary and he ended up being a good mate but I didn't shirk out of anything. I think it's a Ferguson trait; we can be quite mild-mannered but if you push some of the buttons we turn.'

The red card proved costly. Ian Durrant had brought Rangers level at 2-2 just seven minutes earlier but John Robertson earned Hearts a place in the next round when he netted the winning goal with only five minutes remaining. Ferguson only made four more appearances thereafter in what was, in truth, a dismal season at Ibrox. Jock Wallace was dismissed in April and Graeme Souness took over at the helm.

'Jock didn't speak to you, he growled,' recalled Ferguson fondly. 'He had a softer side, though. He would give you a rollicking but would also come and speak to you and tell you that you were playing. He didn't really have a lot of options at the time. The stadium was getting redeveloped so he had to play younger players. That meant the likes of me, Durranty, Shuggie Burns and Dave McFarlane were there at the right time.'

The Souness effect was immediate, with 40,741 people turning up for the 1986 Glasgow Cup Final against Celtic. 'I came on for Durranty but I remember we were heading to Blackpool after the game,' recalled Ferguson. 'After winning the Glasgow Cup we went up to Shawlands in a minibus for a few beers and all the windows got panned in! It didn't stop us going to Blackpool and we ended up on the beach at six in the morning having a game of football. We had to cut it short, though, as the tide was coming in!'

He continued, 'It was instilled in me at an early age that if you work hard, you play hard. Jock took us to Malta when I was 18 and when we got there he told us to put our bags in our room and come back downstairs. He took us into the wee room that had a bar and a piano and he locked the door, he wouldn't let us out! We had a squad of 18 players, having a drink, on the piano, singing songs. It was amazing.'

On the way home from the seaside there was a detour to Dumfries, hometown of eccentric winger, Ted McMinn. 'We ended up in a wee Rangers Social Club,' said Ferguson. 'I loved going to places like that but it doesn't happen now. It didn't even happen when [younger brother] Barry was at Rangers. We used to go to Rangers dances all the time; that was my weekend. I even ended up as guest speaker at the Rangers Rally. I think I was the youngest player to ever speak at it. Now that was nerve-wracking.'

Souness immediately set about establishing his blueprint for success at Ibrox. 'With no disrespect to Jock or John Greig, the standards went up on everything,' said Ferguson. 'The training, the diets, totally different, it just went to another level. We stayed in hotels before games too, every home game and every away game; we had only experienced that for cup finals. His preparation was meticulous.'

He continued, 'When Souness first spoke to us he made no bones about it; there were going to be a lot of players moving on. You think to yourself, "Am I going to be one of them?" but the next day I was asked to go up to the office and he put another two or three years on my contract and more than doubled my wages.'

Recruitment was stepped up too, with Terry Butcher and Chris Woods brought in from the English First Division. It did not take long for them to realise the magnitude of the club they had just joined.

'Me and Durranty are going to take the plaudits for that,' said Ferguson with a smile. 'As young guys we didn't put them up on a pedestal and we made them well aware of what Rangers was all about. We spoke to them, they had been in our company and we told them that this wasn't just a football team. It was all about the punters, going to supporters' events, making themselves available.'

After an explosive and uneven start to the season, Souness's Rangers made a statement of intent when they defeated Celtic 1-0 at Ibrox in the first Old Firm league match on 31 August. Playing alongside Ian Durrant, Ferguson was a dominant figure in the middle of the park. It was Durrant who netted the only goal of the game, latching on to a delicious reverse pass from Davie Cooper, but Ferguson was lauded for his contribution.

'I remember the goal and Durranty blanking Coop [when he celebrated],' recalled Ferguson. 'It was a whole different ball game and even Souness was taken aback. I think he then got it, he knew that this was different. A lot of the new guys thought we were a big club, well supported, but how it gets to people? I think they realised that and we played our part in making sure they knew what the club was all about. We then started to get that atmosphere that I had had in the away dressing room with the reserves.'

More Old Firm glory followed just two months later. Rangers met Celtic at Hampden in the final of the League Cup and, with Souness injured, Ferguson was selected alongside Cammy Fraser, Durrant and Davie Cooper in a four-man midfield. Ferguson's display that afternoon ranks alongside the best he ever produced in a Rangers jersey.

'It got Man of the Match but it was a great game, end-to-end,' said Ferguson. 'With five minutes to go [the game was tied at 1-1] we got a free kick. I whipped it in but over-hit it. However, Roy Aitken pulled down Butcher and we got a penalty. As soon as Coop got the ball I knew we had won it. That was my first medal.'

The match also saw Ferguson go supersonic. He recalled, 'Ian got the first goal which meant he got two free tickets to go on Concorde. I went with him but the plane was delayed for about five hours. You can imagine the state we were in by the time we got on to Concorde! I thought it was going to be massive but it was tiny. I don't think there was much left by the end of the flight; anything that wasn't nailed down we took it. When they were flying we were allowed to go up to the cockpit but we were ushered out as soon as possible as we wanted to press a few buttons!'

The after-match party at Ibrox was memorable too, although Durrant and Ferguson were almost responsible for the loss of the League Cup. With a devilish grin Derek said, 'We went back to Ibrox and all the backroom staff were there; the lassies from the kitchen, the folk that did the washing, all the groundsmen. I loved that. Me and Ian didn't have steady girlfriends at the time so we could enjoy ourselves, not just with the players but we could go out and celebrate with all the punters. The cup was sitting on one of the tables and Durranty said to wee Dougal, who helped the groundsman and did odd jobs, to take it home with him. About half an hour later some pictures had to get taken with the cup but it had gone. There was a panic as we couldn't find it. There were no mobile phones then so we searched everywhere before someone asked where Dougal was. It turned out he had just wandered down to The District Bar, which is about a mile-and-a-half down Paisley Road West, with the League Cup!'

Reward for his stellar displays came in the shape of Ferguson's first two caps for the Scotland U21s and a run of games in the Rangers engine room. Twelve successive first-team starts between November and January witnessed Rangers in swashbuckling form, 23 goals and just one conceded propelling Souness's side to the summit of the Premier Division. Ferguson then returned to the reserve team for a spell, earning praise for being 'in a class of his own' in one match against Dundee United.

Ferguson recalled, 'Souness's fitness was still phenomenal so it was always going to be a big ask [for Ferguson to play every week]. At that time I wasn't doing what he thought I was [going out socialising on a regular basis] but he used to look into the dressing room and we would all be laughing and joking and I think he always thought we had been out. But half the time we weren't; we were just having a carry on. It wasn't just Souness I was up against; there were lots of top players like Cammy Fraser too.'

The match-winning mentality that season was nurtured on the training pitch. The Rangers players were encouraged to train as they would play, which led to a number of bruising sessions at The Albion, which lay in the shadows of the imposing red brick Ibrox facade.

'At my age I should have been coming back in the afternoons with a few of the other guys, working on things, being in the gym,' said Ferguson. 'Durrant was naturally fit; he was an athlete, not just a fantastic footballer. I didn't have that natural athleticism and I should have been working on it.'

He continued, 'Training was good and the quality was unbelievable. We used to have Scotland v England on a Friday and it annoyed me that Graeme used to play for England. I used to think he didn't think we were good enough, that he was looking down on us. So it became a bit tasty. I treated everyone the same and we got torn into each other. Having said that, trying to get near Souness was impossible at times!'

Domestic appearances were supplemented with four appearances in the UEFA Cup and a goal in a 1-0 win over Portuguese side, Boavista, in round two. 'Coop played me in and I just swung my leg at it and it went into the top corner,' said Ferguson with a smile. 'I wasn't a regular goalscorer as that was taken away from me. When I played for my boys' club I used to be a runner that took people on and I loved doing that. But then I had to change my game to become more of a sitting midfielder, dictating things and finding guys that could do the damage. That was my strength at that time and I got just as much enjoyment out of making a killer pass, as other boys maybe couldn't make that pass. But I could see it.'

After his spell in the reserves, Ferguson appeared in six of the last seven league games to chalk up 30 first-team Premier Division appearances for what proved to be a Championship-winning season. However, when the title was clinched at Pittodrie, Ferguson was back at Ibrox playing for the second string.

'It didn't stop me celebrating,' said Ferguson followed by a hearty laugh. 'It was a disappointment but I think Graeme was getting a wee bit irked with me for certain things. However, at that time there was a guy that looked exactly the same as me that was getting in to places like Panama Jacks by saying he was me! I think Graeme listened a wee bit too much to what others were saying and he certainly lost patience with me. Maybe he was looking for better standards and that was part of the reason I didn't get as much game time.'

Derek Ferguson seemed to have the world at his feet. Plying his trade in the first team at Ibrox, he was learning from the very best and season 1987/88 offered him the opportunity to develop further, even though the arrival of the likes of Ray Wilkins meant a regular berth in the first team was not guaranteed.

'Wilkins was brilliant, a class act, and I loved having him in the dressing room,' enthused Ferguson. 'You could just sit and listen to him talk and, even though he had played at the top, he had time for us. Even on the training ground he would give you wee pointers. He had the best first touch of any player I'd played with. We used to test him every day, smashing the ball at him from about ten yards and he'd just kill it dead.'

Such was the burgeoning talent of Ferguson, he was never going to be out of the team for long. Another Man-of-the-Match Old Firm display in the infamous 2-2 draw at Ibrox in October preceded a run that saw Derek miss just four of the remaining 31 Premier Division matches. He earned another League Cup medal too, wearing the number five jersey in the classic 3-3 draw against Aberdeen. By the time it came to the penalty shoot-out Ferguson had been substituted, with his replacement, Trevor Francis, successfully converting one of Rangers' five penalties.

'Until a few years ago I didn't even remember I played in the 2-2 draw,' recalled Ferguson. 'Graham Roberts was talking about it at a dinner I was at and I went home that night and watched it on YouTube and realised I was playing! That felt like a win. At 2-0 down we looked as if we were out of it but the finish to the game was amazing.'

By the end of the season Ferguson had been voted *Rangers News* Player of the Year and international recognition had arrived, with a first full cap against Malta in a 1-1 draw in March 1988.

'I only got two caps for Scotland but at the time I was suffering with a few injuries,' said Ferguson. 'I had some issues with my back that meant I had to go down to Harley Street. I also had problems with my shoulder and I had to change my game a bit and it takes you a bit more time to get back.'

However, just when Derek Ferguson looked to be making serene progress in his Rangers and Scotland career, he hit a rather large bump in the road. Although a new four-year deal was signed in August 1988, he was not part of the first-team picture for 16 of the opening 20 league matches in season 1988/89. When the first team were thrashing Celtic 5-1 at Ibrox, their midfield maestro was playing for the reserves at Parkhead. He was also an unused substitute when Rangers lifted the League Cup for the third successive year in October with a 3-2 win over Aberdeen.

'Graeme Souness eventually ran out of patience with me and told me I was going to move on,' recalled Ferguson. 'He obviously had a change of mind [after offering Ferguson a new deal] but not at any stage did I put in a transfer request. I did respect Graeme but I felt he was trying to shunt me out the club. I flatly refused and there was a conflict. I went through a stage when I was in the first-team matchday squad but wasn't getting selected. My dad would come and pick me up at Ibrox just after 2pm and take me back to Strathclyde Park. Rather than stay and watch the game I'd go for a run for an hour to get it out my system. I was that angry and it was horrible but there was only going to be one winner.'

Ferguson was also elsewhere on the day when Ian Durrant's flourishing career was brought to a shuddering halt. As Durrant and the rest of the first team were at Pittodrie facing Aberdeen, Ferguson was playing in the corresponding reserve game at Ibrox. The absence of mobile phones in those days meant it would be some time before he found out his best pal had had his knee shattered.

He continued, 'After the [reserve] game I went up to the Nile Bar and Durranty and I were going to meet there about 8.30. I remember his brother, Alan, coming in and saying to me that Ian would be a bit late as he had got a bit of a knock [at Pittodrie]. I decided to wait on him but when it came to 9.30, I decided to leave and head for Panama Jacks. I was angry with him because he hadn't turned up and it wasn't like him. I ended up coming out there later on and as I was waiting for a taxi, they were selling the [first edition of] papers. I got a paper and that was the first I knew about how bad Ian's injury was. I went home, slept for a couple of hours then headed up to Ross Hall to see him.'

Three days after the League Cup Final, Ferguson was back in the starting XI for a UEFA Cup tie with 1.FC Cologne. It was during this match that Derek sustained an injury that would dog the last two seasons of his Rangers career.

'I dislocated my left shoulder after about ten minutes but still completed the match,' said Ferguson. 'They put it back in at the side of the park but it was never the same. It came out another eight times before I got surgery. Once in training I went in for a tackle and it popped out again when somebody landed on me. Souness came over and put his foot under my armpit and tried to pull my arm back in. He couldn't get it so I was taken up to the hospital. When it was explained to the doctors what Graeme had tried to do they said he could have permanently damaged the nerves.'

In the dressing room Ferguson was dubbed 'Napoleon' but it would be November of 1989 before he eventually went for an operation on the troublesome shoulder. There was interest at that time from other clubs – a swap deal with Chelsea involving Nicky Walker and Tony Dorigo was mooted – and there was also an unfortunate incident in a kebab shop to deal with.

'Not at one stage did I ask to go,' said Derek. 'I was down at the time, gutted, but I always thought I was lucky to be at Rangers. I thought I would come through the wee storm and have the opportunity to show Graeme that I could do what he wanted me to do. But it wasn't to be.'

On the kebab shop incident he said, 'We always got a Wednesday off so Ian and I went out for a couple of drinks and we were heading back to the District Bar. We went into the kebab shop and Ian had his crutches. There were a couple of guys and girls mouthing off at us and although Ian and I weren't involved in the fight that followed, when the police were called we ended up in the police car. I was standing in front of Ian trying to protect him and they made a bee-line for us. We ended up in Govan police station and although we hadn't been involved, it ended up in the papers and it was the last straw for Graeme.'

Ferguson was fined and banned from Ibrox for a fortnight. In that campaign, 1988/89, he made just 16 appearances in the Premier Division, scoring twice. He scored the winner on Hogmanay 1988 against Hamilton at Douglas Park and struck again in a 2-1 victory at Pittodrie in January. He is often credited with both goals in the latter match, but he said the credit for the opening goal that day should go to Stuart Munro.

The end of season showpiece that season, the Scottish Cup Final, promised to be a cracker. Rangers, going for the domestic Treble, faced Celtic at Hampden but for Derek, it proved an ignominious end to a turbulent season.

'Two weeks ahead of the final, I was fine, I was fit,' recalled Ferguson. 'I thought I had done enough and I was desperate to play. But when we got into the dressing room Graeme named the team and I wasn't in it. I felt sure I'd be on the bench but although his own fitness hadn't been that great, Souness put himself on the bench.'

He continued, 'I was raging as I thought Graeme had taken my place. I think he felt we'd win easily and he'd come on for the last half-hour, showboat and enjoy the occasion. But Joe Miller scored and we lost and in the dressing room, Souness threw his medal away.

I know it was a loser's medal but I wanted to play in a Scottish Cup Final. I lost a bit of respect for him when he did that.'

Despite the cup final frustration, Ferguson appeared in three of the opening seven league matches in season 1989/90. Ironically, he replaced goalkeeper Chris Woods when he dislocated his shoulder in the opening match of the season against St Mirren and followed a run of three reserve games with successive starts against Dundee and Dunfermline. Derek also completed the 90 minutes of the League Cup semi-final against Dunfermline in September. However, after returning from shoulder surgery alongside Souness in a testimonial for Stuart McLean in January 1990, Derek ended up at Dundee on loan.

On return from his loan spell Ferguson played just twice more for the Rangers first team. He replaced David Dodds after 57 minutes in a 2-1 win over Motherwell at Ibrox and the following week lined up alongside Trevor Steven, Nigel Spackman and Mark Walters in midfield as Rangers retained the Premier Division title with a 1-0 win over Dundee United at Tannadice. A ceasefire in the war of attrition with Souness was eventually declared when Ferguson signed for Hearts on 11 July 1990 for a fee of £750,000.

'Graeme would come in to the dressing room and ask if I had spoken to [Hearts chairman] Wallace Mercer and I would say I had told him I wasn't going anywhere,' recalled Derek. 'He would pull me into his office and tell me what he had done with others boys like Graham Roberts. He said he would send me away to play with the reserves but he would put me on the bench. I told him it didn't worry me but it did. It was actually my dad that made my mind up [to leave Rangers].

'He asked me if I really wanted to train all week and not play so I decided to go and speak to Hearts. Another reason for doing that was that Nicky [Walker], Iain Ferguson, Davie Kirkwood and a few of the other Rangers boys were there. Wallace Mercer was brilliant, a fantastic guy, but he wanted me to stay in Edinburgh. I didn't want to do that, which made Souness unhappy, until eventually Hearts agreed that I could still stay in Hamilton with my mum and dad.'

Ferguson made his league debut for Hearts in a 1-1 draw with St Mirren at Tynecastle. In March he scored against Rangers in a 2-1 defeat at Ibrox. He said, 'I never celebrated. It was surreal. I wasn't noted for scoring goals but I was never going to go over and make a gesture to Souness. I had too much respect for him.'

After three seasons in Edinburgh, Ferguson moved to England, signing for Sunderland who were managed by his former captain, Terry Butcher. It did not work out. The loss of his daughter, Lauren, aged just seven weeks understandably had an impact and Ferguson lost his motivation to play football. He came back to Scotland and, convinced by a phone call from former team-mate, Mo Johnston, signed for Falkirk.

'I liked playing for John Lambie but by the end of my second season I had injured my cruciate ligament,' said Ferguson. 'That was just before I was due to move to South Korea but had I done that I wouldn't have had the chance to play against [younger brother] Barry.'

That came to pass on 26 September 1998. By now Derek was plying his trade with Dunfermline Athletic, while the young pretender had been given a new lease of life under Dick Advocaat at Ibrox.

Big brother Derek recalled, 'That was surreal. When you go out on the park and cross that white line you always say that it doesn't matter who it is, you would get stuck in to them. But it's difficult when it is your wee brother, particularly when you've played a big part in him getting to where he was.'

Spells at Portadown, Partick Thistle, Adelaide Force, Ross County, Clydebank, Alloa, Hamilton and Raith Rovers followed Ferguson's season at East End Park before he eventually called time on his playing career at the age of 38 in 2006. He then had a spell in management with junior side, Glenafton Athletic.

'I went there to help out Daz [Gordon Dalziel],' said Ferguson. 'We would train on a Tuesday night at Bellahouston Park and only four or five would turn up but on a Thursday night there would be about 18. Daz then left so I agreed to take the job for a short period of time but I suggested if the players weren't going to turn up for training then that should be docked off their wages. It was a good set-up and a well-run wee club but the players got too much money for doing nothing.'

Today Ferguson is a respected pundit on BBC Radio Scotland. He also does talks in schools as part of the 'Show Racism the Red Card' campaign and is prominent on the after-dinner circuit.

Derek Ferguson was a Rangers supporter who lived the dream. He made 185 appearances for the club and scored 11 goals. He won two Premier Division championship medals (1986/87 and 1988/89), three League Cup medals (1986/87, 1987/88 and 1988/89), two Glasgow Cup medals (both in 1985/86) and a Reserve League Championship medal (1983/84).

'The highlight of my time at Rangers was walking up the marble stairs with my dad and signing a professional contract,' said Ferguson. 'I knew what that meant to my dad, the best player in our family according to him, and to see his face when we walked back down the stairs afterwards was terrific. My only regret is that I didn't score against Celtic for the first team. It wouldn't have mattered if it had been at Parkhead or Ibrox, it would just have been amazing to score.'

Jasper
Ian Durrant (1982 –1998)

Born and raised less than two miles from Ibrox Stadium in Kinning Park, Ian Durrant used to sneak in to home games through a hole in the fence at the back of the old Centenary Stand in the late 1970s. But in 1982 he did not have to slip in hoping he would not be noticed. For that day he had an audience with the Rangers manager, John Greig, as he was about to realise his ambition of signing for Rangers.

'There were eight of us signed on schoolboy forms,' recalled Durrant. 'That included myself, Derek Ferguson, Hugh Burns, Davie McFarlane, Robert Fleck and John Davies. We had lots of jobs and one was to sort out the training kit. Under Greigy and big Jock we would get one set of kit on a Monday to do us the whole week. Sometimes by Friday it would be solid. We had to make sure it was dry for the next day but you knew whose kit was whose. Coop's was always immaculate, but wee Polaris [John MacDonald], his was filthy as he was always on the deck. That all changed under Souness when we got fresh kit every day.'

He added, 'We also had to do the boots. On a Friday the players would wear their match boots for training so we had to make sure they were ready for the game and in the hamper. If it was a wet day on the Friday we had to put the boots on the heaters then scrub them up and paint them. That meant painting the white stripes on the Adidas boots and Derek did numbers 1-10 and I was 11-21. I had the likes of Jim Stewart – his boots were bogging – and John MacDonald but Coisty and Sandy Clark were in the single numbers. At that time Coisty's boots were sparkling as he wasn't playing!'

Tasks like that were commonplace for apprentice footballers in the 1980s and it is something that is sadly absent from the modern game.

Durrant continued, 'About five or six days before pre-season we would have to paint the railings in the Enclosure – four apprentices in each one – and it was hard. But it was your job. We also had to pump up the balls – 12.5 gauge – and put them in a bag. They were all numbered and each player got his own ball for training. It was a £50 fine if you lost it, which was a lot of money back then.'

Durrant soon lived up to his reputation as a talented midfielder. His star was on the rise and, following a successful trial, he was selected in the squad that travelled to take part in the prestigious Croix youth tournament. He was a standout performer and was voted Man of the Match in the 1-1 draw against PSV Eindhoven. An appearance for the reserve team in a 4-0 win over Clydebank prior to the trip to France further cemented Durrant's status as a hot prospect.

'In Croix you never played against teams like Nantes and PSG, you were playing against the likes of the Turkish and Russian national teams,' said Durrant. 'We went from Glasgow Central by train to Euston then got a bus to Dover. From there we got the ferry to Calais then a bus to Croix. What would take you about an hour and a half now on a flight used to take us a full day. The first thing I remember when we arrived at the hotel was this big pot of hot chocolate and croissants. Coming from Glasgow the lads and I didn't know what croissants were in those days but it was a great experience. It was a great learning curve.'

The travelling party would be swelled by iconic figures like Willie Thornton – or 'Bosso' as Durrant referred to him – and Willie Waddell. Bob McPhail was also present when the reserves were in action too.

'Bosso was like a club ambassador even though that wasn't an official role at the time,' said Durrant. 'Bosso, Willie Waddell and Mr McPhail wouldn't travel to the away game with the first team.

Instead they would stay at Ibrox and watch the reserves. Mr McPhail was a quiet man but Mr Waddell would shout at you on the marble stairs if you hadn't played well. You had so much respect for him and when he praised you, you went away feeling amazing.'

Less than a year after signing for Rangers' Durrant had to impress a new manager. And Jock Wallace had been keeping a watchful eye on young Durrant. He played again for the reserves when he replaced Dave Mitchell 18 minutes from the end of a 4-1 win over Dundee at Dens Park on 16 December 1983, scoring the fourth goal in the 72nd minute. A further eight reserve appearances followed and another two goals. But it was in a tournament in Dusseldorf, West Germany, that Durrant really impressed the Rangers hierarchy. Rangers won three, drew two and lost one of the matches they played, with Durrant scoring in wins over Eintracht Frankfurt, Borussia Monchengladbach (2) and Kaiserslautern (2).

'Shortly after that I was asked to train with the first team,' remembered Durrant. 'Both Jock and Greigy were visible presences. Greigy would turn up on a Tuesday night and take training for the 'S' forms with Stan Anderson and Tommy McLean. And whenever he could, big Jock would be at our games and, although there wasn't a youth set-up like there is now, there was a big emphasis on the apprentices.'

Ian spent the majority of season 1984/85 in the second team, making 28 appearances and scoring twice. The chance to pull on a first-team jersey eventually came on 20 April 1985 when Rangers, already out of the title race after a wretched run of form since the turn of the year that had witnessed seven defeats in 11 matches, travelled to Greenock to face Morton. Wallace's side arrived at Cappielow on the back of three successive defeats and the manager clearly felt that an injection of youth was required to try and arrest the slump. Just a fortnight earlier Durrant had been starring again in the Dusseldorf Youth Tournament, scoring in a 1-1 draw with Japan, but now he had been thrust into the first team.

'On the Friday before games we would have a practice match, the Blues against the Reds,' recalled Durrant. 'The Blues was the starting line-up for the game the next day and the day before we played Morton at Cappielow, big Jock threw me the number six jersey. The game lasted about half an hour and when we went back in Jock handed me two comps [complimentary tickets] and told me to get a good sleep as I was playing the next day. On the Saturday I walked from Kinning Park to Ibrox for the pre-match meal in my club tie and a blazer that my dad had borrowed for me. I played for about 84 minutes and it was unbelievable. Coisty got a hat-trick and I had a hand in one of his goals.'

Durrant's stellar display ensured he kept the number six jersey for the remaining five league fixtures. Included in that run of games was his Old Firm baptism, a 1-1 draw at Parkhead, and he also notched a first goal for the first team, a penalty in a 3-2 defeat against Chelsea at Stamford Bridge in a match that was held to raise money for the Bradford City Disaster Fund.

'It was the same for big Jock as it was for Greigy; there was no money to spend as everything was getting spent on the stadium,' said Durrant. 'Nowadays there are about 60 players in the academies but we had eight apprentices so if there were a lot of injuries you would get your chance. Jock would tell us if we got our chance then take it and if we weren't good enough, someone else would come in. I was lucky as I played in the last eight games and established myself in the team.'

On the Celtic game, he added, 'Celtic were the dominant team in Glasgow and Coop and Ally Dawson got sent off so we were down to nine men. But we could have won the match had Coisty squared the ball to me rather than taking a shot. I've still got the newspaper cuttings from after the game where Jock said we were going to build a team round the youngsters and me, Derek and Shuggie [Hugh Burns] were an integral part of it. Jock loved Shuggie and he was the first of us to move up to the first-team dressing room. I was on £36 a week when I started in the first team and you had to play 30 games before your wages got bumped up and you were allowed to move to the first-team dressing room. It was October 1985 before that happened to me and before that I was getting the £36 a week and a win bonus of £200.'

Synonymous with Durrant at that time was a shock of orange hair. This had happened by accident whilst on holiday with Derek Ferguson.

'We were in Magaluf and Derek had these blond tips,' recalled Durrant. 'He was using this thing called Sun In that makes your hair go blonder so, after a couple of beers down the beach one day, I stuck it in my hair and the next thing it was bright orange. I couldn't get it out so the boys called me "Jasper" after the comedian at that time called Jasper Carrot.'

Durrant was now part of the first-team squad and was a mainstay in the starting XI during season 1985/86. He started 30 of the 36 Premier Division matches in what proved a doleful season for the Ibrox club. But along with the goals of Ally McCoist, Durrant's performances were the highlight of the campaign and he ticked another item off his football bucket list on 9 November 1985 when he netted his first goal against Celtic.

'We started the season really well but I got dropped for the first Old Firm game at Parkhead,' recalled Durrant. 'We played Forfar in the League Cup and I was taken off that night and didn't have a good game. The following Saturday we were playing Celtic and I was playing for the reserves at Ibrox. Jock said that I looked tired and it was hard to accept. But it was a wake-up call as I played really well in the reserve game and I was back in. I was supposed to play against Osasuna at Ibrox [in the UEFA Cup] but the pitch was a quagmire. But Jock played me in the away leg and I wasn't out the team after that.'

He continued, 'We were top of the league at the end of September and there was talk of big Jock getting money to spend. He never got it and we went into the Celtic match as massive underdogs [after an impressive start Rangers had won just one of their previous seven league matches]. The game wasn't televised but you can watch it now on YouTube as someone recorded it with a camcorder. I scored the first goal – the ball just sneaked over the line – Davie Cooper scored a great second goal and there's a bit of dubiety about the third. Coisty says it was his goal but Ted McMinn said it was his, although it was eventually given to Coisty. That was the first time I got Man of the Match against Celtic. Where I come from, those are the things that you dream of.'

That victory bought Jock Wallace some time but, by April, Rangers were mid-table and struggling to secure European football for the following season. In a city where first is everything and second is nothing, a predicament such as this only had one outcome. Minus the injured Durrant, Rangers played pathetically in a 2-0 defeat at home to Tottenham Hotspur on 6 April and Wallace was relieved of his duties before the next league fixture.

'The board had already made their mind up about Jock,' said Durrant. 'You don't get the sack on the back of a friendly defeat by Spurs. The crowds were dwindling and we were in a rut. We were a mid-table team. The previous board had said big Jock would be going upstairs and Alex Totten would get the job. In the end Totts, Stan Anderson and Joe Mason left with Jock too.'

It was a sad day for Durrant, who felt he owed a debt of gratitude to the departing manager.

He said, 'I'm eternally grateful for big Jock. Greigy signed me as an apprentice but Jock gave me my debut. You would have run through a brick wall for him. He was ahead of his time. He liked to play 4-3-3, loved two wingers and a centre-forward and you had to be fit too. In pre-season you wouldn't see a ball for ten days, all you did was run. The hardest run was in Bellahouston Park when you were running for over an hour. I was a young boy so could run forever but the older players used to tell me to slow the pace down. But then Jock would pull me aside and say that if he didn't see me up the front he'd smack me!'

Durrant continued, 'I was less than ten stone at the time so he put me on a special diet to get me built up. I had to go in the morning and get porridge – which I hated – so the kitchen staff used to sit there to make sure I ate it. Jock also had me drinking sweet stout for energy. He was old school. When we were away he didn't mind us having a beer but he preferred us to stay in the hotel. One night when we did go out during pre-season Coisty missed the curfew and Jock was waiting in reception. We had to be in the hotel for midnight but Coisty being Coisty was late so Jock took him up to his room and knocked him out and that was it, forgotten about the next morning.'

Chairman Lawrence Marlborough, who had bought a controlling interest in the club and installed David Holmes as chief executive in November 1985, opted for a radical and risky change. Graeme Souness was appointed player-manager and furnished with funds to try and fire Rangers back to the top of the Scottish game. For Durrant, who had grown up supporting Liverpool and idolising Souness and Kenny Dalglish, it was an exciting time. He had emerged as a high-energy, box-to-box midfielder and there was no doubt his game would flourish further under the tutelage of Souness.

The new manager made an immediate impact. After losing 2-1 at Clydebank under the caretaker charge of Alex Totten – Durrant netted his second league goal of the season in the 52nd minute – Rangers suffered a 2-1 defeat against St Mirren and drew with Aberdeen at Pittodrie before Souness arrived for the final league fixture against Motherwell. A win for Rangers would secure a place in the UEFA Cup and that was duly delivered, McPherson and McCoist scoring in a 2-0 win. But if the presence of the new man in charge had helped eke out a victory on that occasion then there is no doubt that it was his arrival that prompted traffic chaos in and around Ibrox six days later. Champions Celtic swaggered into town for the Glasgow Cup Final but, roared on by a partisan crowd of 40,741, Rangers laid down a marker for season 1986/87 by winning 3-2 after extra time.

'Souness came in and told us that there would be a few leaving,' said Durrant. 'He came in to the first meeting, suave in a suit, and basically told us that the club was a joke. He was going to bring in a standard of player that would take the club to where it should be. He also made it clear that he would still be playing. He changed our diet as well. Before he came in we got either fish or chicken, both fried, but all of a sudden there was fruit and salads. We came in for breakfast too and everyone had lunch together.'

He added, 'Souness liked training to be hard as well. We would have the Scotland v England on the Friday and players would end up with cut eyes and gashes down their legs. Graham Roberts would train the way he played and big Butcher would batter us as well. Souness would know if we were up for the game the next day based on how good training was on the Friday. There would be boys sitting there during his team talk with black eyes but he loved that intensity.'

On the Glasgow Cup victory Durrant recalled, 'That match opened Souness's eyes as it showed him what he had to do to pull back Celtic. It was meant to be a meaningless game but the clubs came to an agreement that they'd both play their first teams. I had played in a few finals before that that we'd lost but it was usually a reserve team that played. On the back of that [beating Celtic] we were flying and couldn't wait to get back for pre-season.'

Pre-season 1986/87 took Rangers on tour to West Germany. But before that the headlines were hogged by the influx of talent from south of the border.

'Back then we had about six or seven weeks off so Derek and I went to Magaluf for three weeks,' remembered Durrant. 'There was a guy called Harry Heenan, a former darts player, and he had a pub and we would go there for our dinner. He was a bluenose and he'd bring out the *Daily Record* and show us when we had signed Colin West, Chris Woods and Terry Butcher. Derek and I were sitting in the pub and saying that Souness, Butcher and Woods would all play as would McCoist and Coop and we were using Budweiser bottles to work out the formation and where we would maybe fit into it.'

Both youngsters did fit in and were both in the travelling party bound for West Germany. Durrant played in all four matches, the first and last of which were alongside the new player-manager. It was now Durrant's time to shine and he missed just five league matches in season 1986/87. He made the number ten shirt his own, relinquishing it due to injury between 3 December and 27 December and again on 24 January when suspension counted him out of the 0-0 draw against Aberdeen. He was also in the thick of it on the opening day of the season when all hell broke loose against Hibernian at Easter Road.

'Early in the season I'd either play wide on the right or in the middle but eventually Souness pulled me aside and said I was going to play in the middle with him,' said Durrant. 'He wanted me to play about ten or 15 yards in front of him. After about 18 minutes against Hibs it was carnage but Souness loved that. Although we got beat he told us after the game we'd showed him what we could all do. Two weeks later we lost again, 3-2 against Dundee United. We were playing brilliantly and were 2-0 up but Ian Redford scored with the last kick of the ball to win it for them. We were a brand-new team but you could see signs of how good we could be.'

He added, 'Before that game we stayed at the Grosvenor Hotel, something we did before every home game after Souness came in. We'd have a meal on the Friday night then go for a walk on the Saturday morning. Graeme would then name the team before we went to Ibrox and everything, including our complimentary tickets, had to be done by 1pm. Before that Coisty would still be sitting in the dressing room in his suit at 2.30 writing on envelopes who his comps were for and sending wee Doddie [the kit man, George Soutar] to the front door with them.'

Durrant was revelling in the new team and his game moved on to a higher plateau in the big matches, in particular. It was his goal that put a marker down when Rangers beat Celtic 1-0 in the season's first Old Firm match at the end of August and he netted against Celtic again when the sides met in the League Cup Final.

Durrant recalled, 'If we had lost the Celtic game they would have been something like nine points in front but I was fortunate enough to get the winner. The run I made was just an instinct and it was the best three-yard pass ever from Davie Cooper. He was the best player I played with and he went to another level under Souness. He was given a free role in the final third and he loved that. When the ball was played in to him it was never any more than six inches away from his foot. He was a magician and it was a pleasure to play with him. I still get pelters for blanking him in the celebrations, though, but I saw my brother in the East Enclosure and ran towards him.'

On the League Cup Final victory Durrant noted, 'Souness was suspended and Derek played one of his best games for Rangers. We were centre-midfield with Cammy Fraser and Coop either side. Ted McMinn was up front with Coisty. Dave McFarlane, who had been an apprentice with me, came on in the last ten minutes. For scoring the first goal I got two tickets for a flight on Concorde and for Man of the Match Derek got vouchers for a linoleum company. He got his mum's house decked out in linoleum and the two of us went on Concorde. The flight was delayed for about five hours then it took off in about four seconds. People ask if we went to New York but we were up and back down again in about half an hour.'

'Back at Ibrox after the game everybody was involved in the party. We had the gaffer, Walter and [coaches] Peter McCloy and Donald Mackay, Betty and Kathy from the washhouse, the 'Golden Girls' like Irene and 'Tiny' in the kitchen, Davie Marshall and his four groundsmen, [secretary] Campbell Ogilvie, Mr Waddell, Mr Thornton, Mr McPhail and Stan the commissionaire at the front door.'

Come May the Premier Division trophy sat alongside the League Cup in the Ibrox Trophy Room. After a rather ragged opening gambit to the season, Rangers eventually hit the summit of the league table following a 2-0 win over Hamilton on 17 January 1987. Durrant scored the opening goal that day but was later ordered off. He was soon back in the team, though, and the title was secured when Rangers took a point at Pittodrie and ended an agonising nine-year wait for the country's top honour. The players were swamped at full time as the exuberant supporters sought souvenirs but for Durrant, the euphoria of winning the title was quickly replaced by fear.

'Souness went and got himself sent off again,' said Durrant. 'His team talk was all about keeping our discipline yet he was off after about 20 minutes. That left us up against it but Coop crossed and big Butch scored and that day lives with you. There were fans all over the place and I was looking for my dad after the game. But it was chaos and unbeknown to me my dad had left the game early. Eventually I found my mum and asked where my dad was and she said she had lost him! My dad was showing signs of decline then with a bad heart. He went everywhere to watch me but unfortunately never saw me make my comeback [from injury]. We eventually found him outside. He had met someone he knew and they had taken him for a drink.'

With his family safely back on their bus home Durrant joined his exuberant team-mates on the team bus and the journey back to Glasgow was a memorable one. However, for Durrant and his pal Ally McCoist there was to be a sting in the tail.

'The journey was f*****g brilliant,' recalled Durrant. 'We stopped off in Stonehaven at the hotel we had stayed at the night before and picked up some refreshments. We were up the back of the bus and everybody was flying. Souness called Graham Roberts down to the front of the bus and Robbo came back smiling as he'd been offered a new three-year deal with a wage rise. Next thing Walter comes up and says Souness wants to see me and Coisty. We thought we were set for a new deal but we had been in trouble three months before the game so Souness fined us our win bonus. He told me I'd get my money back if I stayed out of trouble and Coisty would get his money back if he got married. We went back up the bus and Coisty was saying there was no way he was getting married so we started laughing but Souness was raging and I thought he was going to come up and hook us.'

He continued, 'We didn't get our medals that day. It was about three months later when the gaffer came in with a cardboard box and gave us our medals in front of the other players.'

If season 1986/87 had reaffirmed that Ian Durrant was one of the most talented midfield players in the British Isles then season 1987/88 saw him enthralling a new audience as he helped Rangers reach the latter stages of the European Cup. He had made his European debut against Osasuna in Pamplona back in October 1985 and scored his first-ever European goal against Borussia Monchengladbach just over a year later. But it was the matches against Dynamo Kiev, Gornik Zabrze and Steaua Bucharest that had teams across the continent enquiring about his availability.

'That was the best chance we had to win the European Cup in my time at Rangers,' opined Durrant. 'Had we beaten Bucharest, John Brown, Ray Wilkins and Mark Walters would have been available for the semi-final. We should have beaten them at Ibrox. We got a tanking over there but should have scored five or six at home. We won 2-1 but Coisty put one over the bar and I hit the post and missed a real sitter late on.'

In truth, form had to be good that season as Souness continued to recruit to bolster the Rangers squad. As a result, absence from the team through injury could lead to a prolonged spell on the sidelines even when fitness had been regained.

'I came in one morning for a fitness test before we played Hearts,' recalled Durrant. 'I shouldn't have played but when I walked into the dressing room there was Ray Wilkins, another midfielder. I patched myself up, played and scored the winner.'

But the season was not without its challenges for a sometimes impetuous 21-year-old. In October 1987 he was transfer-listed at his own request and asked not to be considered for a match against Dundee United at Tannadice. However, before the end of the month he returned to action to create the last-gasp equalising goal in a 2-2 draw with Celtic and turn in an imperious performance in the League Cup Final against Aberdeen.

'I was a bit of a naughty boy at times but I felt Souness was picking on me,' said Durrant. 'It came to a head one day when he hooked me in training and knocked me out. I asked him if he wasn't going to play me what the future held for me and he threw the *Rothmans* [*Football Yearbook*] at me and told me to "go and pick a f*****g team". I was adamant I was going. We never spoke for a month and I moved down to the away dressing room and I was training with the reserves.

'He tried to pull me out the Scotland squad when I made my debut against Hungary but I played. After the game I met the Sheffield United manager, Dave Bassett, as I was coming down the stairs at Hampden and he asked if I was still up for transfer. Souness heard about it and he pulled me in the next day and I got hauled over the coals. There was also speculation about me going to Manchester United in a swap deal for Norman Whiteside. Everyone had their price at that time and if they felt it was for the benefit of the club you would have been sold.

'But on the Thursday before the Old Firm game Souness and Walter got me into a room and said they needed me to play. I was back in the team and playing well so Souness offered me a four-year contract.'

Everything in the garden seemed rosy again and Durrant signed his new contract in January 1988. But he fell foul of his manager again before the season ended, with Souness dropping him for the last three league matches, citing a lack of professionalism as the reason. Nonetheless, season 1987/88 was Durrant's best thus far in a Rangers jersey. In 40 league appearances he scored ten goals and added a further five in the domestic cup competitions. Despite his form, though, it was Hibernian's John Collins who scooped the PFA Scotland Young Player of the Year award.

'I came second twice,' said Durrant ruefully. 'I should have won it three seasons in a row but for some reason I didn't. I wasn't big-headed but I was the best player in the country and probably should have won Player-of-the-Year. In 86/87 Robert Fleck won it and in 87/88 John Collins got it even though I'd played more games than him and scored more goals.'

The summer of 1988 found Durrant and Rangers in the idyllic surroundings of the Tuscan hills for pre-season training. It was as hard, if not harder, than anything experienced under Jock Wallace.

'We did more running but we did see the ball a bit earlier,' noted Durrant. 'Souness had been to Il Ciocco with Sampdoria and had been introduced to high-altitude training. We used to get the bus up a wee windy road to the pitch and it was a bit scary on the way back down as you felt one wrong turn could take you down the side of the mountain. But it was fantastic and when you came back for the first game of the season you felt your lungs were massive and you were ready to go.'

With the number ten jersey back in his possession, Durrant and Rangers started season 1988/89 intent on bringing the Premier Division title back to Ibrox. And they started off with a bang, walloping Celtic 5-1 at Ibrox in just the third league fixture. But Ian's season – and indeed his career – was ripped asunder just six weeks later. There had been no love lost between Aberdeen and Rangers throughout the 1980s and when the two clashed there was always the potential for an explosive 90 minutes. On this occasion the fire had been stoked further by the fact that Neale Cooper, a Pittodrie hero who had recently signed for Rangers from Aston Villa, was making his debut for Rangers. It was a bruising encounter. Ally McCoist required stitches in a head wound and John Brown also had a gash in his leg sewn up. Mark Walters also limped out of the action and was replaced by Davie Cooper at half-time. However, the worst injury of the day was sustained by Durrant after just eight minutes.

'Up until October I was absolutely flying,' recalled Durrant. 'Then came the tackle and two-and-a-half years in the wilderness. I had 14 operations and 3,000-odd stitches. I ruptured three of the four knee ligaments and partially stretched the other one. My medial, anterior and posterior were gone and my lateral was stretched.'

An operation at Ross Hall Hospital followed two days later and what proved to be a long road to recovery began. The initial prognosis was that Durrant would not play again in season 1988/89. In actual fact it would be almost 500 days before he pulled on a Rangers jersey again. That was for a Reserve League Cup tie against Hearts at Ibrox on 10 February 1990 – after a 0-0 draw Rangers lost 7-6 on penalties, with captain-for-the-day Durrant netting the fifth of Rangers' six from the spot – but it would be another 12 months before he was back in the first team. The process had an effect on Ian physically and mentally.

He said, 'It was a dark time. I made the conscious decision to stay away from the club but I hit a major depression. I didn't know how to cope with it or speak to people about it. Alcohol became my friend for about three or four months. Nothing seemed to be getting better. I had the operation but I kept looking at my knee and it was this odd shape as I had no muscles in my leg. I became a bit of a loner and sought solace in drink. I even got jailed one night for something that was later unproven. I broke down in front of the gaffer and Walter but then I heard about Grant Downie at Lilleshall. I spent eight months there and it became like a double rehab as they worked on me psychologically as well.'

Ian Durrant finally donned his coveted number ten jersey for the first team again on 6 April 1991 when Rangers drew 0-0 with Hibernian. A week later he scored his first top-team goal since 17 September 1988 when he grabbed the opening goal in a 3-0 win over St Johnstone. The goal – a precise finish from the edge of the box – was scored with what was perceived to be his weaker left foot.

'After the injury I had to learn how to work with my left foot,' recalled Durrant. 'Although I'd lost a bit of my pace, I could still get about the park. But I didn't have that injection of pace any more so I became more of a passing player.'

Although not anywhere close to being 100% match fit, having Durrant available for action was welcome, particularly as Rangers, still reeling from the departure of Graeme Souness to Liverpool, faced a titanic title-decider against, of all teams, Aberdeen on 11 May. Although he did not start the match, Durrant replaced the injured Tom Cowan in the second half and played his part as Rangers made it three-in-a-row with a 2-0 win.

'We had heard rumours [that Souness was leaving] and to be honest that was the only job he was going to leave Rangers for,' recalled Durrant. 'I think he was just sick of having his run-ins with the SFA but I think he regrets leaving now. It was a sad day for me and I had total respect for him for what he did for me when I was injured.'

But if Durrant thought his injury woes were behind him he had another rude awakening on the horizon. He made a goalscoring start to season 1991/92, scoring in a 6-0 win over Queen's Park in the League Cup, but after donning his favourite number ten jersey for a 3-2 win over St Johnstone on 12 October, it would be the end of February before he would see action for the first team again.

'Without being big-headed I had gone from being one of the first names on the team sheet to having to graft for my place again,' said Durrant. 'I was told that I wouldn't be able to play every game due to the severity of the injury. I would fall out with Walter [due to lack of first-team games] but I needed game time so he put me in the reserves as he wanted me to get at least 60 minutes regularly.'

The spell in the second string was certainly beneficial. Durrant seemed back to his best, running games from midfield and scoring goals, and the campaign ended on a high, with Durrant starting six of the last seven league games and making the starting XI for the 2-1 win over Airdrie in the Scottish Cup Final.

Durrant was back orchestrating Rangers' play in the midfield engine room and season 1992/93 saw him consistently reproduce the form he had shown prior to his injury. He made 30 Premier Division appearances, scored twice against Celtic and played in both cup finals as Rangers won the domestic Treble for the first time since 1978. But once again he reserved his best performances for the European arena, scoring crucial goals against Lyngby, Brugge and Marseille.

'That was the year at Rangers when I played the most games after my injury,' said Durrant. 'We had a team that knew how to win games and never give up. We had great camaraderie but that was the case with Greigy and big Jock too; we always had a great dressing room. That's the biggest thing you miss when you're finished with football.'

But that campaign would be the last in which Ian Durrant would be recognised as a first-team regular at Ibrox. Like so many others in the squad he was bedevilled by injury in season 1993/94, spending almost four months out of the first team between mid-December and early April. Prior to that Durrant had shown flashes of his brilliance, notably in the League Cup Final against Hibernian.

'I seemed to play in the bigger games at that time,' recalled Durrant. '[The cup final] was all about Super Ally again though. He was just coming back from his broken leg and on the Friday Walter told me I was playing but didn't tell Coisty he was only on the bench. He was livid and took the hump but then he did what he does best, came on and scored the winner.'

It was fitting that Smith's sixth successive trophy had been secured thanks to the two longest-serving players on the books. The Durrant-McCoist 'bro-mance' began in the mid-80s and had grown over the years such that they both recognise each other as brothers.

'Coisty was always up to something and was the main man in the dressing room,' laughed Durrant. 'He would always arrange the days out at Christmas and fancy-dress parties. You had to pick your costume out a hat and for a couple of years I got uniforms that were about six sizes too big for me! We used to play 'It's a Knockout' with the massive boxing gloves as well. It was chaos. And he loved scoring goals. The goalscoring instinct never leaves you. Your legs go but even now I go and watch Coisty playing five-a-side and he's still banging them in.'

As season 1994/95 dawned Durrant was still struggling to sustain a regular run of games in the first team. Although he appeared in five of the opening six league games it seemed like his Rangers career was over when he was sent south to talk to Everton in October 1994. He went to Merseyside with Duncan Ferguson and when neither party could agree a permanent switch, a loan period was arranged. Durrant would stay for a month, with Ferguson signing on for three months.

'I wasn't getting a game and Walter told me Everton had put a bid in for me,' recalled Durrant. 'I was never going to pass the medical so I went on loan instead for an initial three-month period. But due to injuries at Rangers I was called back. I did enjoy it at Everton, getting games in the Premier League, but I came back and scored against Dundee United [in a 3-0 win at Tannadice].'

Durrant was now back in favour at Ibrox and, after replacing Charlie Miller in the 1-1 draw against Celtic on 4 January 1995, Ian appeared in all but one of the last 17 league games. He added to his goals tally too, with the last of his four league goals coming in the 3-1 win over Hibernian at Ibrox that clinched Rangers' seventh successive Premier Division title. That run of games afforded Durrant the opportunity to play alongside one of the most skilful players ever to play for Rangers, Brian Laudrup.

'In terms of ability Laudrup was a phenomenon,' said Durrant. 'We used to try and kick him in training but we couldn't get near him! In the five-a-sides you hoped you were on Laudrup's team. He came in and grasped what the club was all about. He became part of the gang and was a great boy.'

Rangers were now just two titles away from the holy grail of nine-in-a-row. But although they achieved their goal in the two seasons that followed, Durrant made just 23 appearances across the two campaigns. Although he added a Scottish Cup medal to his collection when he came as substitute in the 1996 final against Hearts and scored in a 4-1 Champions League defeat against Ajax in Amsterdam in October 1996, Ian spent most of his time cooling his heels on the sidelines.

There were still some highlights in that spell, though, notably at Parkhead in March 1997. Rangers travelled to the east end of Glasgow looking to make it four league wins out of four over their Old Firm rivals and Durrant was pitched into action, the first time he had played a first-team game since 2 November 1996. He laid on the winning goal for Laudrup and a few games later, the title was secured and the stage was set for another epic bus journey, this time back to Ibrox from Tayside.

'You were just trying to take it all in,' said Durrant. 'It was sensational and you felt like you were on the bus for about three days. By the time we got back to Ibrox there must have been about three or four thousand people there.'

With season 1997/98 being the final year of his existing contract, it looked certain that campaign would be Ian Durrant's last in a Rangers jersey. As Walter Smith, who announced in October that this would be his last campaign at the helm, tried to guide his team to a then unprecedented tenth title in a row, Durrant was once again peripheral. He made only one start in the Premier Division and there were a further seven appearances from the substitute's bench. He watched as new signing Marco Negri initially blazed a goal-scoring trail – he scored in each of the first ten league matches and had netted an incredible 36 goals before Christmas – only for Smith's side to have a sticky start to 1998. Buoyed by the return of the evergreen McCoist, Rangers got back on track and they were ahead of Celtic following a 2-0 win at Ibrox in April. But subsequent defeats against Aberdeen and Kilmarnock ultimately proved costly and the pursuit of ten-in-a-row ended when Celtic finished two points ahead.

'Had we maybe got one or two more players in we might have made it,' said Durrant. 'We were running on empty but money had been promised to [incoming manager] Dick Advocaat. It was a shame to finish on such a low note after having the level of success we did. But you wouldn't have swapped it for anything.'

There was one last hope of ending arguably the most successful era in the club's history with silverware when Rangers faced Hearts at Parkhead in the Scottish Cup Final. Durrant, who had played in the quarter-final replay win over Dundee, sat alongside McCoist on the bench and, with Smith's men trailing 2-0, he was brought into the action when he replaced Stuart McCall. Inevitably McCoist got on the scoresheet but even he could not resuscitate Rangers on this occasion.

Durrant noted, 'I was only in the cup final squad because big Jorg [Albertz] got sent off at Tannadice the week before. In hindsight

Walter should have thrown me on earlier! Coisty came on at half-time for Staale Stensaas, who was a great boy but he couldn't handle playing for Rangers.'

With Dick Advocaat set to take over as manager, Durrant spent the summer contemplating life after Rangers. He was offered a one-year deal by the new manager but decided to move on. Ian was only a few months shy of his 32nd birthday so his career was far from over and he had an opportunity to move to Montpellier but his wife, Angela, fell pregnant. In the end he elected to take up an offer from former team-mate and then Kilmarnock manager, Bobby Williamson.

'Bobby had been badgering me to sign for Kilmarnock for about six months,' recalled Durrant. 'Signing for them was one of the best decisions I made.'

Initially Durrant enjoyed a resurgence. He was imperious as Kilmarnock thrashed Scottish Cup holder Hearts 3-0 at Rugby Park, reigniting his partnership with McCoist, who netted a hat-trick. Indeed, his form was so good that he got himself back into the Scotland team, with almost half of the 20 caps he won for his country earned while a Kilmarnock player.

'I had said to Bobby that I couldn't play all the time because of my knee,' said Durrant. 'But he told me not to worry; if he could get 25-30 games out of me, he'd be delighted. I ended up playing 62 games in the first season and 50 games in the second season!'

But eventually injuries took their toll and in April 2002 Ian Durrant hung up his boots. He moved into coaching – guiding Kilmarnock to success in the Scottish Youth Cup – and he even had a single match in charge of Rangers at the end of the ill-fated Paul Le Guen era.

'Walter still tells me I'm the worst manager in Rangers' history,' laughed Durrant. 'Alex McLeish asked me to come back as a coach and I was doing scouting as well. I found [being in charge] very hard. All of a sudden Mr Le Guen left and some of the players he had brought in declared themselves unfit. Le Guen had killed the dressing room so it was tough. But we should have beaten Dunfermline. We were 3-0 down but eventually lost 3-2. Barry [Ferguson] hit the post and Kris Boyd hit the bar and missed a header from four yards to take it to a replay.'

Durrant remained as part of the backroom team when Walter Smith returned and he enjoyed a thrilling UEFA Cup run in 2007/08 and three successive SPL titles between 2009 and 2011. When Smith stepped down in 2011 to be replaced by Ally McCoist, Durrant became assistant manager. But any hopes of the dynamic duo repeating the success from the playing days were dashed in February 2012 when a Scottish institution found itself mired in a financial meltdown.

Durrant remained on the staff as Rangers journeyed back from the bottom tier of Scottish Football but left Ibrox in 2015. Since then he has taken on other coaching roles, the most recent of which was as assistant manager to Stephen Aitken at Dumbarton. He is still a Ranger to the core, though, and like others in the Rangers family, he is excited by the start Steven Gerrard has made to his managerial career.

'It seems to be going the right way,' said Durrant. 'I only hope the board can match what Steven wants. Steven is getting players that want to come in and play for Steven Gerrard. It was the same with Souness and Walter. Butcher knocked back Manchester United to come to us and Walter managed to get Gascoigne for £4 million and Laudrup for £2.5 million. How much would you have to pay for them nowadays?'

Ian Durrant made 419 appearances for Rangers and scored 58 goals. He won six Premier Division titles (1986/87, 1988/89, 1992/93, 1993/94, 1995/96 and 1996/97), three Scottish Cups (1991/92, 1992/93 and 1995/96) and four League Cups (1986/87, 1987/88, 1992/93 and 1993/94).

Sid

Ian Ferguson (1988–2000)

Despite being brought up in the shadows of Celtic Park in Glasgow's East End, Ian Ferguson is Rangers through and through. A tough-tackling midfielder who had the capability to strike the ball with venom from distance, he arrived at Ibrox in March 1988 for just shy of £1 million. He had endeared himself to Graeme Souness during his time with St Mirren, where he won a Scottish Cup medal, his goal being decisive in the 1987 final against Dundee United. But the genesis of his football career started a little further north, where he had to overcome rejection from one of the leading managers in the Scottish game in the 1980s.

'I started on an 'S' form with Aberdeen and the time eventually came when Alex Ferguson had to decide if I was being kept on,' recalled Ferguson from his home in Australia. 'The feedback I got suggested I was being kept on as a YTS player but when I got into the office I was told I wasn't good enough. I was too small and wasn't what Aberdeen were looking for. When I left I went to work at a place called Dunn and Moore's in Glasgow. They had a works team so I played about three or four games for them. A man called Dougie Liddell used to coach the team and he went to the owner of Dunn and Moore's, Mr Dunn, who provided the sponsorship, Solripe, for Clyde. He came along and watched one of the games and told me to go down to [Clyde's home ground] Shawfield.'

He added, 'When I got there, I had to ask for Mr Craig Brown who was the manager at that point. I started training with the reserves and ended up playing six or seven reserve games. The one game that sticks in my mind was playing against Celtic, who had a really good team, and I got Man of the Match. I was called in after the game and Craig Brown signed me on a part-time contract for Clyde FC.'

Clyde were in the old First Division when Ferguson signed for the club. They had finished eighth in the league in season 1983/84, a position they would also occupy at the end of Ferguson's debut season. Ferguson made his first-team debut as substitute in the penultimate fixture against Kilmarnock on 4 May 1985 and made his first start the following week in a 3-2 home defeat against St Johnstone.

'There were experienced players there and, as a young boy, I just listened to what these guys said,' noted Ferguson. 'Once I was in the first team they made me feel part of it, which was great. I really enjoyed it. I played a number of games, then St Mirren came in with a bid of around £45,000 which Clyde said no to. The bid went up to £65,000 and that's when I got the move.'

The bid was submitted early in season 1986/87. Ferguson had made 19 league appearances for Clyde in the previous campaign, netting his first senior league goal in a 1-1 draw against Forfar Athletic on 18 January 1986. He also had the distinction of scoring in the final league match played at Shawfield on 28 April 1986, the ground having been Clyde's home since 1898. His performances stimulated interest in his services but the Paisley side were not the only ones who were showing an interest in the promising midfielder.

'I had the opportunity to speak to Wimbledon and I met with Kenny Dalglish who was manager of Liverpool,' said Ferguson. 'Kenny said I had potential but I wouldn't be going straight into the first team. To be honest I didn't expect to go straight into the first team at any club. The opportunity to go to Liverpool excited me and to have a player of Dalglish's stature coming in for you was a big boost.'

He continued, 'I then met [St Mirren manager] Alex Miller, ironically at Ibrox after a Scotland game. He took me into the Blue Room and told me he planned to put me straight into the first team and would give me 10-12 games, regardless of how I played. He didn't expect me to fail as he thought I was a good player. As I was coming from the First Division and the Premier Division was a lot harder, Alex expected it would take a lot of games to settle in.'

It was now decision time for Ferguson. Did he go to the reigning English First Division champions and bide his time in the reserves and hope an opportunity to progress arose or did he opt for guaranteed first-team football with St Mirren? He chose the latter, making his debut on 13 September 1986, just a week after his last league appearance for Clyde.

'Going to St Mirren gave me a chance to play at Ibrox, Parkhead and up at Aberdeen,' said Ferguson. 'My first game was against Hibs at Easter Road and we won 1-0 and I was fortunate enough to get the goal. It was a great strike from an acute angle past Alan Rough so it was a great start to my St Mirren career. I really enjoyed my time there. I was up against the likes of Ian Durrant, Paul McStay and John Collins and it was a great challenge for me as a young boy.'

St Mirren never flirted with relegation in the mid-1980s and often chalked up notable victories over the bigger teams in the top flight. They also enjoyed some good cup runs but none more so than in the 1986/87 Scottish Cup when they went all the way to the final and beat Dundee United 1-0 after extra time. The match-winning hero was Ian Ferguson.

'[The cup final] was probably one of my worst games for St Mirren,' remembered Ferguson. 'I was only about 20 years old and going to Hampden and playing in front of a full house was great. Getting the winning goal was amazing too.'

The winners' medal was the icing on the cake for Ferguson after a fine first season in the top flight. He made 35 league appearances and added a further three goals to his debut strike against Hibernian. Included in that haul was the winning goal against Aberdeen on 25 February 1987. Ferguson continued to excel in season 1987/88, making 22 league appearances and scoring six goals. He scored against Rangers too at Love Street in November 1987. His 85th-minute strike earned St Mirren a 2-2 draw and arguably put the wheels in motion for his transfer to his boyhood heroes. And in March 1988 the dream of pulling on a Rangers jersey became reality.

'I got a phone call from a journalist who told me there was interest from Rangers and would I be interested in going,' recalled Ferguson. 'I had had this kind of thing before, including one of my mates pretending he was Alex MacDonald asking if I would like to go to Hearts. I thought a prank was getting played on me again so I told him if Graeme Souness wanted me then he should phone me. Within five minutes Graeme Souness called me and confirmed he was interested.'

He continued, 'I felt it took forever [to get the deal done], about three months. In that time the St Mirren board did everything possible to stop me going to Rangers but I wanted to go to Ibrox. Graeme was turning Scottish football around and it was an exciting time and I wanted to be part of that. It was a tough time as I was getting stick from the St Mirren fans and some of the players. I was a bit naïve and a bit young and was probably a bit selfish too.'

The stand-off continued, with the board looking for Ferguson to speak to Alex Ferguson about a move to Manchester United. Tottenham Hotspur manager, Terry Venables, was interested in signing him too.

'I agreed to go and speak to them but, in the car, my gut feel was that it didn't feel right,' said Ferguson. 'It didn't excite me like Rangers did. Getting the opportunity to play for your boyhood heroes was something special. I told my agent to turn the car round and I phoned up [St Mirren manager] Alex Smith and told him I wasn't going to Manchester and made it clear I only wanted to go to one club. Within two or three days Alex told me to go to Ibrox as a bid had been accepted and I had permission to speak to Rangers.'

The transfer fee was £850,000, a sizeable sum for a player in Scotland at that time. Ferguson had only been on the scene for just over two seasons and had played just 57 times in the Premier Division, the last of those appearances ironically coming against Rangers at Ibrox on 13 February 1988. The pressure was on and Ferguson found the early days of his Rangers career challenging.

'Nothing was ever spoken about as to whether I'd be guaranteed a first-team game,' noted Ferguson. 'I just wanted to play for the club, whether that was starting in the reserves, on the bench or in the team. With the likes of Derek Ferguson, Ian Durrant, Ray Wilkins and John Brown competing for places you had to go in every day and train at a very high intensity to show the manager you wanted to be there.'

'I did feel pressure [regarding the transfer fee] but I shouldn't have as that was nothing to do with me. Two teams negotiate and come to an agreement over what is paid for a player, but it stuck with me a bit. I think Celtic started the big money stuff when they signed Joe Miller. That meant for other Scottish clubs if Rangers or Celtic wanted their players that drove the price up. Was I worth it? No, I don't think any player is worth that but that's what the clubs negotiated. But it was a burden as people kept saying I wasn't worth it.'

Having played in St Mirren's 3-0 defeat at the hands of Clydebank in the Scottish Cup third round, Ferguson was not eligible to make his Rangers debut against Dunfermline Athletic in the fourth round. Instead his debut came at Tannadice on 27 February 1988 in a 1-1 draw against Dundee United.

'I was in the stand [for the Dunfermline game] and it wasn't a good game to go and witness,' remembered Ferguson. 'We lost 2-0 and at half-time I saw the real wrath of Graeme Souness for the first time. He let the players know in no uncertain terms that it wasn't good enough. A couple of teacups, a tray and a jug of milk went flying, probably not the first time that that had happened under Graeme. I'll be honest, I didn't mind that [approach]. There are two things you can do; either throw your dummy tit out the pram and sulk like a wee baby or decide that you were going to show him he was wrong. Graeme wanted commitment and effort in every game and the players Walter and him brought in had that in abundance. You can't be a shrinking violet if you want to play for Rangers. It is a heavy, heavy strip to wear and if you can't carry it, you won't be there long.'

On his debut at Tannadice he added, 'Playing for Rangers was obviously a new experience for me in front of a full house. It was a massive game for us but we went 1-0 down. I was fortunate, though, to get a flick-on for Mark Walters's goal. A cross came in and I knew

Mark was behind me so I nodded the ball towards him and he took a touch and scored. It was great for me as I could now say I had played for Rangers which was very special. My family were there and I was very proud to get on the park wearing the blue jersey.'

Another appearance in a 3-0 win over Dunfermline at East End Park followed before Ferguson made his home debut in a turgid 1-0 win over Motherwell. As was their wont at that time, Motherwell defended stoically but in the 59th minute, Ferguson delivered a wonderful through-ball for Ian Durrant to net the only goal of the game. That, and other contributions to Rangers' attacking play, earned Ferguson the *Rangers News* Man of the Match award. He played a further five league matches after that but missed the final three games. In that run of games he netted his first goal for the club, a spectacular scissors kick in a 3-2 defeat at the hands of Morton at Cappielow.

The summer of 1988 would be the first time Ferguson had experienced pre-season training the Souness way. This meant a trip to the salubrious Il Ciocco resort in Tuscany and the players were subjected to brutal sessions in the Italian heat. But Ferguson had already experienced how ferocious the training at Ibrox was in the brief time he had already trained with his new team-mates.

'Training was very intense, very fiery,' recalled Ferguson. 'We had Scotland v England and the Scottish boys used to take the piss all the time. We had about three or four fights over the years which showed how intense it was. Souness would never come in the Scottish side, I think because he had played in England. They had Butcher, Woods, Stevens and Wilkins and we had McCoist, Durrant and John Brown so it was always very competitive. They were great games to be involved in. I loved training because I was a high-tempo player that loved the hustle and bustle and physicality. But you had to be able to play as well.'

On the training in Italy he stated, 'It was hard at the time but once you had done it, you felt like a million dollars once you came back. It was high altitude [the resort is just over 4,000ft above sea level] and Graeme worked us hard. I wasn't a big fan of running on sand and that's what we did our running on. Football is played on grass so I couldn't understand why we were doing it but Graeme's logic was that this would make our muscles stronger. It was very tough but I loved every minute of it and it set you up for the season.'

On their return to Scotland, Rangers played four friendly matches, testimonials for goalkeepers Alan Robertson and Jim Gallacher against Kilmarnock and Clydebank respectively, and outings against Raith Rovers and Ayr United. Ferguson wore the number eight jersey in all the matches as he did in the final warm-up game against Bordeaux at Ibrox. This match was a testimonial for Davie Cooper and in keeping with so many interviewed for this book, Ferguson felt privileged to have played alongside the wonderful winger.

'Coop was a dream, I loved him,' stated Ferguson. 'He gets this tag of "the Moody Blue" but his sense of humour was first class. On the park, the talent that he had, you can't coach it; it was just natural ability from a man that was a genius. He loved Rangers and made that clear and the fans loved him. He was an absolute joy to work with, both in games and in training. He always had a kind word for you and would sit you down and, if you weren't playing well, he would put it across to you in a way that made sense. I have nothing but admiration for the players I played with in that era and Coop is up there with the best of them.'

The match against the French side may have been memorable for Cooper but for Ferguson it had a premature and painful conclusion. He lasted just 25 minutes before he was stretchered off and the injury he sustained sidelined him for the opening four competitive fixtures. But he returned in time for the first Old Firm match of the season on 27 August 1988 and his timing was impeccable. Rangers romped to a 5-1 win and people were purring about Ferguson's display. The *Rangers News*, who voted him Man of the Match, said he had been 'quite brilliant' and 'looked every inch a million-pound player, adding verve and aggression to the Rangers midfield'.

Thereafter he was rarely absent from the engine room, enjoying a run of 36 consecutive matches. That spell featured a number of notable moments, including a goal in the League Cup Final and a strike against Celtic on 3 January 1989. Indeed, there are some who feel he doubled his Old Firm tally some three months later in a 2-1 win at Parkhead.

Ian recalled, 'The goal in January took a bit of a deflection so I don't know if [Pat] Bonner would have got it. I just hit it as hard as I could. I remember the celebrations more. I was running towards the Celtic supporters and quickly realised I'd better turn the other way! It's something you treasure; there's nothing better than beating your old rivals and getting a goal is even better.'

On the dubious goal in April, Ferguson is claiming it as his but would happily add it to the array of goals Ally McCoist scored for the club. Ferguson's rasping free kick stung the palms of Bonner and spun into the air towards goal. Ever the predator, McCoist followed in and looked to have nudged the ball over the line with his head.

'I think it's mine and Coisty thinks it's his,' chuckled Ferguson. 'I think it was over the line before Coisty got the touch but he makes a valid point, he was going in to make sure it was in the net as Bonner could have got back to flick it out. I'm happy to give it to Coisty as the most important thing was to get the victory, as it was our first win there in about ten years. To go there and be part of that 2-1 win after all the suffering the Rangers fans had been through going to Parkhead was very special. You could see my old house when the camera was on the Celtic end so it was nice to get the victory and that proved that, under Souness, we had a belief we could go anywhere and win.'

The three victories over Celtic went a long way to ensuring Rangers would reclaim the Premier Division title and for Ferguson, the title win completed the full set of major domestic honours. Having won the Scottish Cup with St Mirren, he added the League Cup in October 1988, scoring Rangers' second goal in an absorbing 3-2 win over Aberdeen at Hampden.

'My goal was like a scissor kick and it was brilliant to score and get a League Cup medal,' said Ferguson. 'I always remember a lovely gesture from Graeme Souness who took me to the Rangers fans and put my hand up. I got a fantastic reception when he did that and it's always nice to feel appreciated.'

Ferguson looked to build on an impressive first full season as a Rangers player in season 1989/90. But when old club St Mirren visited Ibrox on the opening day of the Premier Division season, the midfielder found himself playing out of position.

'In the five-a-side games in training Chris Woods used to like to play outfield and one day we were a goalkeeper short so I went in,' laughed Ferguson. 'I had an absolute blinder, no one could score past me. About two or three days later Woodsy dislocated his shoulder against St Mirren and in those days you didn't have a sub goalie. Terry Butcher came up to me and told me to go in goal and I didn't even think about it, I just did it. I put the gloves on but it wasn't until the play started to resume that I thought, "What the f**k have I done?" It was a different kettle of fish playing in front of 40,000 than it was playing in a five-a-side game, I can assure you. You're scared in case you make a mistake, I don't know the angles of the goals, there was loads going through my head. But they never scored a goal [Kenny McDowall's winner had come about as part of the clash that injured Woods] and that was down to the likes of Butcher and Gough that were playing in front of me.'

Once back in his usual position Ferguson found himself appearing only sporadically, his appearances curtailed by illness and injury.

'The illness was the worst one,' said Ferguson. 'My game was about energy, getting up and down the park, but there was poison going through my system from my glands and it was draining me. I felt really lethargic and I knew something was wrong. We did a lot of tests, which took months, to rule things out but we never got to the bottom of it. I eventually got my tonsils taken out and I felt a lot better after that. That took about four or five months and I was still playing games. Graeme was still picking me and I kept telling him that Rangers were playing with ten men after about ten minutes as I had no energy. He was very supportive but because the test results were coming back negative, we just kept trying to get through it. My fitness and energy levels got better after my tonsils came out and I felt stronger.'

He continued, 'After that I tried to come back too quickly and started picking up injuries, hamstring, quad or calf, and it seemed to be a knock-on effect for a couple of years. You can't throw the towel in, though. You have to keep fighting and doing the best you can. I

Jimmy Nicholl pictured during his second spell at Rangers circa 1987 and, right, with the author in September 2018

Jim Stewart guards his near post during an Old Firm game in October 1982 and, right, with the author in November 2018

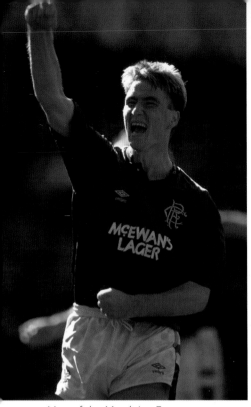

Man-of-the-Match Ian Ferguson celebrates the 5-1 victory over Celtic in August 1988

David Kirkwood in action on his Rangers debut in May 1987

Dave MacKinnon battles through the Celtic midfield in August 1985. Stuart Munro is looking on in the background

The majestic red brick façade of Ibrox Stadium taken from the ash park at The Albion training ground

Hugh Burns in action at Parkhead in 1985 and, right, with the author in September 2018

Mark Walters in action in 1989 and, right, with the author in October 2018

Richard Gough towers above Celtic's Paul McStay and, right, the former Rangers captain with the author in September 2018

Ian Durrant celebrates his goal against Celtic in November 1985 with the late, great Davie Cooper

Derek Ferguson celebrates scoring against Aberdeen at Pittodrie in January 1989

Jock Wallace flanked by Dave McPherson (left) and Bobby Russell

Gordon Dalziel scored on his Old Firm debut but could not reproduce his form for the reserves in the first team

Iain Ferguson (left) and Craig Paterson with the League Cup in October 1984

Captain Ally Dawson lines up before the 1981 Scottish Cup Final against Dundee United

John MacDonald in action against Celtic circa 1980

Colin Miller with Ally McCoist in 2013

Colin Miller in his heyday

Dundee United's Paul Hegarty wins an aerial joust with Derek Johnstone. The Govan Stand is under construction in the background

Stuart Beattie on the training ground with Davie Cooper in the background

look at life and say that there are people a lot worse off than me so I had to knuckle down and take whatever criticism was coming my way. I just had to deal with it.'

When he did pull on a Rangers jersey in season 1989/90 he was part of a team that included a player whose signing had caused consternation. The dynamic Ferguson would be supplying ammunition for a new striker at Ibrox, Maurice Johnston.

'[The signing] was a big shock to be honest,' remembered Ferguson. 'Wee Mo was paraded in a Celtic strip a week before he signed for us. But I remember Graeme telling us after Celtic beat us in the [1989] Scottish Cup Final that Celtic thought they had something but they didn't. I couldn't figure out what he was talking about, none of us could, but when Mo signed, the penny dropped. I'll be honest, I thought Mo did a great job for us. He came in and scored important goals at important times and was a big part of us winning the league that year. I remember goals against Aberdeen, Hearts and Celtic, 1-0 wins, and he was always there to score. He was a top-quality player, probably the number one Scottish striker. It was a great coup for Souness to get him, particularly when Celtic thought they had him. It was a brave decision as Mo wasn't loved by the Celtic fans or many of the Rangers fans and he lived with a lot of pressure every single day. I certainly wouldn't have done it but he scored important goals for Rangers.'

Johnston never missed a league game and was top scorer with 15 goals as Rangers retained the title for the first time in almost 15 years. Despite his illness and injuries, Ferguson made 32 appearances across the four major competitions, scoring twice in the League Cup, once against Arbroath and again in the emphatic 5-0 semi-final win over Dunfermline.

Season 1990/91 followed much the same pattern as before for Ferguson. After playing in the opening two league games, between 1 September 1990 and 9 March 1991 he made only one league appearance when he replaced Trevor Steven in a 4-0 win over Hibernian at Ibrox in November 1990. Despite the long-term absence from first-team duty, Ferguson managed to add a second League Cup winners' medal to his collection when he came on as substitute for Ally McCoist in the 2-1 win over Celtic. And when the title race was entering its final furlong, Ferguson was back in action, starting all but one of the last nine league matches.

'The illness and injuries were frustrating but I still contributed to winning titles and cups,' said Ferguson. 'There was one match against Dundee United and we won 1-0. I got the goal that night with a diving header. That was me just coming back from that spell and that was really satisfying to get back in the line-up and get the winning goal.'

A matter of weeks later that goal took on even greater significance. Having led the title race for most of the season, the two points kept Rangers ahead of Aberdeen. But a 3-0 defeat away at Motherwell on the penultimate weekend allowed Aberdeen to take top spot on goal difference. With the top two scheduled to play each other at Ibrox on the final Saturday of the season, a winner-takes-all showdown was set up.

'I knew we were going to win the Aberdeen game,' recalled Ferguson. 'What cemented it for me was the warm-up, the reaction of the crowd was tremendous and we had their backing straight away. There wasn't an eerie silence or nervousness about the place, it was a good atmosphere.'

One of the enduring images from that day was, with Rangers in the driving seat leading 2-0, Ferguson trotting past referee Brian McGinlay and tapping his wrist to indicate that it was full time. As if acting on instruction McGinlay then blew his whistle and Rangers were champions for the third year in a row.

'I was always on at referees like that,' laughed Ferguson. 'I knew it was near the end. The fans were whistling, the clock on the scoreboard was at 90 so I was just giving him a wee reminder it was time up.'

Season 1991/92 brought a fourth successive Premier Division title but this time under the stewardship of Walter Smith. Graeme Souness had left in April 1991 to take over from Kenny Dalglish at Liverpool and David Murray favoured a 'promotion from within' approach. There were differences between the respective managers, though.

'Graeme was more aggressive and Walter would man-manage a little bit better,' admitted Ferguson. 'Graeme was always the "bad cop" but I loved his style. These days the manager has to please the players whereas in our day, we had to please the manager. I had to please Graeme and Walter in training and in games if I wanted to play. Walter was a different character, more of a calming influence, but if you weren't doing what he wanted you would feel his wrath too.'

Smith's first full season in charge was ravaged by injury for Ian Ferguson. He made just 22 appearances and missed the Scottish Cup Final victory over Airdrie. But he returned to action in time to play an active part in one of the finest seasons in Rangers' illustrious history.

'1992/93 was probably one of the best seasons that I was at Rangers,' stated Ferguson. 'We went 44 games unbeaten and we had a total belief that, no matter who we were playing, we were always in with a chance of winning. That included in Europe too. The confidence within the playing squad came from the games, training and winning. There was also the camaraderie in the dressing room, a special bond between brothers. Most of the squad were British and they all knew what it meant to play for Rangers. You had to try and educate the foreign players that defeat was unacceptable. Later on, guys like Albertz and Laudrup were amazing and took to it straight away. Amoruso and Gattuso also bought in to the Rangers way.'

He added, 'That season was the first-ever Champions League and that was what it should be about, champions. You shouldn't be bringing in who finishes fourth in the Premiership or third in the Spanish league and German league. It should be the Champions League but today it's a bit of a farce. You could get a team that don't win their own league but win the Champions League and, for me, that takes a bit of the credit away.'

The 44-match unbeaten run referenced by Ferguson took Rangers to the domestic Treble and within a goal of the inaugural Champions League Final. Ian made 43 appearances and scored five goals, including the winner against CSKA Moscow in Bochum and the opening goal against eventual Premier Division runners-up Aberdeen in a 2-0 win at Ibrox in March 1993.

With the three major trophies encased in the stunning Ibrox Trophy Room, Ferguson could finally go in and visit what is quite rightly the jewel in the Ibrox crown. He had vowed only to step foot in there when the Treble was won and he was not disappointed when he clapped eyes on the glittering souvenirs contained within.

'I passed by it a couple of times and the door was open but I kept on walking,' recalled Ferguson. 'I really wanted to go in there when the three [major] cups were there and see all the memorabilia. It was an amazing time and I remember walking through the door; I actually get goosebumps even now speaking about it. Seeing Rangers' history and knowing you were part of that was amazing.'

One player who did more than most to ensure the Treble was won for the first time since 1978 was Ally McCoist. He scored 49 goals and would surely have secured a half century had he not broken his leg playing for Scotland in Portugal. As a midfielder, having someone of McCoist's ilk ahead of you made your job easier and Ferguson thoroughly enjoyed playing in the same side as McCoist.

'He was the life and soul of the dressing room and you could guarantee, more or less week in, week out, McCoist would score,' said Ferguson. 'We had an abundance of players that were game winners but McCoist did it on a regular basis. I think he scored more goals than I had games in fact! I can't speak highly enough of Coisty. He was a very passionate man who loved the Rangers and gave everything on the park. There's not many Ally McCoists going about these days.'

In season 1993/94 the Premier Division title was secured for a sixth consecutive year and the League Cup was also added when McCoist's audacious overhead kick gave Rangers a 2-1 win over Hibernian. Hopes of a back-to-back clean sweep of the domestic honours were thwarted by Dundee United in the Scottish Cup Final.

'In the League Cup Final against Hibs, the script was written for McCoist,' recalled Ferguson. 'He'd been out injured, came on at 1-1 and got the opportunity. That's typical Ally McCoist. There was no fluke about it either. People say he's lucky but there's no luck about it, he was just a very good predator.'

The resolute Ferguson made 47 appearances and chalked up winning goals against St Johnstone in the league and Aberdeen in the quarter-final of the League Cup. And he was joined in the first-team ranks that season by another Ferguson, Duncan, who came from Dundee United for £4 million. His stay at Ibrox would be brief and controversial but Ian has fond memories of the centre-forward.

'There are a lot of pressures and expectations at Rangers and you need time,' said Ferguson. 'Lesser people can crumble but I don't think that was the case with Duncan. I just think he needed more game time. After he arrived he ended up with an injury which kept him out for a while and then he struggled to get back in the team. I think if he had got a few more games under his belt, he'd have been a far more effective player. When you see what he did down in England, it was phenomenal. He's still loved at Newcastle and Everton. I think stuff off the field put a heavy burden on him and, in the end, he had to get away.'

Duncan was not the only Ferguson who courted controversy that season. On 11 December 1993 Rangers were hammered 3-0 at home by Dundee United and Ferguson was ordered off for spitting at the United centre-half, Gordan Petric.

'That was stupid on my part, embarrassing,' recalled Ferguson. 'He hit me in the face but rather than hit him back, I went to spit at him. The minute I did it my heart sank. It was one of the most shocking and disgusting things I did in my career and I'm ashamed of it. Walter fined me and told me if it happened again I'd be out the door. That wasn't the Rangers way and wasn't how Rangers players should react.'

The next two seasons, 1994/95 and 1995/96, were again stop-start for Ferguson. A series of niggling injuries meant he could not enjoy a sustained run in the team. However, there were notable contributions to the title wins and cup triumphs in both campaigns. In January 1995 he scored another Old Firm goal in a 1-1 draw and just over a year later he scored a hat-trick in a 10-1 win over Keith in the Scottish Cup.

'My goal against Celtic was right in front of their supporters and I think it's fair to say that I wasn't well liked by them,' said Ferguson.

'I was a Glasgow boy, playing for my boyhood heroes and I knew who the old enemy were. When you did go and play against Celtic, you were doing that for the Rangers fans. If I didn't play, I'd have been in the stands as a supporter but I had an opportunity to go and play and have opportunities to score goals. And when you do score goals it's the best feeling you'll ever get in football. The atmosphere in those games was electric. The Celtic fans hate you and the Rangers fans love you so when you score, you want to show the ones that hate you just exactly how much it means to you.'

He added, 'The hat-trick against Keith was my first and only one in my career. To me it didn't matter who we were playing, you wanted to win. Our boys didn't want to take their foot off the pedal so we created a lot of chances and I was very fortunate to get three goals. Alex Cleland, wee Tefal Heid, got three goals too and he got the match ball. I must be the only player in world football not to have taken home the match ball after scoring a hat-trick!'

When he was stripped for action in the seasons that brought titles seven and eight in succession, Ferguson shared the field with two of the most skilful players ever to play for Rangers: Brian Laudrup and Paul Gascoigne.

'They were probably the two best signings we made [during that era],' opined Ferguson. 'We had two players that could turn a game [in Rangers' favour], two players that could create chances and win you games. To have them on board at Rangers was amazing. I think we got the best out of Paul. He enjoyed his football and Laudrup was the same. They were given free licence to do whatever they wanted to do. The balance was provided by myself and Stuart McCall.'

He continued, 'Gascoigne was always a prankster. It was worse when he was injured as you just didn't know what you'd be coming back to. You didn't know what would be in your shoes or if he had changed over wallets or if your keys were missing. He was always up to mischief. The boys would be going to their cars and trying to unlock them but they had the wrong key. But there's a real nice side to Paul that he doesn't get enough credit for. We would go up to the sick kid's hospital every year and one year, a nurse came up to Gascoigne and asked him to go with her. I went with him as you were never sure if he would go in and press a button on a machine or something daft like that. I stood outside the window and watched as he spoke to a kid, asking what he wanted from Santa Claus. The kid said he hadn't had a chance to write a letter that year and that he'd be in hospital rather than at home. But Paul told him that Santa came to the hospital too so he sat with the kid and they wrote a letter. Paul then went out and bought everything on the list and took it up to the hospital and asked the nurse to make sure the kid got everything. That's what the man was all about, yet he gets slaughtered because of all the issues he has. He's a lovely guy.'

In addition to swelling his number of Premier Division title medals to eight, Ferguson was also part of the team that hammered Hearts 5-1 in the Scottish Cup Final. Brian Laudrup was imperious, scoring twice and providing the assist for each of Gordon Durie's three goals.

'The game really opened up after [Hearts goalkeeper] Rousset let the second goal through his legs,' recalled Ferguson. 'Hearts had tried to sit in and hit us on the counter-attack but from then on it was one-way traffic. Durie and Laudrup were phenomenal. It shows the calibre of Brian that day that he got Man of the Match even though Durie got a hat-trick.'

Rangers now stood on the cusp of history. Another title triumph would mean nine-in-a-row, equalling the achievement of Celtic between 1966 and 1974. For Ferguson, the supporter living the dream, involvement in the title tilt would see him stand alongside Ally McCoist and Richard Gough as the only Rangers players to have played an active part in each of the title wins.

'Nine-in-a-row, for me, was everything,' said Ferguson. 'What a journey it was. The pressure from the fans and the press was unbelievable. As I said, you need to have a strong mentality to play for Rangers. You need to lock yourself away from it so I didn't watch the news or buy a paper. The press would be asking if we were good enough and saying we had an ageing squad. We didn't need the negativity and the boys were brilliant. I've got mates like wee Monty [Billy Montgomery] and Andy Smillie that go everywhere with Rangers and did so long before I was a player. The pride I had that night [at Tannadice when the title was clinched] for them was phenomenal. I was with big Andy in the stand at Tannadice and he was in tears.'

Although the title was not mathematically confirmed until after that 1-0 win over Dundee United, to all intents and purposes nine-in-a-row was secured some weeks earlier when Rangers made it four league wins out of four over Celtic in a typically tempestuous Old Firm match at Parkhead. Two players were sent off and Ferguson became embroiled in a battle with Celtic's fiery Italian, Paolo Di Canio. But Brian Laudrup's goal gave Rangers a 1-0 win.

'That for me was the final nail in the coffin,' stated Ferguson. 'They beat us 2-0 the week before [in the Scottish Cup] and we had a lot of injuries. There was a lot of negative press and a lot of people thought Celtic were going to steamroller us. During the week leading up to the game, the players all sat down and looked back at the cup tie and analysed what we had done wrong. That day Di Canio was one of Celtic's best players and he made them tick. We had let him run the game the week before so, for me, it was about how I stopped him playing. Ability-wise he was away ahead of me but I could compete with him aggressively. I took every opportunity to take his focus off the game by winding him up and getting in his face. He didn't like it and told me he was going to break my leg and would see me in the tunnel [at full time]. Needless to say, he didn't appear.'

If season 1996/97 represented utopia for the Rangers family then the following season was hell on earth. At that time no team had ever won ten successive titles but despite a gallant final push, spearheaded by members of the old guard like Ally McCoist, Rangers fell short of their target. With Walter Smith set to leave in the summer of 1998 along with a number of others in the band of brothers, the campaign just petered out. And, following defeat in the Scottish Cup Final to Hearts, arguably the most successful era in the club's history ended without a silver lining. Unsurprisingly Ferguson, who made just 11 appearances in the league, ranks season 1997/98 as his most disappointing in a blue jersey. He also had the misfortune of conceding a penalty in the opening minutes of the cup final when TV replays clearly showed the infringement had taken place outside the box.

'The Scottish Cup Final was a very emotional day,' stated Ferguson. 'A lot of grown men cried as it was like a family all going in different directions now. There's no doubt it was the end of an era and to lose against Hearts at Parkhead was a sore one.'

Although numerous players were released by new manager Dick Advocaat, the services of Ian Ferguson were retained. He had a year left on his existing contract and he adopted a role under the Dutchman that saw him play fleetingly but have an influence in the dressing room.

'It was about making sure the likes of Gio van Bronckhorst, Arthur Numan and Andrei Kanchelskis knew what it meant to play for Rangers,' recalled Ferguson. 'Defeat was unacceptable and the penny finally dropped after we lost 5-1 to Celtic at Parkhead. There were players laughing in the dressing room after the game and that nearly led to a fight. Some home truths were told and after that everyone knew what was expected at the club.'

Clarity was evidently achieved as Advocaat led Rangers to a domestic Treble in his first season in Glasgow. Although he made just 26 appearances, Ferguson picked up another two winners' medals when he came on as substitute in the League Cup Final against St Johnstone and the Scottish Cup Final against Celtic. It is the latter appearance that he remembers most fondly though.

He recalled, 'I had been out with an ankle injury for about three or four months. No matter what I did, be it rest or treatment, it just didn't go away. There were about six or seven games left when I went in for an operation to remove two bits of floating bone. About two weeks before the cup final I got myself up to a reasonable level of fitness and was involved in training. The gaffer came up to me and said that I wouldn't be involved in the squad [for the cup final] but he wanted me to be part of it. We did another training session at the hotel and Dick named his team that night. He said he would name the subs the next day [the day of the game]. We had a meeting in the morning and after he went through a few things on the board, he named the subs and I was one of them. I couldn't believe it and was as high as a kite. We won 1-0 and he put me on with about 20 minutes to go at Hampden and it was great to be part of it as Celtic threw everything at us. It's a memory I'll always cherish as I didn't think I was going to be involved.'

What proved to be Ian Ferguson's last season in a Rangers jersey, 1999/2000, started with the usual spate of pre-season friendlies. But for Ian a home match against Sunderland stood out. In recognition of his service to the club this would be his testimonial match and today, almost 20 years later, he remains the last Rangers player to have been bestowed such an honour.

'When I look back and see the players that have been given a testimonial by the club, it was a great privilege,' said Ferguson proudly. 'I had a lot of great times at Ibrox; won nine championships, got into the Hall of Fame, won two Trebles and, of course, got the testimonial. It means so much to me to have achieved what I did and have been part of the club's history.'

With opportunities even to make the matchday squad becoming more and more infrequent Ferguson looked to pastures new and he joined Dunfermline Athletic.

'I spoke to Dick Advocaat before I spoke to Dunfermline to see what my chances were of getting a game for Rangers,' remembered Ferguson. 'He had just brought in Claudio Reyna so I knew the writing was on the wall but I wanted to hear it from him. I then went and spoke to [Dunfermline manager] Jimmy Calderwood, who was brilliant. He was larger than life and he told me he wanted to get Dunfermline into the Premier League and competing for the top six. I wanted to be part of that and as heartbreaking as it was to go into Ibrox and collect my boots and walk out for the last time, another chapter was starting for me. And I really enjoyed my two years at Dunfermline. We got out the First Division and, under Jimmy, we were probably the third best passing team in the Premier League. After two seasons I was offered a new contract but Jimmy was up front with me and told me there were games that I wouldn't play, particularly against the Old Firm. Those were the games I wanted to play in so I decided to look into going to America or Australia.'

Ferguson opted for Australia and signed for Sydney-based Northern Spirit before finishing his playing career in 2006 after a season with Central Coast Mariners.

'The minute I got to Australia, I loved it,' recalled Ferguson. 'It was a beautiful environment. Bill Collins, who was the physio when I was at Rangers, was in charge at Northern Spirit and he gave me and my family the opportunity to come here and we've never looked back. We've seen a fair bit of Australia, including Sydney, Perth and Queensland, and I look on it as a big adventure.'

During his time with Northern Spirit, Ferguson turned his hand to coaching and he also had the role of assistant coach at Central Coast Mariners. During his time there the Mariners reached two Grand Finals, losing out to Sydney FC in 2006 and Newcastle Jets in 2008. Clearly Ferguson had an aptitude for coaching and when North Queensland Fury were formed in 2009, he was appointed manager. With former Liverpool legend Robbie Fowler in the ranks, Ferguson took the club to within a point of the A-League play-offs. When the Fury became embroiled in financial difficulties Ferguson moved on to work under former Rangers striker Dave Mitchell at Perth Glory. Within a few months he was appointed head coach and he led his side to the Grand Final in 2012.

'I inherited an ageing squad – we had something like 15 players over the age of 30 – so I told the owner that I needed to get some fresh faces in,' said Ferguson. 'We did that and became more consistent. I was the first manager to take Perth Glory to a Grand Final and although we lost [Brisbane Roar won 2-1 courtesy of a contentious injury-time penalty], it was a massive step forward.'

The Grand Final team was then broken up and Ferguson returned to Queensland where he had the opportunity to build a team from grassroots level. The structure he helped develop bred several players who went on to play in the A-League but, in 2017, Ferguson decided to return to Perth where he is now involved with a club called Quinns FC.

Looking back on his illustrious career with Rangers, Ian finds it difficult to pinpoint one particular highlight.

'I had a fantastic time at Rangers,' he concluded. 'Two Trebles, nine-in-a-row, in the Hall of Fame, my testimonial; it would be hard for me to pick out just one of these because they are all very special. But, if I was pushed, then nine-in-a-row was a tough, tough run and a hard, hard journey. I'll never forget it and that would be my main highlight. I'm very proud to be one of only three players to hold all nine medals and that's part of the history of the club that can't be taken away. I was told recently that I'm in the top ten in terms of medal winners in Rangers' history. It's just an amazing feeling for a wee boy from the East End of Glasgow to be part of that.'

Ian Ferguson made 384 appearances for Rangers and scored 50 goals. He won ten Premier Division titles (1988/89 to 1996/97 inclusive and 1998/99), three Scottish Cup medals (1992/93, 1995/96 and 1998/99) and five League Cup winners' medals (1988/89, 1990/91, 1992/93, 1993/94 and 1996/97). He also won nine caps for Scotland.

Spike
David Kirkwood (1987–1989)

By March 1987, David Kirkwood had been earmarked as one of the top young players in the Scottish First Division. Aged just 19, he was over halfway through his third full season with an East Fife side that were flying high in Scotland's second tier. In addition to plying his trade as a footballer, Kirkwood was also studying at college to become an engineer. And it was while on campus that he learned title-chasing Rangers were seeking his services.

'I was an 'S' form signing at East Fife, signing my first professional forms aged 16,' said Kirkwood. 'I was 19 when Rangers came calling. Aberdeen, Manchester United and Liverpool were also interested in me. But as soon as Graeme Souness became involved, it was a no-brainer. I was doing an HND in Mechanical and Electrical Engineering and the first I knew about signing for Rangers was when there were reporters outside the college. When I got home I went down to Bayview and had a chat with the manager, Dave Clarke, and I was told to travel to Ibrox the next morning to speak to Graeme Souness.'

He added, 'East Fife had played Rangers in the League Cup earlier in the season and we took them to penalty kicks. I played well that night and Rangers also came and watched me when we played Dundee in the Scottish Cup.'

Kirkwood barely had time to get used to his new surroundings before he was off on his travels. Globetrotting would be a hallmark of his early days at Rangers – within 18 months of arriving at Ibrox he had been to Italy, Russia, Poland and Dubai – and on this occasion he was off with the youth team to take part in the Europ Espor Lorraine Youth Tournament in France.

'We had a very good youth side, with the likes of Gary McSwegan, John Spencer, Gus McPherson and Scott Nisbet,' said Kirkwood. 'The calibre of teams we played was really high and the fact we won the tournament just showed the quality we had.'

Once back from France, Kirkwood set about making an impression. He made his first appearance for the reserve team on 21 March 1987 against St Mirren at Ibrox – he was taken off injured after 75 minutes – and made further appearances against Motherwell, Troon Juniors and Clydebank. In the latter match he claimed a goal and an assist in a comprehensive 6-0 victory. He was rewarded for his performances when he was named in the first-team squad for the trip to face Aberdeen at Pittodrie in the penultimate, and ultimately decisive, league match of the season.

'I was 14th man at Aberdeen but I made my debut the following week against St Mirren,' recalled Kirkwood. 'I found out I was going to Aberdeen the Thursday before the game. There were 14 names on the list and mine was the last one. It was bedlam outside with people wanting tickets. I got handed two at 2pm when the team was announced and I knew two guys who were outside so I made their day when I gave them the tickets. And my day was made when the final whistle went and we'd won the league.'

The season ended with a first medal too when Kirkwood was part of the side that defeated Celtic 1-0 in the Glasgow Cup Final. It was evident that the St Andrews youngster had made a real impression in his short spell as a Ranger, witnessed by the fact he was included in the first-team squad that prepared for season 1987/88 with a trip to Switzerland and West Germany. Davie was in the starting line-up for five of the six matches played, playing alongside the likes of Souness, Butcher, Cooper, Durrant and McCoist. And when Rangers returned to Scotland to take part in the Glasgow International Football Tournament, Kirkwood was once again in the starting XI, wearing the number seven jersey in the matches against Real Sociedad and Porte Alegre.

When the competitive action got underway Kirkwood kept his place in the team. He was selected in midfield for each of the opening three league matches and also for the trip to Brockville to face Stirling Albion in the League Cup.

'That wasn't a severe pre-season as it was mostly games we played,' recalled Kirkwood. 'We had some good results and some bad results at the start of the season. We drew with Dundee United and lost up at Hibs and Aberdeen and there was a bit of a hangover after that. But if you had told me a year earlier when I was playing in the First Division with East Fife that I'd be playing in the same team as Graeme Souness I wouldn't have believed it. As the season went on more and more players came in so I ended up back in the reserves. It was hard but you just had to get your head down and keep working away and hope you'd get picked.'

In addition to making headway in the Rangers first team, Kirkwood was also impressing in the international arena. Before the month of August had ended, Davie had netted a hat-trick for the Reds in a 4-3 defeat by the Blues in a trial match in Largs for the Scotland U19 World Youth Cup squad. He did enough to earn a place alongside team-mate Scott Nisbet in the squad bound for Chile. However, Kirkwood was eventually withdrawn from the squad. Instead he would be heading for Kiev to play for Rangers in the European Cup.

'Scotland played against Canada at Motherwell and I was captain of the U19s that night,' recalled David. 'After the game I found out I was going to Kiev and would miss out with Scotland. In a way I was disappointed but what an experience it was playing for Rangers in the European Cup. I wouldn't have changed it for the world.'

Rangers had been drawn against Dynamo Kiev and Kirkwood was on the bench for the first leg in what would eventually become the Ukraine. And, with 65 minutes played in front of an estimated crowd of 100,000, he was asked to replace Avi Cohen.

'When we trained the night before there were about 45,000 people watching us,' remembered Kirkwood. 'When it came to the match all the other subs were out warming up and I was told to stay on the bench. I thought that meant I wouldn't be going on. But I think that was just to calm my nerves as I was told to get stripped and ready to go.'

Two weeks later Kirkwood replaced Cohen again in the return leg. This was one of those magical European nights under the Ibrox floodlights as Rangers overturned a 1-0 first leg deficit to eliminate the Russians.

'That was the famous night when the pitch was brought in,' said Kirkwood. 'They trained on the full pitch the night before then it was brought in. It was totally legal, though. The atmosphere that night was incredible, just wall-to-wall noise. The main difference [between European and domestic football] for me as a midfielder was that, away from home, you didn't see much of the ball. You did get more time on the ball but you were punished very, very quickly for making mistakes.'

He continued, 'I was now part of the first-team dressing room and all the guys made me feel part of it. We did everything together and you were treated like everybody else.'

Although dialogue with Souness was limited, it was apparent what the manager wanted from players like Davie Kirkwood.

'He demanded respect and would respect you if you respected him,' said Kirkwood. 'Graeme didn't really get involved in the dressing room but he was vocal in training. Walter Smith was the link man between the manager and the dressing room and he did most of the coaching. But Graeme would never ignore me if I passed him in the tunnel or went past his office. None of the staff did that.'

He added, 'Graeme's team talk ahead of one game against Celtic was simply, "Watch Paul McStay, he's a good player." He didn't need to get us up for games like that. We had guys like Terry Butcher and Walter Smith to fire us up but Graeme knew we were good players and didn't need to tell us how to play the game. The brawl at Easter Road [in the opening game of season 1986/87] was Graeme looking to see who would back him up in a fight. He knew then that his players would look after each other. He got 100% every day in training and we did everything together. If someone was to be punished then everyone got punished. You couldn't do it now as you'd have a revolt in the dressing room but we had so much respect for each other that you would never question it.'

Before the year was out Kirkwood also journeyed to Italy, Monaco and Dubai. His trip to Italy was for the Casale Monferrato Youth Tournament. Kirkwood scored the equalising goal in the 1-1 draw with Juventus in the opening match and was also part of the side that defeated Inter Milan 4-0 in the semi-finals and Torino 2-0 in the final. The excursions were completed when Kirkwood was in the squads that went to the French principality for a first-team friendly against Monaco and Dubai for the Dubai Champions Cup match against Everton.

'Dubai was a cracking trip,' recalled David fondly. 'We played Everton and it was the first time I'd played in conditions like that. You could actually kick the ball from the six-yard box into the goal at the other end of the pitch. We were 2-0 down but came back to draw 2-2 before winning on penalty kicks. It was a great experience.'

The last of those matches featured Ray Wilkins, a £250,000 signing from Monaco. Wilkins, with 84 England caps and a CV that included time with Chelsea, Manchester United and AC Milan, had huge respect in the dressing room and was a big influence on the development of Davie Kirkwood.

'Davie Cooper and Ray Wilkins were the best players I played with,' said Kirkwood. 'You learned from them about the high expectations and how to pass a ball properly. You also learned how they wanted to receive the ball and how they wanted to pass it. But it was the high standards that you saw and that didn't just come from them, it came from the likes of Terry Butcher, Chris Woods and Souness too. Players who had been there before were used to the old training methods so it was an eye-opener at the time.'

There would be no further first-team appearances for Kirkwood until the final day of season 1987/88 when he came on as substitute in a 5-0 thrashing of Falkirk. But his game had developed in the reserves and he travelled to the Tuscan hills for pre-season training hoping to become a regular feature in the first-team squad in season 1988/89.

'That was one of the hardest pre-seasons I've ever done,' admitted Kirkwood. 'Unlike the year before when we had played games, this was now about pure fitness. It was a gruelling two weeks and when we came back we went to Lilleshall to do monitoring and fitness testing. That was probably the fittest I've ever been in my life. We would be out first thing in the morning before the sun came out, then again in the afternoon and sometimes at night as well. Players today would turn their nose up and refuse to do it but we all did it.'

Unfortunately, season 1988/89 – the last of his current contract – would be a frustrating one for Kirkwood. Although he was part of a few matchday squads, Rangers accepted an offer from Airdrie for his services in November. Kirkwood, who two months earlier had scored his first two goals for Rangers in a 6-1 win over East Stirlingshire – rejected the opportunity but he remained in the first-team wilderness until he was selected when Rangers faced Dundee United at Ibrox on 2 May 1989. He played against United's city neighbours, Dundee, four days later and came close to being involved in the 1989 Scottish Cup Final when he was included in the squad.

He recalled, 'There were Scotland v England games [in training] all week before the final and I think they cost about three players their place as they got injured. That was the final when Graeme Souness put himself on the bench but we had a massive squad. For me it was an achievement to be in the squad and you still feel part of it even though you don't get on the pitch.'

However, the match at Dens Park would prove to be Kirkwood's last appearance in a Rangers jersey. Although he had changed position in the team – following his return from a month-long loan at East Fife, Souness had redeployed him at right-back – the lack of first-team opportunities meant Kirkwood took the chance to move along the M8 to join a growing contingent of former Rangers players at Hearts.

'There were so many good players in front of me so it was very hard to get a chance,' said Kirkwood. 'I just wanted to play every week. I didn't go to Il Ciocco [ahead of season 1989/90] as I had an illness but I joined up with the first-team squad when they came back and played in a couple of matches with Mo Johnston after he signed. Then I got a call from Graeme Souness who told me there was interest from Hearts. Graeme was happy for me to stay and I had just signed an extended contract but he said I'd probably play most weeks at Hearts. I went and spoke to them and spoke to my family and decided to go. At 3pm every Saturday I just wanted to put a strip on and go out and play.'

He added, 'I was always ready to step in at Rangers. That's what Graeme Souness and Walter Smith wanted. If anyone got injured, you had to be ready. If you weren't they would just go and find another player that was ready. I was never really a right-back, even though I could play there. But I preferred playing in midfield.'

The transfer fee was £100,000 but although he was capped at U21 level for Scotland in September 1989, Kirkwood would last just over a year at Tynecastle. He made his league debut against Celtic on 12 August 1989 and made a total of 28 league appearances, scoring once in a 3-2 defeat against St Johnstone in October 1990. After leaving Hearts he moved to Airdrie and enjoyed a successful spell there under Alex MacDonald. And in season 1991/92 he played in a national cup final when the Diamonds went down 2-1 to Rangers in the Scottish Cup.

'Alex MacDonald was sacked early in season 1990/91 and Joe Jordan came in at Hearts,' recalled Kirkwood. 'I played almost every game under Joe but he was looking for funds to sign players. Airdrie came in with a decent bid in December and, while I wasn't forced to go, Hearts wanted me to go to raise money to sign players. Airdrie were in the First Division but had ambitions to be in the Premier Division by the end of that season. We did that and also had the great experience of the Scottish Cup Final. Rangers weren't that great on the day and if we had played to our potential we could have created an upset. But we only really put a bit of pressure on in the last ten minutes.'

Despite being a regular at Airdrie, Kirkwood decided to join his former Rangers team-mate and reserve-team coach, Jimmy Nicholl, at Raith Rovers in the summer of 1994. And he picked up honours during his time there, although he was absent in November 1994 when Raith defeated Celtic on penalties to lift the Scottish League

Cup at Ibrox. He also scored against Rangers in an enthralling 4-2 defeat at Stark's Park in March 1996.

'I fell out of favour at Airdrie and refused to sign a new contract,' said Kirkwood. 'I trained with Hamilton for about six months but went to Raith in the summer. They used the money they got when Peter Hetherston went to Aberdeen to buy me. [1994/95] was a great season. We beat Celtic in the League Cup Final and got promoted.

'Myself and Danny Lennon missed the League Cup Final through injury. I was coming back from a knee injury and Danny from a foot injury. We both played against Cowdenbeath in a reserve game to get our fitness back up and I ended up injuring my ankle and Danny broke his foot. But fair play to the club, we had played in all the matches up to the final so we got our medals and our bonuses.

'The week after we beat Celtic we played St Mirren in the league and drew. We were something like 15 or 16 points behind Dundee at that time but we didn't lose from then until the end of the season and won the league by one point.'

On scoring against Rangers, he added, 'I never had any issues with the Rangers fans but if you scored against them you could get a rough ride. I never celebrated but it would be tough for the next ten minutes. But you would expect that.'

Kirkwood was forced to hang up his boots in 2000 through injury. He subsequently moved into coaching and had a successful spell as manager of Brora Rangers. He also coached the youngsters at Ibrox. Today he is academy director at Ross County.

'I was playing for Raith against Ayr United and I got injured in a challenge,' recalled Kirkwood. 'I had a wrist injury at the time as well so I was sent up to Aberdeen the following Monday for a scan. The results showed I had broken my wrist which would mean I would be out for three months. But the scan on my knee showed that I had snapped my anterior cruciate ligament and I was looking at a year to two years out. The specialist basically said if I kept on playing I would be in a wheelchair by the time I was 36.'

He added, 'The injury gave me the opportunity to do my coaching badges. I started coaching the Raith U18s and then went to Motherwell before I got the chance to come back to Rangers. They had just moved into Murray Park and I was working with guys like John Fleck, Chris Burke, Allan Hutton, Charlie Adam and Allan McGregor.'

David Kirkwood made 26 appearances for Rangers and scored two goals. Although he did not pick up any first-team honours, he was part of the youth sides that won the Europ Espor Lorraine Youth Tournament in 1986/87 and the Casale Monferrato Youth Tournament in 1987/88.

UP FRONT
THE FORWARDS

Solo
John MacDonald (1978–1986)

John MacDonald loved playing for Rangers. Brought up in Maryhill, John went to see Partick Thistle with his dad in his younger days but a move to Drumchapel when he was five saw a change of allegiance. He started to go to Ibrox to watch Rangers and fell in love with the club. He attended Kingsridge Secondary School, a school that had spawned players like Alex Miller and Danny McGrain, and was soon showcasing his blossoming football talent.

After spending time with Bobby Robson's Ipswich Town, he signed as a schoolboy for Rangers in February 1976 at the tender age of 15. He was much sought after, with Manchester United, Everton and Birmingham City rumoured to be interested in acquiring him. But John wanted to stay in Scotland and he continued to play for his school team before becoming John Greig's first signing in 1978. He was just 17 years old and on 29 July 1978 he realised a dream when he made his first-team debut against Inverness Caledonian. Rangers won 6-3 and just three days later, John netted his first top-team goal in a 2-2 draw against Kilmarnock in a benefit match for Ian Fallis.

'I loved every time I stepped on to the pitch,' recalled John. 'Before making my first-team debut, I was invited to play against Celtic Reserves on a Wednesday night. I was still at school and we had two cup finals on the Tuesday and Thursday that week. But I had to ask the school for permission to play for Rangers and they refused. I went to Ibrox to tell them I couldn't play but when one of the players did not show up [reserve-team coach] Joe Mason told me to get stripped to play. We were not expected to win the match but we won 4-0 and I scored the second goal.'

More appearances for the reserves followed before John made his Premier Division debut in February 1979 when he replaced Davie Cooper in a 3-2 defeat against Hearts at Tynecastle. He featured from the substitutes' bench again in the penultimate game of the season when Rangers beat Partick Thistle 1-0 at Ibrox. But there was a sombre mood among the sparse attendance of 6,087 as just two days earlier Rangers had lost 4-2 against Celtic at Parkhead to surrender the league title. John had fared better against the Celtic second team five days prior to the Parkhead reverse, heading the opening goal in a 3-1 win in the Glasgow Cup Final. He had netted in the semi-final too, Rangers defeating Thistle 4-3 on penalties after a pulsating 3-3 draw.

Still only 18, MacDonald remained in the first-team frame in the pre-season matches for 1979/80 and he featured prominently in a match in which Davie Cooper scored a goal that would later be voted the greatest ever scored in the history of the club.

'We played Celtic in the final of the Drybrough Cup, which was a pre-season tournament,' said John. 'I came on as substitute in both matches before the final and managed to score both goals in the semi-final against Kilmarnock. Our own pre-season tournament [the Tennent Caledonian Cup] was due to take place the Friday and Sunday of the same weekend as the Celtic match. John Greig told me I would not be playing in that, though, as I was starting the Celtic match instead. I couldn't believe it and even on the Saturday I felt he wasn't going to play me. But when he read the team out at 2pm, there I was, starting my first Old Firm match.'

John wore the number 11 jersey and opened the scoring after just 13 minutes. He recalled, 'We totally dominated the match and I felt really confident throughout. For my goal, I remember picking the ball up on the left wing and starting to run at their defence. I managed to open up space and play the ball to Davie Cooper who sent it back to me. I was through one-on-one with Peter Latchford and managed to keep my composure and slide it under him into the corner. I got mobbed by the players and was then physically sick just beside their goal as the atmosphere got to me.'

Twelve minutes later a superb solo effort from Sandy Jardine doubled Rangers' lead – he ran from the edge of his own penalty area, evading several challenges before despatching a powerful shot beyond Latchford – before Cooper provided the *pièce de résistance* with 12 minutes remaining. Receiving the ball from Alex MacDonald with his back to goal, Cooper allowed the ball to bounce just once after juggling it and flicking it over four Celtic defenders and knocking it into the net with his left foot.

A matter of weeks later, John scored again against Celtic, this time in the Premier Division. Ibrox Stadium was in the throes of redevelopment and the new Copland Road stand was opened that August afternoon. From their vantage point in the 7,500-seater stand the patrons witnessed MacDonald open the scoring four minutes into the second half with a header. When Bobby Russell scored five minutes later to double Rangers' lead, it seemed the home side were coasting to victory, but alas, Celtic scored twice in the closing six minutes to snatch a draw and this match was symptomatic of Rangers' season, ragged and inconsistent. John has fond memories of the Old Firm fixture. 'I scored in my first two Old Firm matches which puts me in a wee group of players who have done that,' he said with pride. 'Just playing in these matches gives you a buzz but scoring in one and you win the match, you just can't beat it.'

MacDonald made a further 33 appearances in season 1979/80, scoring eight goals, but he was unable to prevent Rangers lurching through one of the worst campaigns in their history. An early exit from the League Cup was followed by an abysmal Premier Division finish of fifth and Celtic poured salt into the wounds when they won the Scottish Cup Final 1-0 after extra time.

However, in the midst of a calamitous campaign, John had made an impression on John Greig and also his fellow professionals. He was voted as PFA Scotland's Young Player of the Year for 1979/80. He was the first Rangers player to win the recently inaugurated award and only four others – Robert Fleck, Charlie Miller, Barry Ferguson and Danny Wilson – have won it since. 'It was fantastic to win that,' said MacDonald. 'I pipped Alex McLeish to get it and it capped a good season for me.'

There was international recognition too. Having been capped at schoolboy and at U18 level, MacDonald made his first appearance for Scotland's U21s in February 1980 when he came on as substitute in a friendly against West Germany. A further seven appearances at that level followed over the course of 1980/81 and 1981/82, with MacDonald getting on the scoresheet in a 4-0 win over Sweden in September 1981.

Imbued with confidence, young MacDonald started season 1980/81 in fine fettle. Following two goals in a 3-1 Anglo-Scottish Cup win over Partick Thistle, MacDonald was in the starting XI for the opening Premier Division match against Airdrie. A goal in a 1-1 draw at Broomfield was followed by further strikes against Partick Thistle and Dundee United before he doubled his tally for the season with a hat-trick in an 8-1 mauling of Kilmarnock at Rugby Park.

'1980/81 was a good season for me as I started to become a regular starter in the team,' said MacDonald. He partnered Colin McAdam in attack and the duo were prominent in November when Celtic were beaten comprehensively at Ibrox. An impressive start to the season saw Rangers unbeaten after 11 matches – although they had lost rather humiliatingly 3-0 to Chesterfield in the Anglo-Scottish Cup – and MacDonald added to his impressive tally of Old Firm goals when he outpaced the Celtic defence to score Rangers' second goal after 37 minutes. McAdam had opened the scoring following a mistake from Pat Bonner and he added his second and Rangers' third in the 77th minute with a trademark header. 'I started off my career playing alongside Derek Johnstone and learned so much from him that the change to Colin McAdam was like for like,' said John. 'Both were strong in the air and great at holding the ball up. My job was to try and read when they were going to flick balls on so I was ready to make my run behind the defence. That was my style until we started playing smaller guys up front.'

At this point Rangers were thriving and looking a good bet for the league title. However, successive defeats against Morton and Aberdeen ended the unbeaten run and Greig's men won just eight of their remaining 19 league games to finish third, 12 points adrift of champions Celtic.

On a personal level, though, John MacDonald excelled. His missed only six league matches and his tally of 11 league goals was second only to McAdam, who netted 12. However, if his Premier Division return was good, it was in the Scottish Cup he enjoyed arguably his finest moment in a Rangers jersey.

A comfortable 5-0 win over Airdrie was followed by a 3-3 draw against a St Johnstone side boasting the talents of an 18-year-old Alistair McCoist. It had taken a late Ian Redford goal to keep Rangers in the cup in Perth but although McCoist scored in the replay at Ibrox, Rangers progressed to the quarter-final with a 3-1 victory. John missed that match but was back in the number 11 jersey for the last-eight meeting with Hibernian. And he made a scoring return, netting the third goal in a comfortable 3-1 victory in front of a crowd of 26,345. A semi-final win over Morton followed, but when Rangers faced Dundee United at Hampden in the final, John was on the bench. 'Coop and myself had missed the semi-final as the gaffer thought it'd be too rough for us [Greig was right; two Morton players were ordered off for bad tackles in Rangers' 2-1 win at Parkhead],' recalled MacDonald. 'I can't recall why I didn't start the final, though.'

A dour match was dominated by Dundee United but when Cooper and MacDonald came off the bench, Rangers were reinvigorated and they should have won the cup when they were awarded a penalty kick in the last minute. John surged down the wing and when his cross was parried by Hamish McAlpine, Bobby Russell was fouled. Ian Redford stepped up but his effort struck the legs of McAlpine and rebounded to safety. 'I felt sick when he missed the penalty,' recalled John. 'But in hindsight it worked out great for myself and Coop.'

Three days later both MacDonald and Cooper were back in the team and there was a place at centre-forward for Derek Johnstone too. Rangers were now on the front foot and, inspired by a vintage display from Cooper, Rangers won 4-1. Cooper opened the scoring after ten minutes and delivered a swerving free kick to the back post for Bobby Russell to net the second. United halved the lead shortly afterwards, though, when David Dodds scored and the final was now back in the balance. Rangers needed a hero and found one in the shape of their 20-year-old sharpshooting forward. A defence-splitting Cooper pass put John through one-on-one with McAlpine and he despatched the ball into the net with his left foot and he scored a second after the interval to seal the victory. 'For me, managing to score two goals in a cup final was fantastic and that was the only Scottish Cup Final I won out of four,' said MacDonald. 'Coop was magnificent in the replay. He was fantastic to play with. If you made a run he'd find you as he did with my first goal in the match. His teasing of players was brilliant and he was also a great guy off the park too.'

Buoyed by his cup final heroics, MacDonald enjoyed arguably his best season with Rangers in 1981/82. He featured in all 36 Premier Division games, starting all but four of them, and scored 14 goals, including another against Celtic in a 3-3 draw in September. 'For a player it's always good to be playing regularly,' noted John, 'and if you're scoring your confidence is so high.'

Despite John's goals and the signing of John McClelland in a bid to shore up the defence, the team could still not garner a consistent run of victories to mount a title challenge. For the second successive season, Rangers finished third, once again 12 points adrift of Celtic. 'Apart from Greigy's first season in charge we seemed to struggle in the league,' recalled John. 'I think a lot of it was down to trying to change the playing staff as a lot of great Rangers players were either retiring or moving on. We blew hot and cold and Aberdeen and Dundee United had good teams in that era. We couldn't string three or four wins together to get us further up the table.'

There was more joy in the cup competitions, though. MacDonald scored five goals in the run to the League Cup Final, including one in each leg of the semi-final against St Mirren. In the final against Dundee United he won the free kick from which Davie Cooper equalised and a fine chip from Ian Redford secured the trophy. A domestic cup double looked to be on the cards when John met Gordon Dalziel's cross with a superb diving header to put Rangers ahead in the Scottish Cup Final against Aberdeen. However, future

Rangers and Scotland manager Alex McLeish equalised to force extra time wherein Alex Ferguson's side scored a further three times to win 4-1.

Season 1981/82 witnessed another notable first for John MacDonald: his first goal in European competition. Having made his European debut as a substitute against Norwegian side Lillestrom in 1979, John marked his first start with Rangers' second goal in the second leg of a European Cup Winners' Cup tie against Dukla Prague. It was the first of five goals MacDonald would score in Europe for Rangers – the other four, including a second leg hat-trick, came against Valletta of Malta in 1983 – but he was utilised infrequently at this level. 'It seemed they wanted to keep it tight in Europe so I was used sparingly,' explained John. 'It was great going away to play in these matches and watching how the European teams played. Against Dukla Prague we were already 3-0 down from the first leg in Prague so we went for it at Ibrox. We lost an early goal – a bad mistake from our goalkeeper Jim Stewart – but we managed to go in at half-time 2-1 ahead. It was great to score my first goal but second half we could hardly get the ball and went out 4-2 on aggregate.'

The recruitment focus ahead of 1982/83 was once again on stiffening the rearguard, with centre-half Craig Paterson brought in for a club record fee of £225,000, while full-back Dave McKinnon was signed from Partick Thistle. John MacDonald was again first pick in the forward line and he scored three goals as Rangers topped their League Cup section to qualify for the quarter-finals. A further four goals were chalked up in an emphatic 12-1 aggregate win over Kilmarnock but John was dropped when Rangers reached the final against Celtic. John Greig had brought Gordon Smith back to the club on loan from Brighton and Hove Albion and he was handed MacDonald's number 11 jersey. John was understandably disappointed. He recalled, 'To play in all the matches and get left out of the starting 11 was disappointing. Taking a chance on someone who just arrived at the club even though he had played there before [Smith had signed in 1977 and left for England in 1980] was a risk.'

It was a risk that backfired. Celtic were 2-0 ahead after half an hour and although Jim Bett's second-half free kick galvanised

Rangers and John came on to replace Bobby Russell, they could not find another goal. Greig's men reached the Scottish Cup Final too, for the fourth successive year. MacDonald scored the winning goals against Forfar Athletic in round four and was in the starting XI for the final against Aberdeen but he was replaced by Gordon Dalziel prior to extra time. Eric Black's goal four minutes from the end of the additional half hour ensured the Scottish Cup would join the European Cup Winners' Cup in Aberdeen's trophy cabinet.

With ten goals amassed in 30 league appearances, John was once again top scorer at the club. He may have netted more but for an enforced absence from the team following a match at Pittodrie in January. 'I was substitute that day and got on after an hour,' noted John. 'I got the ball just inside their half and started to make towards their goal. As I was running I got grabbed round the neck by Dougie Bell. I turned round to vent my anger and he came up close to me. Our heads got close to each other and he pulled his head away as if I had head-butted him. A melee erupted and in that, players did worse than what I did. I got sent off and ended up with an extra four-match ban.'

Yet again the league challenge petered out. Sandy Clark arrived in March from West Ham United and scored five goals in ten matches but a lack of firepower proved Rangers' downfall. Only four wins away from Ibrox proved costly too and Rangers finished in fourth place, 18 points behind champions Dundee United.

Rumblings of discontent were now reaching a crescendo so John Greig spent £185,000 in June 1983 in a bid to sharpen his attack. Two years after he failed to sign him from St Johnstone, Greig finally secured 20-year-old Alistair McCoist and a legend was born. 'I always tell everybody I've scored more Scottish Cup Final goals than Ally,' laughed MacDonald. 'When Ally first arrived John Greig told me I wouldn't be the player to get dropped for Ally. Ally was great to play alongside but he mainly played in midfield in his first few years. His work rate and goal ratio even then was fantastic.'

However, despite scoring a hat-trick in an 11-0 win over Arlovs, netting a brace against Norrstrands in a pre-season tour of Sweden and adding a Glasgow Cup winners' medal to his collection, John started just one of the opening 11 Premier Division matches. 'Some managers bring guys in and they always prefer to play them,' said John. 'Managers then didn't tell you that you weren't going to play and I wasn't one for going chapping on their door. I just got on with it and tried to work my way back into the team.'

During his time on the sidelines, MacDonald earned the nickname 'the Magistrate' for the amount of time he was spending on the bench. This temporarily replaced his usual nickname in the dressing room, 'Solo'. 'Dave Armour gave me that in my younger days in the reserves,' said John. 'As a winger in those days I liked to go on a dribble and Dave shouted one day "just give the ball to Solo" and he called me it that much it stuck.'

From the bench, John watched as Rangers made a wretched start to the season. Five of the first nine league matches were lost and following a 2-1 home defeat to Motherwell on 22 October, John Greig resigned. Although there had been success in the cup competitions, the Premier Division title remained elusive and that is what ultimately led to a parting of the ways. Despite his lack of game-time, MacDonald was sad to see Greig go.

'John Greig gave me my chance at Ibrox and I will be forever grateful to him for that,' said MacDonald. 'It's never nice to see a manager you've worked with for five years leave. A few years later, after I'd retired, my wife's cousin got a tour of Ibrox with his friend who was then the manager of the Australian national team. They met Greigy and he told them that after we played Arsenal in a friendly in 1980 [John scored both goals for Rangers in a 2-0 win] they had put in a bid for me which was rejected, something I never knew about.'

After Alex Ferguson and Jim McLean turned the job down, Jock Wallace returned to the helm and his return galvanised Rangers. After losing his first match 3-0 against Aberdeen at Pittodrie, they embarked on a 15-match unbeaten run in the Premier Division. The League Cup Final was also reached, with John scoring twice in the 11 appearances he made. One of those appearances was in the final against Celtic at Hampden wherein Ally McCoist scored a hat-trick to ensure the trophy returned to Ibrox for the 12th time. However, John's appearances were less frequent in the Premier Division.

Despite scoring his 99th goal for the club when he netted against Hearts at Ibrox in December and scoring prolifically in the reserves (including four in an 8-0 win over Dundee), he only made a further 15 appearances, all but one of which was from the substitutes' bench. 'When Jock arrived I thought "new manager, new start" but it didn't turn out that way,' said John.

Despite a lack of game time MacDonald was included in the travelling party as Rangers embarked on a world tour at the end of 1983/84. The tour was a memorable one for the diminutive front man, both personally and professionally. He recalled, 'The tour was fantastic although very long. I have family who stay in Melbourne so I got to see a lot of them as we were based there for two weeks. I also scored my 100th goal for Rangers, against New Zealand, which was brilliant and a good end to that part of the trip.'

Following the impressive unbeaten run in the league and a punishing pre-season on the sand dunes of Gullane, there were high hopes around Ibrox that season 1984/85 would be the one that would see the league championship return to Ibrox.

'Gullane was an experience you were glad only happened once a year,' recalled MacDonald. 'Two hours running up and down the sand dunes was the hardest training. You had to follow the steps that the experienced guys made or you would get a clout around the ear. By the end of it you were crawling!'

Having also focussed on building his upper body strength in the gym, John MacDonald hoped the rigorous pre-season would help him re-establish himself as a first-team regular. Competition for places was high, with McCoist, Clark and Mitchell in contention for the forward berths in the preferred 4-4-2 formation in addition to new signing Iain Ferguson and youngsters Robert Fleck and Eric Ferguson.

However, despite starting the first league match of the season against St Mirren and scoring his first league goal of the season against Hibernian in September, MacDonald had to wait until October for his next start. After another spell in the reserves he returned to the first-team fold for a run of games in December, January and February but when John replaced Ted McMinn in a

2-0 defeat against Hearts at Tynecastle on 23 February, he made his final first-team appearance of the 1984/85 season. An exasperating spell was rounded off when he was red-carded in the 68th minute of an Old Firm reserve game at the end of March.

'That was the time when I did ask for a transfer,' admitted MacDonald. 'Jock said okay but I never knew if he put it about to other clubs or not. I was frustrated so I just kept playing in the reserves and hoped someone would come in for me.'

John continued, 'In January Jock took not well and [assistant manager] Alex Totten took the team for a few matches. We happened to be playing Morton in the Scottish Cup and Alex liked me so I started the match and scored. I scored in the replay too but when Jock came back I was back as sub and then eventually out the squad altogether. I'd have played anywhere at that time to get a game. I didn't care where I played as I started out as a winger, then a striker and had also played midfield.'

John MacDonald spent most of what would prove to be his last season with Rangers playing in the reserves. He scored 20 goals in 32 appearances for the second string, partnering Robert Fleck in attack. However, an operation on his collarbone which kept him on the sidelines for two months and the form of Ally McCoist in particular, meant opportunities in the first team were limited. He made four appearances, the last of which, against St Mirren at Love Street in April, was played out under the watchful eye of the club's new assistant manager, Walter Smith.

The romantic reunion with Jock Wallace had not borne fruit and Rangers were struggling to finish in the top half of the Premier Division in 1985/86, far less challenge for the title. Decisive action was taken; Wallace was sacked and Graeme Souness was appointed player-manager. Walter Smith, assistant manager at Dundee United, took on a similar role at Ibrox.

The arrival of the new regime did not reignite the Rangers career of John MacDonald. 'Twelve players were released that summer but I wasn't one of them,' said John. 'I was signing month-to-month contracts, though, and the manager asked to see me in September. He told me to get myself a club as Rangers were letting me go.'

Still only 25, MacDonald looked to England for that club and almost ended up in London. He said, 'I went to Charlton for two months and they were in the top division at the time. London wasn't the place for me, though, so I took an offer I got from Barnsley. Alan Clarke was manager there and I loved that place to bits. The guys I played with were great too.'

Remarkably Barnsley, struggling in the Second Division, was paying MacDonald a higher wage than Rangers and he stayed at Oakwell for three years. He scored 20 league goals, including one from the halfway line in a 1-0 win against Grimsby Town in February 1987. A short stint at Scarborough followed before John returned to Scotland. He signed for Airdrie in December 1990, three months after they had recruited former team-mate, Ally Dawson. MacDonald scored in his first two games, 2-2 draws against Ayr United and Clyde, and added another against Forfar Athletic in April as the Broomfield side earned promotion to the Premier Division. After making 14 appearances in his first season, John did not feature at all in the following two campaigns and signed for Dumbarton in September 1993. He scored twice in six appearances for the Sons before leaving to see out his career in the Highlands with Fort William and Caledonian Thistle. Short stints coaching the U18s at Partick Thistle and the U16s at St Mirren followed before John drifted away from an active involvement in the game.

'I have no regrets about my Rangers career,' said John. 'Although I had tears in my eyes when I left the stadium for the last time, it was a boyhood dream to play for them. I'm back now playing in legends matches and it has given me a new lease of life. I've been keeping fit and it's great getting to play with guys I've recently watched playing for Rangers.'

In total, John MacDonald made 292 appearances for the Rangers first team and scored 106 goals. He won a Scottish Cup winners' medal (1980/81), two League Cup winners' medals (1981/82 and 1983/84), two Glasgow Cup winners' medals (1978/79 and 1983/84), two Reserve League Championship medals (1983/84 and 1985/86), and a Drybrough Cup winners' medal (1979/80). He also won eight U21 caps for Scotland, scoring one goal.

Daz
Gordon Dalziel (1978–1984)

Since 1872 numerous footballers have lived the dream and played for the Rangers first team. There are, however, few who can lay claim to having scored a goal after just five minutes of their Old Firm debut and then picked up a winners' medal in a domestic cup competition the following weekend. One who can, though, is Gordon Dalziel, a free-scoring youngster in the early 1980s whose time at Ibrox was brief but memorable.

'I signed straight from school the year after we won the Treble and was on 'S' forms since I was about 14,' said Dalziel. 'When I turned 16, I left school and the following Sunday I played a game at The Albion. After the game John Greig took me into Ibrox and signed me on my first full-time contract. There were international footballers there at the time like Sandy Jardine and Derek Johnstone. I was still a kid and I wanted to learn my trade in the reserves and try and break into the first team and get an odd game. That was the way it worked in those days.'

Dalziel made his first-team debut when he replaced Chris Robertson during a League Cup tie against Clyde on 1 September 1979. His league debut followed two months later when he was in the XI that faced St Mirren at Love Street.

Gordon recalled, 'I was picked for the Scotland U18s and after the game I was to fly out to Monte Carlo with the squad. I turned up at the Rangers game with my Scotland suit on as my family were picking me up and taking me to the airport. We lost the game 2-1 and as I was walking out the door Greigy said to me that I wasn't going [with the Scotland squad] and to come in for training on Monday. We were due to play Aberdeen the following weekend and I don't know if it was the disappointment of losing or that we had injuries, but he felt he had to keep me part of the squad. I had always wanted to go to Monte Carlo but, at that age, I was more interested in playing for Rangers.'

When Dalziel took part in those training sessions with the first team, he did so in the company of some of the finest players ever to wear a blue jersey.

'We had real quality players at that time and you didn't know how good they were until you went against them in training,' said Dalziel. 'In my first couple of weeks at the club I played in a practice match and I couldn't believe how good Alex MacDonald and Bobby Russell were. Coop was different class but these guys were just as good. Bobby was probably the best uncapped player, ability-wise. He was incredible, a fantastic talent.'

Dalziel did not play for the first team again in season 1979/80 after his 90 minutes against St Mirren but he was selected in the squad that travelled to Canada to take part in the Red Leaf Cup in June 1980. Rangers played four matches, drawing with Nancy (3-3) and Botafogo (1-1) and beating Ascoli (1-0). Dalziel came on as substitute against the Italians and started the match against Botafogo. He was in the starting XI again for the final against Ascoli, which Rangers lost 2-0. It was a memorable experience for young Dalziel, although his abiding memory is of a horrific injury sustained by a team-mate.

'It was absolutely fantastic but I couldn't believe how warm it was,' recalled Dalziel. 'We came off the park and got on the team bus and, as these were the days before sports science, all you were doing was drinking gallons of stuff like Coca-Cola. I remember playing in one game and you could actually feel your arms burning as it was that warm. What always sticks out, though, was the Ally Dawson incident [when he sustained a fractured skull]. We were all very much concerned about him but thankfully he got himself back playing again.'

Although he had been involved with the touring party, Dalziel was still serving his apprenticeship in the reserve team. Indeed, in season 1980/81 he made just one appearance for the first team, scoring Rangers' goal in a dour 1-1 draw against Chesterfield in the Anglo-Scottish Cup. Thereafter Dalziel endured a spell when he picked up niggling injuries, like a knee injury that required a cortisone injection, which meant he was in and out of training. When he played for the reserves he was in free-scoring form. This is perhaps best illustrated by events on 4 October 1980. With Colin McAdam struggling to be fit for the Premier Division match against Morton at Cappielow, Dalziel was placed on standby. However, McAdam declared himself fit so Dalziel played in the reserve fixture at Ibrox; he promptly scored four goals in a 6-0 win.

As the old saying goes, 'good things come to those who wait' and this rung true for Gordon Dalziel as he looked to be graduating to the first team in season 1981/82. Although yet to turn 20 he made five appearances in pre-season, playing against leading English sides Liverpool, Everton and Southampton. The latter match, played at Ibrox, was a testimonial for Sandy Jardine and Dalziel scored the only goal of the game.

'Playing Liverpool was the biggest eye-opener I've ever had in my life,' recalled Dalziel. 'It's the only time I've ever played – and I was on the park for 70 minutes – and never actually touched the ball. They were just a different class. I remember Greigy's team talk when he talked about Ronnie Whelan, who I think had just come into the team, as being the weakest point. After about ten minutes Jimmy Stewart, a big unit who covered every angle, came running out of his goal and Whelan chipped him. We knew then that if he was the weak link, we were in trouble! They were by far the best team I've ever played against. They were magnificent but it was a great experience.'

A return to the reserve team followed but November 1981 proved to be a month to remember. Dalziel followed up a substitute appearance against St Mirren with his Old Firm debut and by the end of the month he was clutching his first winners' medal.

'I always wanted to play in an Old Firm game but I didn't think I'd be playing that day,' said Dalziel. 'In those days the younger boys carried the hampers so I thought that's what I'd be doing. I was sitting with my suit on when Coop came up to me and told me I was playing. I thought he was joking!'

Dalziel was always sick with nerves before games and this match, unsurprisingly, was no different. Nevertheless, he donned the number ten jersey and when he took to the field he was met with a wall of noise.

'We could hardly hear each other so I went across to Coop and asked him what I was supposed to do as I had never experienced anything like it,' recalled Dalziel. 'He looked at me and said, "Just run, I'll find you." I had a terrific first half. I scored after five minutes [a diving header at the back post] and I set up Jim Bett's goal too. I had a hand in wee John MacDonald's goal before wee Murdo [McLeod] scored an absolute cracker to make it 3-3. It was some game and to score on my debut was incredible.'

Silverware was at stake the following weekend when Rangers faced Dundee United at Hampden in the League Cup Final. Buoyed by Old Firm heroics, Dalziel kept his place in the team.

'After the Celtic game I knew I had played very well and I got a lot of good press,' said Dalziel. 'On the Thursday before the game I realised I was going to play and it was great. We went a goal down and Paul Sturrock had a goal chalked off for United. What a goal it was – into the roof of the net – but John Holt, the right-back, was offside. It would have counted today, though, as he wasn't interfering with play. We got back in the game with Coop's free kick and Ian Redford came on and won it with a lob over Hamish McAlpine.'

He continued, 'That was my first real taste of playing in a cup final and winning a medal, it was terrific. It's amazing how things go in football as Reddy [Ian Redford] came on for me as sub that day and came on as sub for me again for Raith Rovers in the League Cup Final against Celtic [in 1994].'

The opening goalscorer that day, Davie Cooper, was a stalwart of that side and he and Dalziel had a terrific relationship. Cooper did not drive at that time so Dalziel, who stayed five doors down from him in Motherwell, used to take him to training every day.

'Coop was great to me,' said Dalziel. 'I used to go over in the morning and he'd have tea and toast ready for me. I would take him in to training and afterwards, because I wouldn't take petrol money off him, he'd take me for lunch. You didn't get anything to eat at Ibrox so we would go for lunch then back to his mum and dad's for tea and a cake. After that he would go and put on his [bookie's] line and watch the racing on the telly. He was a terrific guy.'

He continued, 'He would walk in [to the dressing room] and people would always be polite and say "good morning". Coop would always answer "What's f*****g good about it?" I think it was a character he played, though. He was fun, a good laugh who liked a joke.'

Dalziel remained in and around the first-team squad for the remainder of season 1981/82. He tasted Old Firm victory for the first time on 9 January when Rangers beat Celtic 1-0 at Ibrox. And a week later he added another goal to his tally in a home match against Dundee United. After a spell on the substitutes' bench – which witnessed another goal against Morton – Dalziel appeared in nine of the last 12 Premier Division matches. And in the penultimate one, against Dundee at Ibrox, he chalked up his first career hat-trick.

'That was a good afternoon's work as they say,' said Dalziel with pride. 'I had never scored a hat-trick for Rangers and it was nice to do it.'

The season culminated with the Scottish Cup Final and appearing in the showpiece match was becoming an annual event for Rangers. This was their seventh successive final and Alex Ferguson's Aberdeen stood in the way of the Light Blues retaining the trophy. Dalziel, who had only just turned 20, made it two cup final appearances for the season when he was given the number nine jersey.

He recalled, 'Aberdeen were a real good side and they were getting the better of us, especially at Pittodrie. When it came to the final we went one up [Dalziel's cross from the right wing was clinically despatched by John MacDonald] but the turning point of the game was when McLeish scored the curler from the corner kick [to make it 1-1]. I was right behind it and big Alex would never do that again in another 20 years. It gave Aberdeen a boost and a lift at that time.

They had some really good players coming through and they were a dominant side at that time.'

Although he did not end the season with another winners' medal, Dalziel had made an impression in the first team. He ended season 1981/82 having made 30 appearances and scoring seven goals. It seemed he had now earned a place in the first-team squad.

He made a goalscoring start to season 1982/83 too, netting twice in a 6-3 win over Swansea City in Tam Forsyth's testimonial. Remarkably, though, rather than cementing a place in the first team, he found himself back in the reserves. It was November before he made his first league appearance of the season – notching a double in a 4-0 win over Motherwell – and between 18 December and 5 February, the name Dalziel was conspicuous by its absence on the first-team team sheet. His lack of game time can be attributed to an altercation with John Greig in the wake of the 1982/83 League Cup Final defeat at the hands of Celtic.

'I was told on the Tuesday before the game that I was playing,' said Dalziel. 'We went down to the Marine Hotel in Troon and on the Thursday afternoon after training, Gordon Smith came in. I was wondering who was going to be left out [to accommodate Smith in the team] and it became evident it was going to be the youngest one, me. Looking back, I can totally understand it. I can see why Greigy did it as he was under a bit of pressure to get some results. But Greigy and I drifted apart when, on the Saturday morning, I was pulled aside. My family were going to Hampden so I thought I would be told I'd be on the bench. Instead I was told to drive up to Ibrox and play for the reserves [against Dundee]. When I arrived [reserve-team coach] Joe Mason asked what the f**k I was doing there, he couldn't believe it.'

While the first team lost 2-1 at Hampden, Dalziel scored twice – with a close-range finish after 22 minutes and a header from a Kenny Lyall cross 11 minutes from time – as the second string won 3-0.

He continued, 'On the Monday Greigy pulled me in. It never worked [the return of Smith] and we lost the cup final. Greigy told me not to speak to any journalists but I was so angry that I spoke to someone. He then came on the phone and went crazy at me. I was then dubbed the Rangers Rebel by Jimmy Sanderson [of Radio Clyde] and for about three weeks I was brought in every afternoon and told to run round the track by myself. Joe Mason would run me until I couldn't run any more. That was my punishment and I don't think Greigy and I ever recovered after that. I think if he had taken me to Hampden, I wouldn't have been happy but I would have understood. Looking back, I regret it. Greigy is a great guy, a legend, with his statue outside Ibrox but, at the time, his decision was a sore one to take.'

Following the League Cup Final, Dalziel remained in the reserves. Andy Kennedy was selected at centre-forward and when Sandy Clark arrived from West Ham United in March 1983, it looked like Dalziel would slip even further down the pecking order. Clark, Player-of-the-Year in Scotland in 1982, had netted ten goals in 34 appearances for the Hammers so had a goalscoring pedigree at the highest level. He played in each of the last ten Premier Division matches, scoring five goals. In contrast, despite playing 11 of the last 15 matches, Dalziel netted just once, against Hibernian in a 1-1 draw in March. He made what proved to be his final appearance for Rangers when he came off the bench to replace John MacDonald in the 1983 Scottish Cup Final against Aberdeen.

It was evident that Gordon Dalziel's footballing future lay away from Ibrox. He was consigned to the reserves for the opening gambit of season 1983/84, but even his glut of goals there dried up. He scored just four times in 15 appearances and even a change of manager could not provoke a change in fortune.

'Big Jock came in and he was great to me,' said Dalziel. 'He told me big Billy [McNeill] had been on the phone from Manchester City and asked if I wanted to go down and talk to them. He told me I couldn't do anything until I phoned him. I went down and spoke to Billy and then I phoned Jock. He asked what my heart was telling me. I told him I wanted to sign for City and he said he would get it sorted.'

He continued, 'My dream had been to play in an Old Firm match. As a young boy I used to kid on I was playing in them and scoring against Celtic. To have the opportunity to do that, play in cup finals and play against that Liverpool team, it was a good time when you look back. I made a lot of good friends and played with a lot of fantastic footballers. Bobby Russell was one of the most underrated footballers and there were guys like Willie Johnston, Alex MacDonald and Tommy McLean too. I was very fortunate.'

Dalziel joined City in November 1983 for a fee of just £25,000. He played alongside former Rangers Derek Parlane and Gordon Smith and Scotland stalwart Asa Hartford but his time in Manchester was brief. Dalziel felt he was played in the wrong position – in a wider area rather than as a centre-forward – and admits to living the high life, socialising with the likes of Alex Higgins and George Best. Less than a year later he was back in Scotland, firstly joining Partick Thistle then East Stirling. His career seemed to be drifting. He had lost his way but the kiss of life for his footballing career was provided by Frank Connor. He signed Dalziel for Raith Rovers in 1987 and he never looked back. By the end of his first season in Kirkcaldy he had netted 25 goals in 42 matches and had also encountered Graeme Souness's Rangers in the Scottish Cup.

'That was the match Rangers went for a 0-0,' laughed Dalziel. 'Souness came on [as sub] and he was giving the back four pelters. At that time we were on a bigger draw bonus as the replay [at Ibrox] meant the club would get more money. Rangers started just passing the ball about at the back so Colin Harris, who was playing up front with me, sat down in the middle of the park. The game just petered out after that.'

Rangers won the replay 4-1, thanks to a double from Ian Durrant and solitary strikes from McCoist and Walters, the latter's being his first goal for the club. However, 12 months later the clubs were drawn together again and this time Dalziel got himself on the scoresheet.

'I always wanted to score against Rangers,' admitted Dalziel. 'You were maybe trying to prove a point that you were decent and you deserved to play with a club like Rangers. I scored at Stark's Park with a header and we drew 1-1 after Ian Ferguson scored a terrific equaliser.'

Rangers triumphed in the replay again – 3-0 on this occasion – but Gordon Dalziel's football career was now back on track. He was First Division Player of the Year in 1991/92 and 1992/93 before he reached the zenith of his career in season 1994/95, scoring in the League Cup Final and lifting the trophy as Raith Rovers captain.

'I was captain and we were promoted from the First Division that year,' recalled Dalziel. 'We played Celtic in the Coca-Cola Cup Final at Ibrox and they were 2-1 up with seven minutes to go. I remember saying to Ally Graham on the halfway line that we would get one more chance. He looked at me as if I was stupid but we got that chance. I scored it and when that went in I believed we were going to win the cup.'

With no further scoring in extra time the final would be, to coin the phrase used in the match programme, decided on kicks from the penalty mark. Dalziel, by now on the sidelines having been substituted through injury, could not bear to watch.

'I had been struggling with a calf knock and I got a bang on it ten minutes into extra time,' said Dalziel. 'I never watched a penalty kick and to this day I've never seen them, apart from the one Paul McStay missed. I knew we were going first so I stood up the tunnel with [BBC reporter] Chick Young and I looked over at our supporters so I could tell if we had scored or not. Even as a manager I never watched a penalty kick, it was a superstition I had.'

Dalziel left Raith at the end of that season to join Ayr United and after ending his playing career, he cut his managerial teeth in Ayrshire. He did well and holds the distinction of being among a select band of managers who has led the Somerset Park side to a league title. But that triumph is not the enduring memory of his time with Ayr.

'My biggest achievement was to take a First Division team to Hampden for a final [in the League Cup] then take them back six days later for a semi-final [in the Scottish Cup],' said Dalziel. 'Unfortunately, we played Rangers and Celtic and they were far better than anything we had. But just to achieve that was fantastic for a club of that size. Ayr were known at that time as a cup team and we had beaten the likes of Motherwell, Hibs, Dundee and Dundee United.'

He continued, 'In the League Cup Final against Rangers we held our own until Tore Andre Flo opened the scoring. I could see it coming too. My midfield player dropped the runner and I was screaming for my centre-half not to come out. But by the time I got down to the technical area, Flo had put the ball in the net. I went from a 0-0 half-time team talk which would have been all positive, to going in and the boys' heads were down and you had to try and lift them. The pure class of Rangers told in the end, though.'

Dalziel left Somerset Park in 2002 and, following two years in charge of junior side, Glenafton Athletic, he returned to take the helm at Raith Rovers. Thereafter he returned to Glenafton and held the role of director of football at Airdrie up to January 2018. He is now one of the regular pundits on Radio Clyde's *Superscoreboard*.

Gordon Dalziel made a total of 62 appearances for Rangers and scored 15 goals. He picked up a League Cup winners' medal in 1981/82.

DJ
Derek Johnstone
(1970– 1983, 1985–1986)

As the New Year bells rung to welcome in the 1980s, Derek Joseph Johnstone had been there, done it and got a cupboard full of medals as a Rangers player. A first-team debutant at 16 and a League Cup Final winning goalscorer a few weeks later, the big Dundonian had also picked up two domestic Trebles, a Scottish First Division title and a Scottish Cup winners' medal. And to cap it all off Johnstone, aged just 18, had been at the heart of the Rangers defence when they won, to date, their only European trophy.

'I was only a matter of months out of school when I made my debut,' recalled Johnstone. 'Most people think my debut was against Celtic when I scored the winning goal [in the League Cup Final] but it was a few weeks earlier, a game at Ibrox against Cowdenbeath when we won 5-0 and I scored twice. That told me I was now a professional footballer.'

On his Roy of the Rovers heroics in the League Cup Final he said, 'I found out the day before the game that I'd be playing. I was in the dressing room when big Jock came in and took me through to the boot room. Willie Waddell was there and he told me I was playing and to go home and get a good night's sleep. In those days you didn't go to hotels the night before a game. The gaffer gave me four tickets and I told him I'd need more than that as I had six brothers! At that time Rangers hadn't won a trophy for four or five years and in the

271

papers that day, the captains of the teams in the old First Division were asked who would win and 19 of them went for Celtic. It was a fantastic game to play in. Just under 107,000 were there and it was an absolutely magnificent atmosphere.'

Johnstone was coming into a Rangers side packed with experienced players who had endured a tortuous few years as Celtic dominated the Scottish game. His captain was a man who would later manage the club and be voted the Greatest Ever Ranger: John Greig.

'One thing that a club needs is a leader, on and off the park, and Greigy was the leader for Rangers,' said Johnstone. 'When people's heads were down and they needed a lift from somebody, he was the man that did that. He would either kick you up the backside or put his arm around your shoulder. It was a good environment and it was an experienced side to play in. Celtic were in the middle of their nine-in-a-row and the crowds weren't great at Ibrox simply because we were only really winning the odd cup here and there. But the big one is the league and it was then that I learnt that certainly in Glasgow, first was fantastic but second was no use. That's still the case today.'

He added, 'It was drummed into us by the likes of [first-team coach] Jock Wallace that we were here to win things as that's what the club was all about. Basically, if you weren't a winner, you wouldn't be at the club long. The fans and the management team demand that.'

Johnstone's first full campaign in the Rangers first team was season 1971/72. Although the club continued to toil domestically they found form in the European Cup Winners' Cup. Entering the competition by virtue of the fact they had been runners-up in the Scottish Cup against league champions, Celtic, Waddell's side defeated Rennes, Sporting Lisbon, Torino and Bayern Munich to reach the final. There they would face Moscow Dynamo in the iconic Camp Nou in Barcelona.

'1971/72 was the season that we didn't get a sniff of anything domestically,' said Johnstone. 'I don't know if, psychologically, because we were doing so well in Europe we put all our eggs in one basket. Rangers had been to a couple of finals and lost [in 1961 and 1967] so this was the chance for the likes of John Greig and Sandy

Jardine who had been at the club then and won everything apart from a European trophy. After the game Willie Waddell said that people would be talking about this for years to come and we are now coming up to the 50th anniversary of our win. I was part of the only Rangers side that has won a European trophy and that's a wonderful feeling.'

Johnstone, still only 18, had featured in the four ties that immediately preceded the final. He wore the number eight jersey but for the showdown in Catalonia that jersey was handed to Alfie Conn. This did not mean that young Johnstone missed out. Instead he was moved to the heart of the Rangers defence after injuries to Ronnie McKinnon and Colin Jackson. Throughout his career at Rangers, Johnstone would prove his versatility by playing in a number of positions but his first appearance at centre-back came in a league match in Ayrshire.

'That happened when I was 17 and coming back from injury,' he said. 'I was on the bench against Ayr at Somerset Park and Colin Jackson went down injured so Willie Waddell asked me if I'd ever played in defence. I told him I'd play anywhere. I'd played all over the park at school and with my boys' club so I was willing to have a go. I played well and after the game Waddell told me that if I couldn't get a game up front then there was every chance I would get a game at the back instead. As it transpired, I played in midfield as well so I played in all three areas.'

He continued, 'I loved playing centre-half because you were facing the ball all the time. With Dave Smith alongside me, we became one of the first clubs to play the ball out from the back. We wouldn't get the ball and just hoof it forward. In Barcelona it was the first European game that Dave and I played together. Ronnie McKinnon had broken his leg against Sporting Lisbon and Colin Jackson was injured so we were paired together. Dave was a great talker so he talked me through the game. Before it he said just to go for everything and if I missed it, he'd be at my back and that gave me great confidence to go and try and win the ball. I actually managed to get forward and have two or three shots at goal. They played without a centre-forward so Dave and I were left with the ball quite a lot. And when you think about two of our goals it was Dave pushing forward that set them up. They had obviously watched Sandy Jardine and Willie Mathieson and how they liked to attack so decided to play two wingers to stop them coming forward. I watch the game every now and again. We were coasting at 3-0 but took the foot off the gas. They got two goals which gave them a lift but in the end it would have been a travesty if we had been beaten because we were by far the better side. There's no doubt in my mind that it was the best day of my career.'

Johnstone's excellent display earned him a regular berth in the first team in season 1972/73. All but seven of his 45 appearances came at centre-half and he ended the season with a first-ever Scottish Cup medal, Rangers defeating Celtic 3-2 in a match watched by Princess Alexandra.

'In those days the results of the Old Firm games usually decided what was happening in Scottish football,' recalled Johnstone. 'If you won both games in the league [prior to league reconstruction in 1975, teams only played each other once at home and once away each season] you would most likely win the league and if you beat them in the cup, there was every chance you would win the cup as well.

'It was different in the early 1980s when the competition was ferocious. Apart from Celtic, the 'New Firm' of Aberdeen and Dundee United were dominant. Aberdeen won the European Cup Winners' Cup and United won the Premier Division championship in 1982/83 so there was a real challenge then. Celtic were the kingpins as they had the best players but although we had the likes of McCloy, Jardine, Jackson, Russell and, of course, Coop, there were a lot of players coming to the end of their career.

'Maybe the club could have freshened things up a bit earlier and we did bring in the likes of Ian Redford and some other young players. But other teams strengthened as well. Winning cups is great and we did that but as far as Rangers were concerned, it was getting harder and harder to win the league. In the end something had to be done as, apart from the Celtic games, the support was dwindling. People want to see a winning Rangers side and the board realised that, which kick-started the Souness revolution.'

Johnstone added a First Division title medal to his collection in season 1974/75 and another six medals followed when he was an integral part of the teams that secured the domestic Treble in 1975/76 and 1977/78. By the latter part of the decade he played more often than not at centre-forward and in 1977/78 he was top scorer in the Premier Division with 25 goals. A further 12 goals in the two cup competitions earned Johnstone the inaugural SPFA Player-of-the-Year award.

'It was a fantastic season, probably my best,' remembered Johnstone. 'But what a team we had, probably one of the best Rangers sides ever. We had Tommy McLean on one wing and Davie Cooper on the other and that's what I needed. I was never going to be the player that picked the ball up 30 yards out, beat three men and hit the ball into the net from 20 yards. My game was getting in the box and when wingers got to the by-line and crossed the ball in, I had to be on the end of it. I depended on ammunition coming in from both wings and I got that.'

He continued, 'We were one of the first teams to play a 4-4-1-1 formation as Gordon Smith never played up alongside me. He used to play in behind me and in that season we scored 63 goals between us. Smithy was a great foil for me because any time big Peter [McCloy] would lump the ball forward, he would read the situation knowing I was going to knock the ball on. He would make his run and nine times out of ten, he would stick the ball in the back of the net. The Treble side were fantastic. We never gave in and we were relentless. That's what big Jock instilled in to us.'

Season 1977/78 was the debut season at Ibrox for Davie Cooper and, in common with the majority of players from that era, Johnstone rates the winger as the best player he played with.

'It's a question I'm always asked but, without a shadow of a doubt, Coop is the best I've played with,' stated Johnstone. 'He was just a genius with the ball. He wasn't great in the air, wasn't the quickest and didn't have a right foot but I tell them that neither did [Jim] Baxter.

'He's one of the best players that ever played for the club. Umpteen times he'd get the ball and get you out of trouble by taking the ball, beating three men then laying it off for someone to score. He was just magnificent at doing that.'

Despite such a successful campaign both individually and collectively, the summer of 1978 saw the winds of change gusting through Ibrox. Jock Wallace abdicated his throne and joined Leicester City, captain John Greig replaced him at the helm and Johnstone was contemplating a future away from Rangers. He eventually resisted offers from Arsenal to stay at Ibrox and he was appointed as captain by the new manager.

'I've heard stories that I was only going to stay if I was captain but that's nonsense,' said Derek emphatically. 'In the first team I was never a big shouter. If I didn't get the ball in from a wide situation I would have a quiet word with the wingers but I was never like Greigy who was very passionate, getting in and about players. Being made captain didn't appeal to me but when I was offered it I said yes. It was a real honour. When you look at the players that have captained the club, it's great to say that you were once the captain as well. When you go into the Blue Room [at Ibrox] there are paintings of all the captains of the club and my face is up there, which is wonderful.'

Under his leadership, Rangers won a cup double in season 1978/79 – Johnstone scoring twice in the Scottish Cup Final second replay against Hibernian – but he was a reluctant leader. The first trophy he held aloft, though, was the League Cup and an incident in the final against Aberdeen can be pinpointed as the starting point for the bad blood that still exists between the clubs to this day.

'Doug Rougvie took me out, it's as simple as that,' stated Johnstone. 'It was a sending off without a shadow of a doubt. Alex Ferguson absolutely slaughtered me and said that's why Aberdeen lost the final. A manager will always stick up for his players but he knew what happened, I knew what happened and, more importantly, the referee knew what happened.'

He added, 'It was always good to win the Scottish Cup as you go away on holiday on a high and come back on a high. The first two games [against Hibernian] were just hard-fought games. Hibs were a good side and we felt we could hit them on the break but it didn't work. The third game was a terrific game and I was fortunate enough to score two goals. The winning goal was an own goal by Arthur Duncan. He went to clear the ball but put it in his own net. I was waiting just behind him to complete my hat-trick. We had a really good party after that at the Orchard Park Hotel in Giffnock but I think we were glad we had finally won it. We didn't want to come back for a fourth time which would have happened as back then there wouldn't be penalties to decide the winner.'

Season 1979/80 was, by comparison, abysmal. Rangers finished fifth in the league, lost 5-1 on aggregate to Aberdeen in the third round of the League Cup and were denied a third successive Scottish Cup by Celtic in a final marred by crowd trouble. Johnstone made 47 appearances and scored 21 goals, one of which was in the Scottish Cup semi-final against eventual Premier Division champions, Aberdeen.

'The Scottish Cup semi-final was at Celtic Park and it was a great game,' said Johnstone. 'I think it was the first time the Rangers fans had been in "the Jungle" and I scored the winner. I got the ball and turned Willie Miller on a sixpence and hit the ball into the net. It took a slight deflection but it was going in anyway. I remember running over to "the Jungle" to celebrate with the Rangers fans but I wouldn't have done that in an Old Firm game as the Celtic fans would have been there!'

The one shining light in an otherwise dismal season was the final of the Drybrough Cup against Celtic. Rangers won 3-1 in a match that was illuminated by a flash of brilliance from Davie Cooper.

'People tend to forget that that day Sandy Jardine ran fully 50 yards with the ball and cracked it in the back of the net,' recalled Derek. 'But Coop's goal was just exceptional. The way he just lobbed it over the heads of the defenders and stuck it in the net was absolutely magnificent. Unfortunately, there was a television strike at that time so the game wasn't televised. But someone had a camera behind the goal and managed to film Coop lobbing the three players and scoring.'

He added, 'Coop was a wee bit like Kenny Dalglish. When Kenny was interviewed people would see him as being dour and Coop was like that, but like Kenny, he had a great sense of humour. You always knew if Coop was going to have a good game as we had a TV in the dressing room and he always had a bet on the 2pm race. If his horse won you knew you were going to get a good game from him that day! He was a genius but he didn't just do it in the big games, he did it in all the games. That was the attitude he had. Ruud Gullit, who was one of the top three players in the world at that time, rated Coop that highly that he said he could have played in any team in the world.'

For the majority of the following season, 1980/81, Johnstone played at centre-half with Colin McAdam, a summer signing from Partick Thistle, at centre-forward. However, when it came to the Scottish Cup Final replay against Dundee United, Johnstone was pushed forward.

'I was dropped for the first game,' recalled Derek. 'There was a supporters' function the Sunday before the game that I went to and when I came in for training on the Monday, I was a wee bit under the weather. Greigy sent me home from training and left me out of the cup final.'

He continued, 'In the replay Bobby Russell was just superb. For two or three seasons when he played well, we played well. He was absolutely outstanding when we beat PSV Eindhoven in the European Cup in 1978. He demanded the ball and the way he used it and passed it was magnificent. Bobby and Coop had a wee rapport with each other. When Coop had the ball, Russell would make a run forward and Coop would always find him. He didn't have to look at times, he knew where he was.'

Rangers were captained to victory by Ally Dawson. Johnstone had relinquished the armband at the start of the season after a meeting with John Greig.

'I suggested Greigy would have been better getting one of the young lads to do it and he chose Ally,' remembered Derek. 'At that time we were doing well in cup finals but were finishing third and fourth in the league. We were so far behind. In the 82/83 season we brought in John McClelland, Jim Bett and Robert Prytz, better players, but we still didn't do well enough in the league. There were six or seven really good sides in the league which made it really competitive. You win the league because you are consistent. Even when you're not playing well you've still got to take the points and Celtic were one of the best teams at doing that.'

He continued, 'What also didn't help was that the stadium had to be redeveloped, particularly after the disaster in 1971. It had to be done but it was probably the biggest reason we weren't successful as we couldn't spend big [in the transfer market] as money had to be invested to build the new stands.'

Rangers struggled again for that consistency Johnstone spoke of in season 1981/82 although they did reach both cup finals. In the Scottish Cup Greig's side succumbed to Aberdeen after extra time but in the League Cup, the other half of the 'New Firm', Dundee United, were vanquished 2-1 thanks to a late goal from Ian Redford.

'He was a smashing player,' said Johnstone who played against United but missed out against Aberdeen. 'He came from Dundee but was a young lad that wasn't frightened of coming to a bigger club. He loved a tackle, even in training. He took training as if it was a game on a Saturday. He would get stuck in and would have shots at goal from daft angles. His goal [against United] was a cheeky wee goal but we weren't surprised when it went in because he did that kind of thing in training. It wasn't the greatest of games but we got the cup and our medals, and our fans went home happy and had a good weekend because they'd just watched us win the cup.'

He added, 'To play against Aberdeen and their two big, solid centre-backs, McLeish and Miller, you had to be physically good enough to challenge them or you would struggle. We needed players that were 100% and I don't think I trained that well that week or even trained at all. I didn't complain about it [not being selected] because I realised myself that I wasn't fit enough to start the game.'

Although Rangers were struggling on the field this did not have a detrimental effect on the dressing room dynamic at Ibrox. There was always a camaraderie amongst the players and Johnstone loved the atmosphere created by the 20-plus players that made up the first-team squad.

'The main thing you miss [when you finish playing] is the banter in the dressing room,' noted Johnstone. 'The fun you have is unbelievable and that's what you miss. It's wonderful playing in the games but an hour in the dressing room, whether it's during the week or before or after the game, was great. That's why most footballers have a sense of humour; you have to, you have to learn quickly or you would get absolutely slaughtered. It was just players having a dig at one another, there was nothing personal in it. It was just having a laugh.'

He continued, 'Even when we were struggling the dressing room was good. It has to be. You'll always get the odd fight as you'll never get everyone getting on and players got angry with each other. There was at least one fight a week, either in the dressing room or on the training ground. Big Jock realised that and knew we had to get it out of our system. In training there might be a hard tackle and the players would grab each other's shirts but big Jock was really clever when it happened. He would let them go and have their spat but then make sure when they were done it was finished. He handled players so well.'

In season 1982/83 Johnstone donned the number nine jersey for 11 of the opening 13 league matches. But thereafter he played just five times in the Premier Division. His time at Ibrox appeared to be at an end.

'I had a lot of injuries and had my ankle strapped up for training every day and my knees needed strapping up at times too,' recalled Derek. 'I think Greigy realised I was in the treatment room more than I was on the training ground. It was inevitable that I was going to leave. It was probably the worst feeling I ever had in the world, leaving the club, but when your time was up, your time was up. You can't go on forever.'

He added, 'Like he did with all players, Greigy spoke to me privately in his office. He said he had a lot of younger players coming through and I wasn't going to get many games. He said he had spoken to Chelsea who wanted to come up and have a look at me so he was going to play me in the next couple of games.'

Johnstone must have impressed as he signed for a Chelsea side who, under John Neal, were languishing in the old Second Division. But Derek realised fairly quickly that his move to London was the wrong one.

'I realised after a couple of training sessions how much I missed Rangers Football Club and everything about it,' said Johnstone. 'I think I only got three or four games for Chelsea. The injuries continued down there, they were never going to go away. I enjoyed the London scene and, like the Rangers fans, the Chelsea supporters were very passionate. But I wanted to play. At Rangers I never really sat on the bench but it was happening a lot at Chelsea. So when I got the chance to come back to Scotland I grabbed it with both hands.'

Johnstone's return to Scotland was a month-long loan at Dundee United. He made his debut against Morton at Tannadice on 26 October 1983, scoring twice in a 3-0 win. Derek made a total of six appearances in tangerine, with the spell affording him an opportunity he had never had up until that point in his career: to play against Rangers.

'The last game of the loan spell was against Rangers at Ibrox,' recalled Johnstone. '[United manager] Jim McLean asked me if he picked me was I going to try! I told him that of course I would try so he put me on the bench. It was 0-0 midway through the second half and Jim asked me if I wanted to go on so I went out and did my warm up. When I came back I actually went and sat in the Rangers dugout by mistake. As I sat down big Jock said to me, "Hey you, get tae f**k." The punters behind the dugout were laughing and I got some stick from them. Eventually I got on but didn't really get a chance and it ended up 0-0. The Rangers fans were great to me but, although it was only for 15 minutes or so, it was still strange to play against Rangers.'

Although the loan spell at Tannadice gave Johnstone the opportunity to get some game time it did little to enhance his chances of making more appearances for Chelsea. He eventually made his first-team debut on 25 February 1984 against Carlisle United, coming on as substitute for Tony McAndrew, but he was a bit-part player as the London side secured their return to the First Division. His only other appearance that season was also from the bench, a 2-1 win over Blackburn at Stamford Bridge. Over a year after signing, Johnstone eventually made his first start for Chelsea in a 1-1 draw against Sheffield Wednesday on 8 December 1984. But when he appeared as a substitute the following weekend it would be the last time he would wear a Chelsea jersey. A month later he answered a call from a former manager to sound him out about a return to Ibrox.

'Jock called me and asked me if I wanted to come back,' stated Johnstone. 'He said to me that I might not get a lot of first-team games but he was going to try and use me to bring the kids through in the reserves. He said it was great having a coach on the park talking to players and that appealed to me. I thoroughly enjoyed it. He said I would cover in the first team if there were suspensions and injuries but I was essentially an on-field reserve-team coach.'

Johnstone's second stint at Ibrox amounted to 23 first-team appearances and one goal, the second in a 2-0 win over Morton at Ibrox in February 1985. He made his second debut against Aberdeen at Pittodrie and it was an inauspicious return.

'I think I only won there a couple of times as a player,' recalled Derek. 'Normally after the game you would go straight into the dressing room and into the bath but that day, Jock told us all to sit down. He said he was fed up telling us how to do things properly so he wanted us to tell him what had gone wrong that day. He started with Peter McCloy and said he didn't want anyone else joining in. He went right through the team and everyone was making excuses and saying it wasn't their fault. The last player to speak was Davie Cooper. He stood up and said he wanted to apologise to the boss, the management team and all the players because he must have had a f*****g nightmare. He was the only one to say it was his fault and everyone then started laughing.'

The goal against Morton may well have been Johnstone's last league goal but it wasn't his last goal for the club. That came in a reserve game at Lesser Hampden against Queen's Park from the penalty spot.

'That was the only penalty I've ever taken,' stated Johnstone. 'It was 1-1 and we got the penalty in the last minute and I scored. It was in front of about 500 fans.'

The principal penalty-taker at Ibrox at that time was one Alistair McCoist and he and Johnstone struck up a friendship that endures to this day. The banter between the two has been well publicised. From McCoist flashing his MBE only to be shot down when DJ showed him his European Cup Winners' Cup medal to the ongoing debate about why McCoist scored more goals than Johnstone, the repartee has been razor sharp. But there is a mutual respect too and Johnstone rates McCoist as one of the best goalscorers Scotland has ever produced.

'In his early days, it wasn't happening for him and he was missing chances,' recalled Johnstone. 'The one thing about Ally was he might have missed chances but he always came back to miss another one. He wasn't one of these players who hid if it wasn't going for him. He would always put himself forward, get involved with the play and work even harder if it wasn't going well for him. You would always find if he missed a couple of chances, he'd score with the third. That's why he scored 355 goals for Rangers because he didn't give in.'

He added, 'He's not the biggest player in the world – about 5ft 9in or 5ft 10in – and wasn't the best in the air. The majority of his goals were on the ground but he scored different goals, goals from 25 yards, tap-ins. He was one of these centre-forwards who was always in the right place at the right time and when he got half a chance he stuck it in the back of the net. For me, without a shadow of a doubt, he is the best striker Rangers have produced. If you compare Alfredo Morelos and Ally, Morelos is a more physical player and is a pest for centre-halves. He has to battle as he's up against two centre-halves every week. They are different types of player; Ally was a natural goalscorer and while Morelos misses chances like Ally did, Ally put the majority of his chances away. That's the main difference between them.'

But while McCoist would be an integral part of the new era when Graeme Souness arrived in 1986, Derek's time as a Rangers player was up for a second time.

'I remember his words to me,' said Johnstone. 'He used to change in the referee's room at Ibrox and he brought me in and said I'd had a fair shot at it but he was going to rebuild the side. He said we were going to be great again but to do that he needed to build a young team. I accepted that and it was a disappointment. But I knew what he was trying to do and it worked as in his first season Rangers won the league playing a lot of great football.'

After leaving Rangers Johnstone stayed in Glasgow, moving to Partick Thistle, where he took on the role of player-manager. When trying his hand at management, Derek could draw on the experience and management styles he himself had encountered as a player. He had played under Willie Waddell, Jock Wallace, John Greig, Jim McLean and John Neal, but Wallace was the man who stood out above all the rest.

'If we weren't doing it and were being beaten at half-time, he would give you a roasting,' said Johnstone. 'He had me by the throat a couple of times because I'd cost us a goal or missed a chance. But when you got back into training on the Monday morning it was all forgotten. He would come over and give you a hug and he never held grudges. You would get your telling off and then you would move on. Everybody got it at one stage during a season but by the following week it was finished. He would even give you a wee kiss sometimes.'

One thing Johnstone was averse to when it came to Wallace, though, was his training methods, particularly on the undulating sand dunes at Gullane.

'I absolutely hated it,' was his assertion when the topic came up in conversation. 'If I could get out of it I did, and I managed that once. I had a wee niggly injury so I phoned up and say that I was ill but he absolutely slaughtered me for it. The next day when I went in, while everyone else got a relaxing day, he took me out on to the track at Ibrox and he ran the bollocks off me. I never missed another one after that. It was hard. Going up and down the sand dunes takes so much out of you. In those days you probably had six weeks off so most of the single lads would be away in Spain on burgers and beer. You had to obviously work hard to get the extra weight off so after three or four days running round the track, he would take you to Gullane. It was hard at the time but you felt so much better for doing it. Rangers won so many games in the last ten minutes because we were fitter than most teams and that was down to Jock.'

He added, 'If we didn't have a midweek game we used to have a Monday off. On the Tuesday we would come in and do a 40-minute running session round the track. During that you never walked at all. Your rest periods were when you jogged. We would go up and down the terracing as well. But by the end of the week you would feel great. Jock would know when we had had enough, though. Sandy Jardine and Alex MacDonald led the two groups and they set the pace as they were the two fittest players at the club. He could gauge if they got tired then we had to stop.'

But Johnstone's time in charge at Firhill did not work out. He lasted just eight months.

'I realised very quickly that it [management] wasn't for me,' said Johnstone. 'I had never gone down to [the SFA Coaching Centre] Largs and got any certificates or had experience of handling players. But I got a call one day from Ken Bates who owned Chelsea and Thistle. He asked me to come in as a player-coach which suited me. I brought John Haggart, who had been at Rangers and Hearts, in and he did most of the coaching. My injuries were still bad so I didn't play that much and we didn't win too many games. If you don't win games, you're under pressure and that's exactly what happened.'

Johnstone's active involvement in football ended when he left Thistle but he had already started eking out a career in the media before that. He had been working with Radio Clyde alongside Richard Park since the end of season 1985/86 and today, over 30 years later, he is still an integral part of the *Superscoreboard* team. He is also back at Ibrox, having been appointed as a club ambassador in June 2018.

'It was 50 years since I had signed an 'S' form for the club so it was great when I got the chance to be an ambassador,' stated Derek proudly. 'I'm enjoying the job and I've come in at a great time. With Steven Gerrard and Gary McAllister, I'm certainly looking forward to the coming years.'

Derek Johnstone made 643 appearances for Rangers and scored 229 goals. He won three league titles (1974/75, 1975/76 and 1977/78), five Scottish Cup medals (1972/73, 1975/76, 1977/78, 1978/79 and 1980/81) and four League Cup medals (1975/76, 1977/78, 1978/79 and 1981/82). He also won a European Cup Winners' Cup medal in season 1971/72.

Fergie (2)
Iain Ferguson (1984–1986)

The Rangers career of Iain John Ferguson was short, and for one season at least, sweet. Signed from Dundee at the age of 22, Ferguson had shot to prominence the previous season with several stellar displays against the Light Blues, scoring twice in a 3-2 league win for Dundee at Dens Park in October 1983, the equaliser in a 2-2 Scottish Cup fifth-round draw at the same venue in March and then another brace in the replay as Dundee denied Rangers a ninth successive appearance in the Scottish Cup Final with a 3-2 win. The fact he also had a good track record against Celtic – including a double in an emphatic 5-1 win for Dundee when he was just 16 – added further evidence that Rangers had seemingly snared themselves a sharpshooter.

'I signed for Dundee on my 13th birthday on schoolboy forms and was top scorer there for about three or four years,' recalled Ferguson. 'There were no youth teams at that time so after a couple of years I went straight into the reserves and was eventually good enough to go to the first team. It was a great learning experience and it was a great place to start playing professionally. We had the likes of Cammy Fraser, John Brown, Stewart McKimmie and Tosh McKinlay playing for us and Willie Wallace, one of the Lisbon Lions, would take us for shooting practice.'

Ferguson's goals were soon generating interest from other clubs, amongst them his boyhood heroes, Rangers. And following a day on the golf course and a night on the town with his Dundee team-mates, he received the call to go to Ibrox.

'There had been a lot of paper talk about Rangers coming to sign me,' said Ferguson. 'Archie Knox was the manager at Dundee and he was in my fourball down at Gullane golf course. At the time Brian Clough, the Nottingham Forest manager, had also been linked with me but Archie told me to ignore what was in the papers as no one had been in touch. He wanted me to sign a new contract but I decided to take a chance and try and get a move.'

He continued, 'After the golf day we went back to Dundee for a few drinks and I got back to my digs about 3 or 4 in the morning. My landlady woke me at 9am and said I had a phone call. She didn't know who it was but it was [Rangers assistant manager] Alex Totten. He told me big Jock wanted me to come down and sign for Rangers so I went upstairs, had a shower then drove down to Ibrox.'

On arrival at Ibrox Ferguson was met by Messrs Wallace and Totten and asked if he wanted to sign for Glasgow Rangers. When he said 'yes' he was presented with a contract and asked to sign it.

'I had only ever signed one contract before in my life, which was a four-year deal with Dundee,' explained Ferguson. 'That had come to its conclusion so I went into Ibrox on my own – there were no agents in those days – and signed without knowing what the terms were. I left Ibrox and drove to my parents' house, still unsure what had happened. I went in and my dad asked how I was doing and if everything was okay and I told him I was reasonably certain I had just signed for Rangers!'

Iain Ferguson's signing broke the mould. In this pre-Bosman era he was the first player to sign for Rangers under freedom of contract. The transfer fee was eventually set by a tribunal at £220,000. And Ferguson barely had time to draw breath before he was getting suited and booted and going on tour with his new team-mates. A boys' holiday in Ibiza was kyboshed and instead of travelling to the party paradise, Ferguson joined his new team-mates for a world tour of Australia, Canada and New Zealand.

'The good thing about the tour for me was getting to know the boys,' recalled Ferguson. 'I knew Coisty and big Nicky [Walker], who is my daughter's godfather, and a couple of the other boys having played with them for Scotland U18s and U21s. It started with a 23-

hour flight from Heathrow to Melbourne and the first thing we did when we landed was to go out and have a few drinks. It was a good way to meet the boys and I got a few games under my belt.'

Ferguson played in eight of the nine matches, scoring his first goal for the club against Australia B, and he continued on the goal trail on the pre-season tour of West Germany. He scored five goals against Einsiedeln, a double in a 5-1 win over FC Grenchen and the opening goal against 1.FC Kaiserslautern. And back on Scottish shores it was Ferguson's penalty that got Rangers on the scoreboard in a 2-2 against Gary Lineker's Leicester City.

Rangers had been somewhat shot-shy in season 1983/84. Only 53 league goals had been scored, only three more than third-bottom Dundee, while champions Aberdeen scored 78. Top scorer was Sandy Clark with a meagre nine goals. It looked, however, that Jock Wallace had unearthed the answer to his side's goalscoring problems.

However, the spate of goals from Iain Ferguson soon dried up. He chalked up just two in the opening 19 Premier Division matches, one against former club Dundee in September and the other against St Mirren in October.

'When I went through phases in my career when I scored goals I always gave the credit to the players that were giving me the ball,' said Ferguson. 'At that time, though, we weren't scoring many goals as a team and the other strikers like Coisty, Bobby Williamson and John MacDonald, really good players, didn't have a great goalscoring record either. As a collective unit we probably had too many players that didn't click at the right time. For example, Cammy Fraser and I had a great relationship at Dundee but we couldn't reproduce the same with Rangers. One of the other reasons why we weren't successful was the number of permutations we had up front; we never really had a settled partnership.'

Iain found more favour with the cup competitions, though. A goal in the first leg of the he Skol League Cup semi-final against Meadowbank Thistle, his first competitive strike at Ibrox, was the prelude to the winning goal in the final against Dundee United. In the UEFA Cup he was Man of the Match as his brace of goals helped a valiant Rangers beat Inter Milan 3-1 at Ibrox.

'The first trophy that was available was the Skol Cup and we won it so we couldn't have been doing everything badly,' said Ferguson. 'The biggest factor was when John McClelland left. He was looking for £10,000 a year for a four-year deal but he didn't get it. We had beaten United on the Sunday and John made his final appearance against Inter Milan on the Wednesday. I don't think he was really replaced.'

However, less than three weeks after the match-winning display against a giant of the European game, Ferguson was playing in the Rangers reserve team. He featured against Aberdeen in the semi-final of the Reserve League Cup, missing a penalty in the shoot-out, and was on the scoresheet when his header earned the second string a point against Dundee United on 1 December.

'I've heard people say that the strip can be too heavy for you but I don't think that was the case with me,' said Ferguson. 'I was the type of striker who could link up play – I had a good first touch – and then I would get in the box and try and score. When things went badly I think I paid the price more than most. Maybe I lost my place in the team and others kept theirs because they did run around the park more than I did. In the League Cup Final I got substituted even though I scored the winning goal. And against Inter Milan, when we needed a couple of goals to go through, big Jock took me off again.'

He continued, 'We played a game against Aberdeen and I had been out the picture for a while. I didn't think I'd even be on the bench. I had put a bet on something like four races between 2pm and 3pm and I was planning to watch them on the TV we had in the dressing room. But big Jock put me on the bench and I lost a stud out of my boot on the way out. I came back in to get one and when I came back out the tunnel I got a huge cheer. The Rangers fans were always good to me.'

Ferguson was on the mark again a week later, netting twice in a 4-1 win for the reserves over Hearts at Tynecastle, and he added another double in a 3-2 loss to Morton. This scoring streak earned him a return to the top team and Ferguson notched the opening goal in a 4-2 win over Dumbarton at Boghead on 29 December. A double followed at his old stomping ground, Dens Park, in January and it looked like the spell in the reserves had reinvigorated Ferguson. However, when he scored Rangers' only goal in a 2-1 defeat against Hibernian at Ibrox a week later, this would prove to be his sixth and last Premier Division goal of the season.

'Our reserve team would have beaten the first team at that time,' said Ferguson. 'We had the likes of Cammy Fraser, Derek Johnstone, Robert Prtyz, Ted McMinn and Bobby Russell so they would never have played both teams against each other. They would put both teams up in the dressing room and there was one game when I was only on the bench for the reserves. I wasn't happy but I didn't kick off. Big Jock and Rangers Football Club had all my respect.'

Ferguson was hampered by a hamstring injury that sidelined him for three matches early in 1985 but he returned to the first-team fold in time to face former club Dundee in the fourth round of the Scottish Cup. He came off the bench to replace John MacDonald but could not muster an equalising goal as Rangers exited the competition, losing 1-0 in a match that was the nadir of Ally McCoist's Rangers career.

'Coisty was a phenomenon but that day all the chances fell to him and he had a day to forget,' noted Ferguson. 'Coisty had a suit of armour but no matter what I did the ball just wouldn't fall for me. If I ran to the front post, the ball would go to Coisty at the back post.'

Ferguson scored again for the reserve team as they lost in the Second XI Cup against Motherwell two days after the cup exit and then played in eight of the final ten Premier Division matches. In total Iain made 39 appearances for the first team in his first season and scored 11 goals. Rangers managed to muster just 46 league goals in a dismal campaign that resulted in a fourth-place finish, a mammoth 21 points adrift of champions Aberdeen.

Things did not get much rosier in the Ferguson garden at the outset of season 1985/86 either. He did not play at all in any of the first-team friendlies; instead he was in scoring action for the reserves against North Uist, scoring twice in a 13-1 win, and four times in a 10-0 victory over Wigtown. A brace in the final friendly for the second string against Falkirk followed but the scoring burst could not nudge Iain ahead of McCoist and Williamson in the first team. He only played in one of the opening 24 Premier Division matches and, in the League Cup, he only turned out as sub against Clyde before starting the goalless draw against Forfar Athletic. By the time that match went to penalties, Rangers winning 6-5, Ferguson had been substituted.

'Big Jock put me on the transfer list but a move away didn't happen,' said Ferguson. 'I know having spoken to Walter Smith that Dundee United were interested and that Jim McLean had always wanted to sign me but I don't think they met Rangers' asking price.'

No matter how well he did in the second team, Iain Ferguson could not earn a regular slot in the first XI. He netted 12 goals in 24 reserve-team appearances and picked up another winners' medal, scoring the fifth goal in a 5-0 win over Queen's Park in the Glasgow Cup Final. First-team appearances were at a premium, though, and over the course of the campaign, Ferguson made just six appearances, starting only twice.

After a couple of substitute appearances in the early months of 1986, Iain made a return to the first-team starting XI in April for a friendly against Tottenham Hotspur. It proved to be a fateful Friday for the man who signed him for Rangers, Jock Wallace. After an abysmal 2-0 defeat Wallace was sacked and replaced by Graeme Souness. The arrival of Souness could, however, have offered Iain Ferguson a chance to resurrect his Rangers career. But initial signs were not positive.

'Truth be told, I don't think any of us thought we had a chance [of staying at Rangers],' said Ferguson. 'Souness walked in and said that everyone apart from Coop was being sold. My football career had stagnated at that time and it was made very clear to me that I wasn't going to get a game. I really didn't see any light at the end of the tunnel.'

Ferguson was not part of the first-team party that travelled to West Germany for the pre-season tour and instead played for the reserves, notably scoring a hat-trick in a 4-0 win over Troon Juniors at Portland Park. Those goals did nothing to help in his fight for a first-team place and when Rangers opened up their Premier Division campaign against Hibernian in Edinburgh, Ferguson remained in Glasgow. He was not playing for the Rangers Reserves, though; he was coming on as substitute for Dundee in their 1-0 defeat against Celtic at Parkhead.

'I went to Dundee on loan because wee Fleckie [Robert Fleck] knocked them back,' remembered Ferguson. 'He was supposed to be going for £25,000 and Fleckie asked me about the move. I told him if he went there and did well it could be a stepping stone for him. He gambled and decided not to go and it worked out well for him. [Dundee manager] Jocky Scott, who I'd played with at Dundee, asked about me instead. I was supposed to be there for a year but I only played three games.'

He added, 'I got a phone call from Walter and he told me that Rangers had accepted an offer for me from Dundee United. I was a Dundee boy so I told him I wasn't going there. Walter convinced me to go and talk to Jim McLean, though, and he offered me a four-year deal. I still didn't want to sign but I went and had a medical. When I got back to my digs, Jocky Scott phoned and asked if I was still playing for Dundee that night [against St Mirren]. I said I was and went out and scored!'

Jim McLean was not one for giving up easily, though. His pursuit of Ferguson continued until he eventually convinced him to swap a blue jersey for a tangerine one.

Ferguson said, 'I played for Dundee on the Saturday against Hibs and scored again only for Walter to call and say the loan had been cut short and I was to be back at Rangers on the Monday morning. I had got my confidence back and walked back into the first-team dressing room at Ibrox to see the likes of Terry Butcher and Chris Woods there. But Walter came in and told me to go down to the reserve dressing room. Even then had someone told me Rangers wanted me I would've stayed.'

Ferguson played in a reserve game soon after his return – the striker injured his ankle – but after the game Walter Smith came to see him in the dressing room. Jim McLean had been in attendance and had intimated to his former assistant manager that he still wanted Ferguson to go to Tayside.

'I was still adamant that I wasn't going to United,' said Ferguson, 'but eventually I decided that I would go as I needed to be playing games. I drove up to Tannadice and left my girlfriend in the car as I thought I would only be about ten minutes. McLean asked me if I wanted to sign for Dundee United and when I said "no" he said "good answer, because if you had said yes I was going to send you away". He told me to go and get my girlfriend while he put the kettle on then come back and he'd tell me why I should sign for United. People were critical of him but had he come to Rangers [when he was offered the manager's job in October 1983] Ibrox would have been a completely different place.'

The move to Dundee United revitalised Iain Ferguson's career. By the end of the 1986/87 season he had scored 16 league goals in 36 appearances. He also found the net against Rangers in the Skol League Cup semi-final and netted memorable goals against Barcelona – he remains the last Scot to score in the Nou Camp – and Borussia Monchengladbach as United made it to the UEFA Cup Final. A double against former club Dundee in the Scottish Cup semi-final further ingratiated him with the United supporters.

'When I left Rangers I was happy to leave but I would have walked straight back,' said Ferguson. 'Big Jock bought me for Rangers but didn't play me. I never asked him why. I had huge respect for him and wouldn't say a bad word about him. But I think I proved at United that had I been given the opportunity at Rangers, there is no reason why I couldn't have done the same thing. Having come there as the big signing, I don't really think I was given the opportunity. I'm not bitter, though.'

He added, 'That year [1986/87] there was a chance I could have gone from Rangers to sign for the West German team, Rot-Weiss Essen. They were a massive club but had just been relegated from the Bundesliga. I went out for a trial spell for two days. It was a fantastic set-up and I did well but they didn't make me an offer. That same season Rangers played Borussia Monchengladbach in the UEFA Cup. They lost and United played Borussia in the semi-finals. I scored the first goal in Germany and we won 2-0 and I'd like to think the guy at Rot-Weiss Essen was watching. Things happen for a reason but I have no doubt that my style of play would have suited their football better than it did in Scotland.'

Ferguson spent season 1987/88 at Tannadice too, netting 11 league goals, including the winner against Rangers in October. He scored in a 3-0 win over Dundee in the second replay of the Scottish Cup quarter-final and struck again to oust Aberdeen in the semi-final. However, for the second successive year United lost in the final, despite leading for the majority of the match.

Iain left Dundee United for Hearts in the close season of 1988 for a fee of £350,000 and continued his knack of scoring high-profile goals in his two seasons at Tynecastle. He scored in Hearts' 2-0 win over Rangers in December 1988 and thundered in a 25-yard winner in a UEFA Cup tie against Bayern Munich. However, the return of John Robertson from Newcastle United effectively ended Iain's time in Edinburgh and he moved to Motherwell in 1990.

'I had been signed to replace Robbo and was top scorer in the league when he came back,' said Ferguson. 'Alex MacDonald pulled me aside the night before he came back and told me I had done really well but Robbo was coming back and I was being moved on. I knocked back Aberdeen and went on loan to Bristol City and Charlton. Joe Jordan wanted to sign me for Bristol Rovers but the deal fell through and my time at Charlton was cut short when I got brought back to Tynecastle when Wayne Foster got injured.'

Ferguson was part of the Motherwell team that won the Scottish Cup in 1991, demonstrating again his ability to turn up for the big occasions by scoring in the final which, ironically, was against Dundee United.

'I wasn't everybody's cup of tea as a player but I proved a point most of the time,' said Ferguson. 'In big games I turned up. I didn't play any differently in games against the bigger teams than I did against the smaller teams but some boys just couldn't play in front of full houses. I had been used to that since I was 15 when I played for Scotland schoolboys at a packed Wembley. Admittedly I'm disappointed I never got a goal in the Old Firm games, although I only played in about three or four of them.'

Ferguson left Fir Park in 1993 and had spells at Airdrie and Portadown before coming full circle and having another season with Dundee in 1996/97. Today he is business development manager at

Rock Sport Radio and is involved in matchday hospitality at Ibrox. He is also part of the commentary team for Rangers TV.

'I don't ever talk about my time at Rangers being bad,' concluded Ferguson. 'It was a fantastic opportunity and although it might have come too early in my career, there's never a bad time to sign for Rangers. I'm proud to have played for Glasgow Rangers and there are not many people out there that can say they've scored a winning goal in a cup final. Once you've made history, no one can ever take it away.'

Iain Ferguson made 71 appearances for Rangers and scored 23 goals. He won a League Cup winners' medal in 1984/85 and a Glasgow Cup medal in 1985/86. He was also part of the team that won the Premier Reserve League Championship in season 1985/86.

Flash
Mark Walters (1987–1991)

Mark Everton Walters arrived in Glasgow to sign for Rangers on 31 December 1987. Born in Birmingham on 2 June 1964, Walters had been on the books at his boyhood heroes Aston Villa since his school days, making his first-team debut at the age of 17. But he was tempted north by Graeme Souness, who beat off competition from Everton and Derby County to secure the Englishman's signature for £500,000.

'In my first year at Villa we won the First Division and I trained a couple of times with the first team,' said Walters when we met in East Kilbride while he was promoting his autobiography, *Wingin' It*. 'In the second year I always trained with the first-team lads who went on to win the European Cup. I made my debut against Leeds United a month before Villa played in the European Cup Final. On the day of my debut I walked to the ground from my mum's house as I didn't have a driver's licence at that time. I was named as sub and when I came on I touched the ball about three or four times and I remember the crowd shouting my name.

'I was supposed to be going to Germany a few weeks later to play for the youth team but I was hoping I wouldn't get picked so I could go instead with the first team to Rotterdam [for the European Cup Final]. But I didn't make the final squad.'

Mark made more inroads to the Villa first team in season 1982/83 and was part of the squad that faced Barcelona in the final of the European Super Cup.

'They had Maradona at that time but fortunately for us he wasn't playing as he was injured,' recalled Walters. 'Without him Barcelona weren't as good and we beat them.'

Performances such as that against the Catalans shot Walters to prominence and he was soon regarded as one of the top players in the English top flight. By 1987 teams were starting to show an interest in him and, from a personal point of view, the time was right for the winger to make the next move in his football career.

'After the first three years when we were successful, Villa went into a bit of a downward spiral,' said Walters. 'The team got broken up and we were no longer challenging for the league or qualifying for Europe. Their ambition was no longer matching mine and my contract was expiring. I had a bad injury in season 1986/87, the year we got relegated, so I was a bit disillusioned. What made my mind up to move was when the chairman offered me a new contract but told me I would have to take a pay cut as I had been injured so much. I had been there since I was ten and I thought this was a bit disloyal.'

He continued, 'Watford and Spurs were interested in me and so were Everton. But there was an attraction to signing for Rangers. English clubs were banned from Europe and I had watched Rangers play Dynamo Kiev a few weeks earlier. I was so impressed with the crowd and the atmosphere. I went up to speak to Graeme Souness and he showed me round Ibrox. Although it was empty, when he put the lights on it was very impressive.'

Although the stadium was awe-inspiring, training facilities were a tad more spartan. Mark noted, 'The facilities at Villa were probably among the better ones in the country at the time. [At Rangers] we used to train at The Albion which was basic and the facilities weren't as good as what I had been used to. We knew that it was only temporary and that eventually the club would get something like Murray Park but I didn't get to experience that.'

Walters made his Rangers debut against Celtic at Parkhead on 2 January 1988. It proved to be an inauspicious start for the new boy for a number of reasons. Celtic won 2-0 and Mark was subjected to vile racial abuse throughout the match.

'Souness warned me what to expect,' recalled Walters. 'I had never played in front of 60,000 in a league game before and got that kind of abuse. That was shocking. When I had the ball I was always looking infield but when I ran back to defend I could see all the stuff that had been thrown at me. There were darts, golf balls and pig's legs. Fortunately, nothing hit me. I didn't even bring it to the referee's attention; I just carried on playing as I was so determined to play for Rangers that nothing would have stopped me giving it a go.'

Walters eventually found his feet and was soon entertaining the Rangers supporters with his stunning array of skills and tricks. After scoring his first goal for the club against Raith Rovers in a Scottish Cup third-round replay on 10 February, he found the net in his next three games. This scoring spurt allied with his ability to ghost past defenders, tying them in knots with his twisting and turning, earned Mark the Player-of-theMonth award in February 1988.

'I was treated fantastically at Rangers,' said Walters. 'From the girls in the canteen right up to the chairman, Mr Holmes, everyone treated me well. I felt it was like a home from home.'

Although Mark's first goal helped earn a 4-1 win over Raith, Rangers exited the competition in the next round when they lost 2-0 at Dunfermline, a defeat that offered Walters the chance to sample the wrath of an incandescent Graeme Souness.

He remembered, 'It didn't matter if it was the captain or a young lad making his debut, the manager would give the same critique. He treated everybody the same and if you weren't playing well he would make that point. At Villa under Tony Barton and Billy McNeill, players picked the team, which I couldn't understand. We couldn't expect to be successful when the older players had so much influence. That's what I admired about Walter and Graeme; they were in charge.'

Between his debut against Celtic and the final Premier Division fixture against Falkirk, Walters made 21 appearances and scored eight goals. There would be no silverware for him as Celtic won the league and cup double in their centenary year. But Walters was a stand-out performer when Rangers exacted revenge on their Old Firm rivals just three league matches in to season 1988/89.

'It was a fantastic day, a beautiful day weather-wise,' was Walters's first recollection of the day Rangers inflicted a 5-1 defeat on Celtic. 'They scored first but, like any team that has character, that winds you up and you play even better. The second goal from Ray [Wilkins] was massive for us. It got the crowd going and the players' confidence grew. For my goal [Rangers' fifth of the afternoon] Coisty got fouled and the ball broke to me and I was able to just tap it in. Although I played out wide, I always enjoyed scoring goals.'

There was one embarrassing moment for Walters, though. After tormenting Mick McCarthy on the right wing, Mark's exquisite cross into the box was bulleted into the net by Kevin Drinkell to make it 4-1. As the players celebrated the camera panned to Walters who proceeded to show off his gymnastic ability with a forward roll.

'I rolled over like a sack of spuds,' he recalled laughing. 'It wasn't very elegant but you do things instinctively when celebrating a goal. That one was a bit embarrassing, though.'

Walters's goal that day was the first of seven he would net in Old Firm derbies. He thrived in those matches and got more opportunities to showcase his ability.

'You got a lot more space in those games,' said Walters. 'In other games we had the ball most of the time but it was tight and compact. But because Celtic would attack more, you would get more space, particularly in the latter stages of the game. If you give any decent player time and space he'll create and score goals so that's why I did so well in those games.'

Walters also enjoyed playing at Hampden Park and he had his first experience of the National Stadium in September 1988 when Rangers faced Hearts in the last four of the League Cup. Walters netted twice in a 3-0 win and was part of the side that claimed the trophy a month later in an enthralling final against Aberdeen.

'I joined Rangers to get to cup finals and win trophies so it was a dream come true to be in the final,' recalled Walters. 'It was another box ticked for me but it was a bit of a whirlwind so I don't remember too much about the game.'

But season 1988/89 was not all plain sailing for Walters. On 10 December he was ordered off in a 2-0 defeat by Hearts at Tynecastle, the first of two red cards he would pick up against the Edinburgh side. They were almost a year apart – the second one was on 2 December 1989 – and both were borne out of frustration at the rough treatment he had received from the Hearts defenders.

'I had a bit of a run-in with one or two of their players, particularly Walter Kidd,' said Walters. 'The fact we were losing didn't help and I got sent off for a couple of tackles. Walter Smith told me after the game that I wasn't good at tackling so it wasn't worth trying to start now!'

The ordering off earned Mark a two-game ban but he was back in position when Celtic visited Ibrox in January 1989. Celtic had won the season's second derby 3-1 at Parkhead – Walters netted Rangers' goal – but just as they had done back in August, the home side dished out another heavy defeat, winning 4-1 on this occasion with Walters scoring twice.

'That was a great game,' said Walters. 'I spoke to the kit man, Jimmy Bell, before the game and he said if I scored I should kiss the Rangers badge. I scored a penalty in front of the Celtic fans and did it and got a lot of stick from them. But it helped continue my love affair with the Rangers fans too.'

The performances of Walters on the wing meant less game time for Davie Cooper. Although he was approaching the veteran stages of his career, Cooper was still a valuable member of the first-team squad and Walters, who many observers felt had been bought to replace Cooper, was disappointed the pair did not get more opportunities to play in the same team. Cooper wore the number seven jersey and Walters 11 when the former made his 600th appearance for Rangers – both players scored in a 4-0 win over St Mirren in February 1988 – but that would be one of just 15 occasions when they appeared in the same Rangers starting XI.

'When I came in I thought I was going to be playing with Davie Cooper,' said Walters. 'Along with Paul McStay, who I'd played against all the way from schoolboy football, he was a Scottish player I really admired. One of the reasons I joined Rangers was to play with the likes of McCoist, Durrant and Davie Cooper. I used to stalk him in training and I watched how he used to angle his body so he could shift the ball quickly from his right foot to his left. We used to play head tennis in the morning and in the two years he was at Rangers with me I did well if I got a point off him.'

Season 1988/89 ended with a first league championship medal for Walters. In an era when assists were not published, his only recorded contribution to Rangers' attacking effort was 17 goals, including the only goal against Polish side Katowice on his European debut. However, he must have also been in double figures when it came to setting up goals. And in season 1989/90 he would be supplying ammunition for another forward of some repute, Maurice Johnston.

'At the time we thought he had signed for Celtic as he'd done all the media stuff but when he came to us there was a big uproar,' said Walters. 'He was one of the best players in Europe, in my opinion, at that time and he improved the squad.'

With Johnston and McCoist a deadly duo and Walters also chipping in with his fair share of goals, season 1989/90 saw Rangers retain the Premier Division title. The League Cup was relinquished – Walters scored from the penalty spot as Rangers lost 2-1 against Aberdeen in the final – and the foray into Europe was brief – a heavy defeat at home to Bayern which featured another penalty goal from Mark put paid to any aspirations of a European Cup run – but Rangers were now emerging as the dominant side domestically.

The glut of Old Firm goals continued for Walters too, with another penalty in a 3-0 win at Ibrox in April. The winger had missed the previous two matches after picking up a hamstring injury in the Old Firm Scottish Cup quarter-final defeat but he was back with a bang when his shot from 12 yards squirmed past Bonner in the Celtic goal. However, when Rangers were awarded a second penalty in the match, a record-chasing Ally McCoist claimed the ball.

'In football you have a designated penalty-taker and, at that time, it was me,' recalled Walters. 'But Coisty told me he needed a goal to beat a record [he was on the verge of becoming Rangers' highest post-war goalscorer in league football] so I gave him the ball. He absolutely loves scoring goals and that was his job so I didn't have a problem giving it to him.'

He added, 'Coisty was just instinctive. We used to call him "Golden Bollocks" and he just knew where the ball was going to bounce. You can't coach that and he scored so many goals because of that instinct.'

In season 1989/90 Walters scored 11 goals in 36 appearances. And ahead of his third full season in a Rangers jersey, 1990/91, it emerged he would be providing supply for a different type of centre-forward. The blue-chip signing in the summer of 1990 was Mark Hateley, a tall, rumbustious striker who had made a name for himself at Coventry City, Portsmouth, AC Milan and Monaco.

'As a winger it was easier putting balls in for guys like Mark,' said Walters. 'I just needed to put it in an area for him whereas with Coisty you would have to try and thread in passes. There are very few strikers like Mark around now – maybe Lukaku at Manchester United – and it's maybe going out of fashion.'

Walters and Hateley would combine to devastating effect on the dramatic final day of the league season but, before that, Walters claimed his second League Cup winners' medal. He seemed to like the competition as he plundered ten goals in 13 appearances during his Rangers career. And he was on the scoresheet again when Rangers defeated Celtic 2-1 at Hampden, pouncing to thunder a shot into the net from the edge of the penalty area.

Walters was joined on the lap of honour by the Dutch winger, Pieter Huistra, who came off the bench to pick up his first medal since arriving in the summer from FC Twente Enschede. He offered competition for places in the wide areas but rather than breed animosity, Walters and Huistra developed a strong friendship.

'At any successful club you need competition for places and he was a great player,' said Walters. 'We got on really well and I went to his wedding. We also went to Holland to watch Manchester United against Barcelona [in the 1991 European Cup Winners' Cup Final] and we became very close. I treated him with respect, the way Davie Cooper treated me.'

Walters scored again when the Old Firm met at Ibrox in January 1991. This one was something of a fluke, though, coming directly from a corner kick. Walters scuffed his kick but the wind that day carried the ball in a trajectory that caught out Pat Bonner. Mark Hateley sealed a 2-0 win in the second half and Rangers looked set for a comfortable run towards a third successive title. But things started to go awry in March when Rangers lost 1-0 at Pittodrie then suffered heavy back-to-back Old Firm defeats at Parkhead. The first of those, a 2-0 Scottish Cup defeat, achieved notoriety as Rangers had three players dismissed by referee Andrew Waddell. Among the trio was Mark Walters.

A matter of weeks later Graeme Souness was gone too. He resigned and took over from Kenny Dalglish at Liverpool and Walter Smith became the ninth manager in Rangers' history.

'Walter was very good at man-management and also had a big influence on the tactical side of things under Graeme,' said Walters. 'They were a great partnership and they worked well together. I was pleased that Walter got the opportunity [to become manager] as he was so influential.'

On the departing Souness he said, 'I was always brought up to do whatever the manager wanted to the best of your ability and as long as you did that with Graeme, you had no problems with him. He would get involved in training, usually in the Scotland v England matches. They were very physical – Graeme broke his ribs one day – and he'd smash a few people then get smashed himself.'

Rangers now had to try and stabilise themselves and ensure the title was secured. However, in the penultimate league match, the applecart was well and truly upset. Rangers were at Fir Park looking for a win to keep their noses in front. However, instead they were beaten 3-0, a defeat that not only allowed Aberdeen to draw level on points but also edge ahead of Rangers on goal difference. But it could have been different had the normally reliable Walters found the net with a second-half penalty.

'I was really disappointed with myself,' said Walters. 'Firstly for not playing well and secondly with the result. We had a lot of injuries and we weren't at the races. Motherwell played relatively well but didn't have to do much to beat us as we were so poor that day.'

A titanic title decider had now been set up. For the first time since 1965 the two teams who could win the title faced each other in the last round of fixtures, with leaders Aberdeen travelling to Glasgow looking for only a point to claim the championship. For Mark and his Rangers team-mates, the days before the match were filled with tension.

He recalled, 'We were wondering who was going to be fit and, to be honest, I don't think anyone was 100% fit that day. That made us nervous but once the game got going and we scored the first goal [Walters supplied a sumptuous cross that was bulleted into the net by Hateley], the crowd got behind us. We were dropping like flies but the crowd got us through it. I tore my hamstring but had to stay on as John Brown ruptured his Achilles. He takes the piss out me for that, saying that his injury trumped mine.'

Aside from his goals and assists there were two other hallmarks of Walters's time with Rangers, his 'Double Shuffle', a skill he had honed since his childhood, and the wearing of his football socks inside out.

'I had been wearing my socks like that since school,' recalled Walters. 'We had three teams in my year – A, B and C – and they all wore the same socks. They would eventually get worn out so by turning them inside out they looked a bit better. It became a superstition for me throughout my professional career.'

On his signature move, he noted, 'I learned to do the 'Double Shuffle' from watching Johann Cruyff. He did something similar in the 1974 World Cup and as we had no garden where I lived, I would go to the local park to practice. It was the perfect skill for me. I was [naturally] right-footed but I could use both feet. That meant I was capable of going both inside and outside and the defender wouldn't know where I was going.'

The summer of 1991 was a time of change in the footballing fraternity. UEFA had introduced the 'three-foreigner' rule which meant, in European competition, only three players from outside a club's home country could be selected. With the first-team pool at Ibrox filled with a cosmopolitan collection of players, Walters and Rangers mutually decided the time was right to move on.

'I spoke to [England manager] Graham Taylor and he said playing in Scotland wouldn't help me get picked for England,' recalled Walters. 'But I told him I loved playing for Rangers and wasn't going to go back to England only for that reason as it still wouldn't guarantee I'd get picked. The 'three-foreigner' rule changed my mind, though. I was still under contract at Rangers but I didn't ask for a transfer. In the end it was a mutual decision. I was told Graeme [Souness] was interested in me and Rangers accepted an offer [of £1,250,000] so I went to talk to him. If Rangers had said no to the offer from Liverpool then I would have stayed. Looking back now I regret not waiting a bit longer [after years of lobbying the rule was eventually abolished in December 1995].'

In the end the move to England did not signal the start of a flourishing international career. Walters was capped just once for England while, ironically, still a Rangers player. He was selected to play in a 1-0 win over New Zealand in Auckland, becoming the 1,092nd player to represent his country in the process.

Walters spent four-and-a-half seasons at Anfield, winning the FA Cup in 1992 and scoring Liverpool's first-ever Premier League goal, before enjoying spells at Southampton, Swindon Town and Bristol Rovers.

Mark Walters made 163 appearances for Rangers and scored 57 goals. He won three Premier Division titles (1988/89, 1989/90 and 1990/91) and two Scottish League Cups (1988/89 and 1990/91).

Summing up his time at Ibrox he concluded, 'I joined one of the best clubs in the world at the time and one of my biggest highlights was my first goal for Rangers. I was a frustrated centre-forward so I always liked scoring goals and I'd gone five or six games without scoring. The goal against Raith Rovers will always stick out and it was a good goal as well, as I chipped the keeper from the edge of the box.

'In terms of players, Chris Woods was one of the best goalies I've played with and although Stuart Munro wasn't highly rated, he was an unsung hero. I really enjoyed playing with him and, obviously, McCoist with his goals. Before he got injured Ian Durrant was a world-class player and Ray Wilkins was great too. But the one who epitomised the team spirit at the time was Richard Gough. He wasn't just a good defender, he could provide goals too. Being a forward I would admire defenders like Richard who could read the game well. He would lead by example and put his head in anywhere.'

Statistics

Honours in the 1980s

Scottish Premier Division Champions	2	1986/87, 1988/89
Scottish Cup Winners	1	1980/81
Scottish League Cup Winners	6	1981/82, 1983/84, 1984/85, 1986/87, 1987/88, 1988/89
Glasgow Cup Winners	4	1983/84, 1984/85, 1985/86, 1986/87

Final Premier Division Placing (full seasons only)

1980/81	3rd
1981/82	3rd
1982/83	4th
1983/84	4th
1984/85	4th
1985/86	5th
1986/87	1st
1987/88	3rd
1988/89	1st

Scottish Cup (full seasons only)

1980/81	Winners
1981/82	Runners-up
1982/83	Runners-up
1983/84	Quarter-final
1984/85	Fourth Round
1985/86	Third Round
1986/87	Third Round
1987/88	Fourth Round
1988/89	Runners-up

Scottish League Cup (full seasons only)

1980/81	Third Round
1981/82	Winners
1982/83	Runners-up
1983/84	Winners
1984/85	Winners
1985/86	Semi-final
1986/87	Winners
1987/88	Winners
1988/89	Winners

Premier Division Record
(1 January 1980 to 28 December 1989)

Overall League Record					
Played	Won	Drawn	Lost	For	Against
376	187	95	94	603	358

Home Record					
	Played	Won	Drawn	Lost	For	Against
1979/80	8	5	2	1	11	6
1980/81	18	12	3	3	33	10
1981/82	18	10	5	3	34	16
1982/83	18	9	6	3	32	16
1983/84	18	7	8	3	26	18
1984/85	18	7	6	5	21	14
1985/86	18	10	4	4	34	18
1986/87	22	18	2	2	45	6
1987/88	22	14	4	4	49	17
1988/89	18	15	1	2	39	11
1989/90	10	8	1	1	18	5
TOTAL	188	115	42	31	342	137

Longest Unbeaten Run   29 November 1986 – 4 April 1987 (19 matches)
Longest Losing Run   15 October 1983 – 12 November 1983 (5 matches)

Away Record					
	Played	Won	Drawn	Lost	For	Against
1979/80	8	2	1	5	11	14
1980/81	18	4	9	5	27	22
1981/82	18	6	6	6	23	29
1982/83	18	4	6	8	20	25
1983/84	18	8	4	6	27	23
1984/85	18	6	6	6	26	24
1985/86	18	3	5	10	19	27
1986/87	22	13	5	4	40	17
1987/88	22	12	4	6	36	17
1988/89	18	11	3	4	23	15
1989/90	10	3	4	3	9	8
TOTAL	188	72	53	63	261	221

Top Tens

PREMIER DIVISION

In the 1980s 90 players pulled on a Rangers jersey and appeared in at least one Premier Division match. The top ten appearance makers were:

		| SEASON											
		79/80	80/81	81/82	82/83	83/84	84/85	85/86	86/87	87/88	88/89	89/90	Total
1	Davie Cooper	15	25	30	31	34	32	32	42	33	23		297
2	Ally McCoist					30	25	33	44	40	19	20	211
3	Ally Dawson	16	22	25	25	28	26	24	7				173
4	Ian Redford	13	35	32	34	32	26						172
5	Bobby Russell	13	28	32	21	31	18	27	1				171
6	Dave McPherson				20	36	31	34	42				163
7	Stuart Munro					5	13	29	43	17	22	20	149
8	John MacDonald	14	30	36	30	18	18	2					148
9	Ian Durrant						5	30	39	40	8		122
10	Chris Woods								42	39	24	16	121

In the 1980s 59 players scored at least one Premier Division goal for Rangers. The top ten goalscorers were:

		| SEASON											
		79/80	80/81	81/82	82/83	83/84	84/85	85/86	86/87	87/88	88/89	89/90	Total
1	Ally McCoist					8	12	25	34	31	9	9	128
2	John MacDonald	4	11	14	10	1	3	0					43
3	Davie Cooper	1	3	3	4	6	5	4	9	1	1		37
4	Robert Fleck					0	0	3	19	7			29
5	Derek Johnstone	4	4	9	6		1	0					24
6	Ian Redford	0	9	2	3	4	5						23
7=	Bobby Russell	4	6	6	1	4	0	0	0				21
7=	Jim Bett		4	11	6								21
9	Ian Durrant						0	2	4	10	2	0	18
10	Mark Walters									7	8	2	17

SCOTTISH CUP

In the 1980s 66 players pulled on a Rangers jersey and appeared in at least one Scottish Cup tie. The top ten appearance makers were:

		SEASON										
		79/80	80/81	81/82	82/83	83/84	84/85	85/86	86/87	87/88	88/89	Total
1	Davie Cooper	6	5	5	5	3	3	1	1	3	3	35
2	Ally Dawson	5	7	6	5	3	0	1	0			27
3	Bobby Russell	5	6	6	3	4	1	1	0			26
4	John MacDonald	6	5	6	3	1	3	0				24
5	Ian Redford		7	5	5	4	1					22
6	Ally McCoist					4	3	1	1	2	8	19
7=	Peter McCloy	6	4	0	6	1	1	0				18
7=	Sandy Jardine	6	6	6								18
7=	Jim Bett		7	5	6							18
10	Derek Johnstone	6	4	4	1	0	1	0				16

In the 1980s 26 players scored at least one goal in the Scottish Cup for Rangers. The top ten Scottish Cup goalscorers were:

		SEASON										
		79/80	80/81	81/82	82/83	83/84	84/85	85/86	86/87	87/88	88/89	Total
1	John MacDonald	4	3	2	2	0	2	0				13
2	Ally McCoist					3	0	1	0	1	5	10
3	Derek Johnstone	3	2	4	0	0	0	0				9
4	Colin McAdam		4	3	0	1						8
5	Bobby Russell	1	3	1	0	2	0	0	0			7
6=	Ian Redford	0	3	1	0	1	0					5
6=	Kevin Drinkell										5	5
8=	Davie Cooper	1	1	1	1	0	0	0	0	0	0	4
8=	Sandy Jardine	2	0	2								4
8=	Mark Walters									1	3	4

SCOTTISH LEAGUE CUP

In the 1980s 68 players pulled on a Rangers jersey and appeared in at least one Scottish League Cup tie. The top ten appearance makers were:

		SEASON										
		80/81	81/82	82/83	83/84	84/85	85/86	86/87	87/88	88/89	89/90	Total
1	Davie Cooper	4	11	9	10	6	4	5	4	4		57
2	Ian Redford	4	11	11	8	6						40
3	Ally McCoist				10	6	4	5	5	4	4	38
4	Bobby Russell	1	9	5	11	5	5	0				36
5	John MacDonald	3	10	11	6	1	2					33
6=	Ally Dawson	0	5	6	10	5	1	3				30
6=	John McClelland		3	11	11	5						30
8	Dave McPherson		1	2	10	6	5	4				28
9	Craig Paterson			9	8	5	4	0				26
10	Jim Bett	4	9	11								24

In the 1980s 25 different players scored at least one goal in the Scottish League Cup for Rangers. The top ten Scottish League Cup goalscorers were:

		SEASON										
		80/81	81/82	82/83	83/84	84/85	85/86	86/87	87/88	88/89	89/90	Total
1	Ally McCoist				9	5	1	2	6	4	4	31
2	John MacDonald	0	5	8	2	0	0					15
3	Davie Cooper	0	1	5	3	0	2	2	1	0		14
4	Ian Redford	0	7	1	1	2						11
5	Mark Walters								0	5	5	10
6	Colin McAdam	5	4	0	0							9
7	Derek Johnstone	1	3	3	0	0	0					7
8=	Jim Bett	0	1	5								6
8=	Bobby Williamson					0	0	6				6
10=	Bobby Russell	0	3	0	1	1	0	0				5
10=	Craig Paterson			2	1	1	1	0				5
10=	Robert Prytz			2	3	0						5
10=	Ian Durrant					0	0	1	3	1		5
10=	Sandy Clark			0	5	0						5

EUROPE

In the 1980s 40 players pulled on a Rangers jersey and appeared in at least one European tie (European Cup, UEFA Cup or European Cup Winners' Cup). The top ten appearance makers were:

		SEASON									
		81/82	82/83	83/84	84/85	85/86	86/87	87/88	88/89	89/90	Total
1	Davie Cooper	1	4	4	3	2	6	3	3		26
2	Ally McCoist			3	4	2	6	6	2	0	23
3	Chris Woods						6	6	4	1	17
4=	Dave McPherson		0	4	4	2	6				16
4=	Stuart Munro			0	1	2	6	2	3	2	16
4=	Terry Butcher						6	4	4	2	16
7=	Ally Dawson	2	4	4	4	0	1				15
7=	Derek Ferguson			2	0	0	4	5	3	1	15
9=	John McClelland	2	4	4	4						14
9=	Ian Durrant				0	1	5	6	2		14

In the 1980s 25 different players scored at least one goal in European competition for Rangers. The top ten goalscorers were:

		SEASON									
		81/82	82/83	83/84	84/85	85/86	86/87	87/88	88/89	89/90	Total
1	Ally McCoist			0	1	0	2	4	0	0	7
2	Dave McPherson		0	4	1	0	1				6
3	John MacDonald	1	0	4	0	0					5
4	Dave Mitchell			3	1						4
5=	Ian Durrant				0	0	1	1	1		3
5=	Ian Redford	0	0	2	1						3
5=	Craig Paterson		0	1	1	1	0				3
5=	Robert Fleck			0	0	0	3	0			3
9=	Terry Butcher						0	0	2	0	2
9=	Robert Prytz		0	2	0						2
9=	Derek Johnstone	0	2	0	0	0					2
9=	Mark Walters							0	1	1	2
9=	Iain Ferguson				2	0					2
9=	Mark Falco							2			2

HEAD-TO-HEAD RECORD

The following shows how Rangers fared against the other clubs they faced in the Scottish Premier Division in the 1980s.

ABERDEEN						
	Played	Won	Drawn	Lost	For	Against
1979/80	2	0	1	1	4	5
1980/81	4	1	2	1	2	3
1981/82	4	0	1	3	2	10
1982/83	4	2	0	2	4	5
1983/84	4	0	2	2	1	6
1984/85	4	0	1	3	3	9
1985/86	4	0	2	2	2	6
1986/87	4	1	2	1	3	2
1987/88	4	1	0	3	2	5
1988/89	4	2	0	2	4	6
1989/90	2	1	0	1	1	1
TOTAL	**40**	**8**	**11**	**21**	**28**	**58**

AIRDRIE						
	Played	Won	Drawn	Lost	For	Against
1980/81	4	1	3	0	4	2
1981/82	4	3	1	0	8	3
TOTAL	**8**	**4**	**4**	**0**	**12**	**5**

CELTIC						
	Played	Won	Drawn	Lost	For	Against
1979/80	1	0	0	1	0	1
1980/81	4	2	0	2	6	5
1981/82	4	1	1	2	5	7
1982/83	4	0	1	3	5	9
1983/84	4	1	0	3	3	7
1984/85	4	0	3	1	3	4
1985/86	4	1	2	1	8	7
1986/87	4	2	1	1	5	4
1987/88	4	0	1	3	3	7
1988/89	4	3	0	1	12	6
1989/90	2	1	1	0	2	1
TOTAL	**39**	**11**	**10**	**18**	**52**	**58**

CLYDEBANK						
	Played	Won	Drawn	Lost	For	Against
1985/86	4	2	1	1	6	3
1986/87	4	4	0	0	16	1
TOTAL	**8**	**6**	**1**	**1**	**22**	**4**

STATISTICS

DUMBARTON						
	Played	Won	Drawn	Lost	For	Against
1984/85	4	3	1	0	9	3
TOTAL	**4**	**3**	**1**	**0**	**9**	**3**

DUNDEE						
	Played	Won	Drawn	Lost	For	Against
1979/80	2	2	0	0	5	1
1981/82	4	3	0	1	10	6
1982/83	4	0	2	2	3	5
1983/84	4	2	1	1	9	7
1984/85	4	1	2	1	5	5
1985/86	4	1	0	3	8	6
1986/87	4	3	0	1	8	2
1987/88	4	4	0	0	8	3
1988/89	4	3	1	0	7	2
1989/90	2	1	1	0	4	2
TOTAL	**36**	**20**	**7**	**9**	**67**	**39**

DUNDEE UNITED						
	Played	Won	Drawn	Lost	For	Against
1979/80	2	1	1	0	2	1
1980/81	4	2	0	2	8	9
1981/82	4	1	2	1	4	4
1982/83	4	1	1	2	4	8
1983/84	4	2	2	0	6	3
1984/85	4	1	2	1	3	3
1985/86	4	1	3	0	4	3
1986/87	4	2	1	1	5	3
1987/88	4	1	2	1	3	3
1988/89	4	2	1	1	4	2
1989/90	2	1	1	0	3	2
TOTAL	**40**	**15**	**16**	**9**	**46**	**41**

DUNFERMLINE ATHLETIC						
	Played	Won	Drawn	Lost	For	Against
1986/87	4	3	1	0	13	2
1987/88	4	3	1	0	7	1
TOTAL	**8**	**6**	**2**	**0**	**20**	**3**

FALKIRK					
	Played	Won	Drawn	Lost	For	Against
1986/87	4	4	0	0	12	2
1987/88	4	4	0	0	13	1
TOTAL	**8**	**8**	**0**	**0**	**25**	**3**

HAMILTON ACADEMICAL					
	Played	Won	Drawn	Lost	For	Against
1986/87	4	4	0	0	8	1
1987/88	4	4	0	0	9	1
TOTAL	**8**	**8**	**0**	**0**	**17**	**2**

HEARTS					
	Played	Won	Drawn	Lost	For	Against
1980/81	4	2	1	1	8	3
1983/84	4	1	2	1	6	5
1984/85	4	1	1	2	4	5
1985/86	4	1	0	3	4	9
1986/87	4	3	1	0	12	3
1987/88	4	1	2	1	5	5
1988/89	4	3	0	1	9	3
1989/90	2	2	0	0	3	1
TOTAL	**30**	**14**	**7**	**9**	**51**	**34**

HIBERNIAN					
	Played	Won	Drawn	Lost	For	Against
1979/80	1	1	0	0	1	0
1981/82	4	1	3	0	5	4
1982/83	4	2	2	0	6	4
1983/84	4	2	2	0	3	0
1984/85	4	1	1	2	5	5
1985/86	4	2	1	1	8	5
1986/87	4	1	2	1	5	3
1987/88	4	2	1	1	4	2
1988/89	4	3	1	0	3	0
1989/90	3	1	1	1	3	2
TOTAL	**36**	**16**	**14**	**6**	**43**	**25**

KILMARNOCK					
	Played	Won	Drawn	Lost	For	Against
1979/80	2	1	0	1	1	1
1980/81	4	3	1	0	13	2
1981/82	4	2	2	0	7	1
TOTAL	**10**	**6**	**3**	**1**	**21**	**4**

STATISTICS

MORTON

	Played	Won	Drawn	Lost	For	Against
1979/80	2	2	0	0	4	1
1980/81	4	2	1	1	8	3
1981/82	4	2	2	0	7	2
1982/83	4	2	2	0	8	1
1984/85	4	4	0	0	10	1
1987/88	4	3	0	1	17	3
TOTAL	**22**	**15**	**5**	**2**	**54**	**11**

MOTHERWELL

	Played	Won	Drawn	Lost	For	Against
1982/83	4	2	1	1	7	5
1983/84	4	3	0	1	9	3
1985/86	4	3	0	1	6	1
1986/87	4	3	0	1	4	1
1987/88	4	4	0	0	5	0
1988/89	4	3	0	1	6	3
1989/90	2	1	0	1	3	2
TOTAL	**26**	**19**	**1**	**6**	**40**	**15**

PARTICK THISTLE

	Played	Won	Drawn	Lost	For	Against
1979/80	2	0	1	1	3	4
1980/81	4	1	3	0	7	3
1981/82	4	2	0	2	5	5
TOTAL	**10**	**3**	**4**	**3**	**15**	**12**

ST JOHNSTONE

	Played	Won	Drawn	Lost	For	Against
1983/84	4	4	0	0	13	4
TOTAL	**4**	**4**	**0**	**0**	**13**	**4**

ST MIRREN

	Played	Won	Drawn	Lost	For	Against
1979/80	2	0	0	2	2	6
1980/81	4	2	1	1	4	2
1981/82	4	3	1	0	11	3
1982/83	4	2	1	1	7	3
1983/84	4	0	3	1	3	6
1984/85	4	2	1	1	5	2
1985/86	4	2	0	2	7	4
1986/87	4	4	0	0	7	1
1987/88	4	3	1	0	12	3
1988/89	4	3	1	0	8	3
1989/90	3	2	0	1	3	1
TOTAL	**41**	**23**	**9**	**9**	**69**	**34**

Scoring Against Rangers

The following former or future Rangers players scored
goals against the club during the 1980s:

Alex O'Hara

03/05/80	Premier Division	Partick Thistle 4 Rangers 3	2 goals
06/08/80	Anglo-Scottish Cup 1st Round, 2nd Leg	Partick Thistle 3 Rangers 2	1 goal
01/01/81	Premier Division	Rangers 1 Partick Thistle 1	1 goal

Colin McAdam

03/05/80	Premier Division	Partick Thistle 4 Rangers 3	1 goal
25/01/86	Scottish Cup 3rd Round	Hearts 3 Rangers 2	1 goal

Davie Dodds

06/09/80	Premier Division	Dundee United 2 Rangers 4	1 goal
07/02/81	Premier Division	Dundee United 2 Rangers 1	1 goal
12/05/81	Scottish Cup Final Replay	Rangers 4 Dundee United 1	1 goal
13/11/82	Premier Division	Dundee United 4 Rangers 2	1 goal
14/02/84	League Cup Semi-final, 1st Leg	Dundee United 1 Rangers 1	1 goal
02/05/84	Premier Division	Rangers 2 Dundee United 2	1 goal
14/05/84	Premier Division	Dundee United 1 Rangers 2	1 goal
14/12/85	Premier Division	Rangers 1 Dundee United 1	1 goal
22/02/86	Premier Division	Dundee United 1 Rangers 1	1 goal
22/11/86	Premier Division	Aberdeen 1 Rangers 0	1 goal
15/08/87	Premier Division	Aberdeen 2 Rangers 0	1 goal
23/10/88	League Cup Final	Aberdeen 2 Rangers 3	2 goals

Alex MacDonald

11/10/80	Premier Division	Rangers 3 Hearts 1	1 goal
10/09/83	Premier Division	Hearts 3 Rangers 1	1 goal
23/02/85	Premier Division	Hearts 2 Rangers 0	1 goal

Ally McCoist

18/02/81	Scottish Cup 4th Round Replay	Rangers 3 St Johnstone 1	1 goal

Sandy Clark

03/10/81	Premier Division	Rangers 4 Airdrie 1	1 goal

Partick Thistle

Partick Thistle, Hearts

Dundee United, Aberdeen

Hearts

St Johnstone

Airdrie, Hearts

16/11/85 Premier Division	Hearts 3 Rangers 0	2 goals
29/03/86 Premier Division	Hearts 3 Rangers 1	1 goal
16/01/88 Premier Division	Hearts 1 Rangers 1	1 goal

Iain Ferguson   **Dundee, Dundee United, Hearts**

17/10/81 Premier Division	Dundee 2 Rangers 3	1 goal
14/04/82 Premier Division	Dundee 3 Rangers 1	1 goal
03/05/83 Premier Division	Dundee 2 Rangers 1	1 goal
15/10/83 Premier Division	Dundee 3 Rangers 2	2 goals
10/03/84 Scottish Cup 5th Round	Dundee 2 Rangers 2	1 goal
17/03/84 Scottish Cup 5th Round Replay	Rangers 2 Dundee 3	2 goals
24/09/86 League Cup Semi-final	Dundee United 1 Rangers 2	1 goal
10/10/87 Premier Division	Dundee United 1 Rangers 0	1 goal
10/12/88 Premier Division	Hearts 2 Rangers 0	1 goal

Maurice Johnston   **Partick Thistle, Celtic**

31/10/81 Premier Division	Rangers 0 Partick Thistle 2	1 goal
17/02/82 Premier Division	Partick Thistle 2 Rangers 0	1 goal
20/03/82 Premier Division	Rangers 4 Partick Thistle 1	1 goal
01/01/85 Premier Division	Rangers 1 Celtic 2	1 goal
22/03/86 Premier Division	Rangers 4 Celtic 4	1 goal

Neale Cooper   **Aberdeen**

13/03/82 Premier Division	Rangers 1 Aberdeen 3	1 goal
22/05/82 Scottish Cup Final	Aberdeen 4 Rangers 1	1 goal

Cammy Fraser   **Dundee**

02/10/82 Premier Division	Rangers 1 Dundee 1	1 goal

Richard Gough   **Dundee United**

13/11/82 Premier Division	Dundee United 4 Rangers 2	1 goal

Bobby Williamson   **Clydebank**

01/09/82 League Cup Sectional Tie	Rangers 3 Clydebank 2	1 goal

Kenny Black   **Hearts**

27/04/85 Premier Division	Rangers 3 Hearts 1	1 goal

Dougie Robertson   **Morton**

26/01/85 Scottish Cup 3rd Round	Morton 3 Rangers 3	2 goals

John Brown   **Dundee**

16/02/85 Scottish Cup 4th Round	Rangers 0 Dundee 1	1 goal
23/11/85 Premier Division	Dundee 3 Rangers 2	3 goals
15/03/86 Premier Division	Dundee 2 Rangers 1	1 goal
20/09/86 Premier Division	Dundee 1 Rangers 0	1 goal

Gordon Durie   **Hibernian**

17/08/85 Premier Division	Hibernian 1 Rangers 3	1 goal
25/09/85 League Cup Semi-final, 1st Leg	Hibernian 2 Rangers 0	1 goal

Ian Redford
16/08/86 Premier Division

Dundee United
Rangers 2 Dundee United 3   1 goal

Dave McPherson
02/04/88 Premier Division

Hearts
Rangers 1 Hearts 2   1 goal

Jim Bett
25/10/87 League Cup Final
(Rangers won 5-3 on pens)
06/02/88 Premier Division
08/10/88 Premier Division
13/05/89 Premier Division

Aberdeen
Aberdeen 3 Rangers 3   1 goal

Aberdeen 1 Rangers 2   1 goal
Aberdeen 2 Rangers 1   1 goal
Rangers 0 Aberdeen 3   1 goal

Ian Ferguson
14/11/87 Premier Division

St Mirren
St Mirren 2 Rangers 2   1 goal

Ian McCall
26/08/87 League Cup 3rd Round

Dunfermline Athletic
Dunfermline 1 Rangers 4   1 goal

Billy Davies
24/09/88 Premier Division

St Mirren
Rangers 2 St Mirren 1   1 goal

Bobby Russell
05/11/88 Premier Division
03/10/89 Premier Division

Motherwell
Rangers 2 Motherwell 1   1 goal
Motherwell 1 Rangers 0   1 goal

Fraser Wishart
07/01/89 Premier Division

Motherwell
Motherwell 2 Rangers 1   1 goal

Gordon Dalziel
29/01/89 Scottish Cup 3rd Round

Raith Rovers
Raith Rovers 1 Rangers 1   1 goal

Index

319